# A STUDY OF SIX PLAYS BY IBSEN

# A STUDY OF
# SIX PLAYS BY IBSEN

BY
## BRIAN W. DOWNS, M.A.

*Master of Christ's College,*
*Professor of Scandinavian Studies*
*in the University of Cambridge*

## OCTAGON BOOKS

A DIVISION OF FARRAR, STRAUS AND GIROUX

New York    1972

First published 1959

Reprinted *1972*
*by permission of the Cambridge University Press*

OCTAGON BOOKS
A DIVISION OF FARRAR, STRAUS & GIROUX, INC.
19 Union Square West
New York, N. Y. 10003

*Reprinted from the original edition in the*
*Wesleyan University Library*

LIBRARY OF CONGRESS CATALOG CARD NUMBER: 72-5255

ISBN 0-374-92262-4

Printed in U.S.A. by
NOBLE OFFSET PRINTERS, INC.
New York, N.Y. 10003

*To*
MY COLLEAGUES AND PUPILS
IN THE
DEPARTMENT OF SCANDINAVIAN STUDIES
NEWLY CONSTITUTED BY THE
UNIVERSITY OF CAMBRIDGE

# CONTENTS

# PREFATORY NOTE

I have chosen the six plays by Ibsen which between them seem to me to illustrate best the various facets of his art and mind. *Love's Comedy*, a fairly early work, shows what comedy and open satire became under his hands. The dramatic poems *Brand* and *Peer Gynt*, vast and complementary, could not be omitted from any study such as I have undertaken, since—apart from the mastery of the verse-form which they have in common with *Love's Comedy*—they give the most perfect idea of what the poet conceived as man's duty and destiny. For a typical example of Ibsen's social plays, the quartette in which a prime concern was to submit to debate acute problems of his day, I have selected *A Doll's House*. *The Wild Duck* inescapably raises the question of the author's use of symbols, which must always interest even when it is no longer thought to have the overriding importance once attached to it. After some hesitation *The Master Builder* (rather than *When We Dead Awaken*) was taken to exemplify the autobiographical strain in almost everything Ibsen wrote.

Besides examining these matters I have endeavoured to collect the relevant material, bearing for the most part on the genesis of the dramas, which different kinds of reader may find helpful to their fuller appreciation.

To avoid misunderstanding I should perhaps add that I would not have selected any or all of these plays had they not, in my belief, been works of art of the greatest power and importance.

Except where otherwise stated, Ibsen's writings are quoted, by volume and page only, from the Standardutgave of his *Samlede Digter Verker* (7 volumes, Christiania, 1918) and, prefaced by the word 'Archer', from the English *Collected Works of Henrik Ibsen* (edited by William Archer, 12 volumes, London, 1907–12); my thanks are due to Messrs Gyldendal and Messrs Heinemann for permission to do so.

B. W. D.

*Cambridge*
*December 1947*

# CHRONOLOGICAL LIST OF IBSEN'S WRITINGS

| | | |
|---|---|---|
| Catilina | Catiline | 1850 |
| Kjæmpehøjen | Warrior's Barrow | 1850 |
| Norma | Norma | 1851 |
| Sancthansnatten | St John's Eve | 1853 |
| Fru Inger til Østraat | Lady Inger | 1855 |
| Gildet paa Solhaug | Feast at Solhaug | 1856 |
| Olaf Liljekrans | Olaf Liljekrans | 1857 |
| Hærmændene paa Helgeland | Vikings in Helgeland | 1858 |
| Kjærlighedens Komedie | Love's Comedy | 1862 |
| Kongs-emnerne | Pretenders | 1863 |
| Brand | Brand | 1866 |
| Peer Gynt | Peer Gunt | 1867 |
| De Unges Forbund | League of Youth | 1869 |
| Digte | Poems | 1871 |
| Kejser og Galilæer | Emperor and Galilean | 1873 |
| Samfundets Støtter | Pillars of Society | 1877 |
| Dukkehjem | Doll's House | 1879 |
| Gengangere | Ghosts | 1881 |
| Folkefiende | Enemy of the Peop... | 1882 |
| Vildanden | Wild Duck | 188... |
| Rosmersholm | Rosmersholm | 1886 |
| Fruen fra Havet | Lady from the Sea | 1888 |
| Hedda Gabler | Hedda Gabler | 1890 |
| Bygmester Solness | Master Builder | 1892 |
| Lille Eyolf | Little Eyolf | 1894 |
| John Gabriel Borkman | John Gabriel Borkman | 1896 |
| Naar Vi Døde Vaagner | When We Dead Awaken | 1899 |

# LOVE'S COMEDY
## (*Kjærlighedens Komedie*)

# 1862

## I

Just for a season let me beg or borrow
A great, a crushing, a stupendous sorrow,
And soon you'll hear my hymns of gladness rise![1]

SO FALK, the hero of *Love's Comedy*, exclaims within a few minutes of the play's beginning. And this, the least solemn or at any rate the most sparkling of his plays, Ibsen wrote during the wretchedest period of his own life. He had come back to Christiania in 1857, to take over the artistic direction of the small theatre in the Møllergate which existed for the purpose of furthering the cause of specifically Norwegian drama and theatre-craft, as did the Norske Theater at Bergen, where he had served his apprenticeship as assistant stage-manager. But the new occupation exceeded his powers; his policy left no impression that one can gauge;[2] financially, the theatre found itself in continual straits and in the summer of 1862 had to give up altogether. Always addicted to his cup, Ibsen haunted low taverns and was often found huddled in the gutter; with creditors harrying him, he was at his wits' end, until the rare coincidence of receiving an invitation to take part in a musical festival at happy Bergen in 1863 and of enjoying there the friendship and patronage of Bjørnson at his most radiant and winning—a coincidence which produced *The Pretenders* as directly as a major work of art can in such terms be said to be 'produced'—restored his self-confidence and almost literally set him on his feet again.

[1]      'Skaf mig, om blot en månedstid på borg
en kval, en knusende, en kæmpesorg,
så skal jeg synge livets jubel ud.'

(I, p. 281; Archer-Herford, I, 299.)
[2] To be sure, the 'second Christiania period' still remains the most obscure portion of Ibsen's life, but would doubtless be less obscure if of greater significance.

I

During the bad years at the Møllergate Theatre, Ibsen's creative power languished.[1] After (1857) *The Vikings in Helgeland* had been completed, he took up once more, only to drop again, the story of 'The Grouse in Justedal' ('Rypen in Justedal'), which he had already turned to some account in *Olaf Liljekrans*, and in 1860 he began a prose play of modern society, to be called *Svanhild*.[2] What posterity has of it introduces four figures who, with the same names and much the same characteristics, were to be revived in *Love's Comedy*: Falk ('a young author'), Fru Halm ('widow of a civil servant'), her daughter Svanhild, and Guldstad ('a merchant'); there is also a Chorus of Gentlemen, a sister to Svanhild, the undergraduate to whom she is betrothed, another engaged couple, together with a son of Fru Halm (who has no counterpart in *Love's Comedy*). Ibsen made no great headway with this play either, possibly because he could not then hit on a medium congenial both to himself and to his subject. The surviving fragment is probably all that he wrote, and forms a first act only. The scheme, however, remained in the author's head and was taken up once more two years later, to be clad in verse and published on New Year's Eve, 1862, as a supplement to the periodical *Illustreret Nyhedsblad*.[3]

Because *Love's Comedy* is a satirical play about love, courtship and marriage, and because the author had fairly recently taken unto himself a wife, it might summarily be inferred that his marital experiences were the root of Ibsen's wretchedness. But that was an erroneous conclusion to which the wiseacres of Christiania incontinently jumped.[4] Eight years later, Ibsen

[1] The period of five years between *The Vikings in Helgeland* and *Love's Comedy* is the longest that elapsed between successive plays in Ibsen's career. Some occasional poetry, as well as his most popular piece of verse, 'Terje Vigen', dates from this time, but its amount is not really bulky and does not suggest either much labour or much imaginative fertility.

[2] The manuscript describes it as 'komedie i 3 Akter'. It was first printed in *Efterladte Skrifter*, I, 449. Blanc says (*Henrik Ibsen og Christiania Theater*, Kristiania, 1906, p. 15) the play was conceived in 1858.

[3] The first edition of *Kjærlighedens Komedie* was printed from a lost fair copy; the foul copy of it is in existence, in the library of Videnskabens Selskab at Trondheim, and has been described and discussed by Landmark, J. A., in *Edda*, xxviii (Oslo, 1928), p. 1. The second edition (1867), which cut down the local allusions and was otherwise altered in minor respects, was published by Gyldendalske Boghandel of Copenhagen and constitutes the established text.

[4] Brandes, G., *Henrik Ibsen* (1858), p. 58; English translation (1899), p. 42.

emphatically belied it with the declaration[1] that his life only began to assume value with his marriage, in 1858, to Susannah Thoresen. This lady—again according to his own statement—furnished the model for the heroine of *The Vikings in Helgeland*, Hjørdis, whose essential character is disclosed when she finally quits the scene in the shape of a valkyrie;[2] and it is she whom he once more put upon the stage as Svanhild, the new heroine whose name deliberately conjures up the heroic age.[3]

## II

The mention made of *Love's Comedy's* predecessor, *The Vikings in Helgeland* (1857), and its successor, *The Pretenders* (1863), prompts a consideration of its place in Ibsen's work as a whole.

Ibsen had proved himself a somewhat slow starter: this was his eighth play; and only the seventh could be said to show truly high promise. Coming to Christiania for the first time in 1850, he had, like many another earnest matriculation candidate, the manuscript of a blank-verse Roman tragedy (*Catilina*) practically in his pocket; eighteen months or so later he had a one-act piece about the Normans in the Mediterranean, *The Warrior's Barrow* (*Kæmpehøjen*), publicly performed. Then, pursuant to his contract with the Bergen Theatre, he turned out for its behoof a fantasia, *St John's Eve* (*Sancthansnatten*, 1852), a costume-melodrama, *Lady Inger of Östraat* (*Fru Inger til Øster-raad*, 1854), and two ballad-dramas, *The Feast at Solhaug* (1855) and *Olaf Liljekrans* (1856); on this had followed *The Vikings in Helgeland*, the fable and style of which owe much to Icelandic sagas.

---

[1] *Breve*, I, 213.

[2] In old Norse myth, the valkyries were supernatural females who not only conducted the heroes, when dead, to the endless potations of Valhalla, but in life urged them on to deeds of valour; they may also be looked upon as filling the *rôle* of Egeria. It may be urged that, if Ibsen were married to a lady whom he likened to a valkyrie, that is no guarantee of matrimonial felicity; but all the evidence goes to show that Ibsen's marriage was a successful one (see his daughter-in-law Bergliot Ibsen's *De Tre*, 1948, *passim*).

[3] According to the 'Hamðismál' of the older *Edda*, Svanhild was the daughter of the great Sigurd and of Guðrun, married to Jarmunrik, who caused her to be trampled to death by wild horses—for which her half-brothers Hamðer and Sørli set out to avenge her.

Ibsen's development was probably retarded by the 'national-istic' programme which the theatres, both at Bergen and in the Møllergate, imposed on him and to which he subscribed at the time.[1] What they required of him was something *norsk-norsk*,[2] as it was called, something tangibly associated with the heroic past, or the folk-lore, or the struggle for independence, or the ancient balladry, of the Norwegian people—subjects which the mature Ibsen touched on but rarely and then only in a satirical vein. At the same time Hettner[3] had impressed on him the necessity of being modern, actual, if his plays were to be truly effective, though, as an admirer of Shakespeare, the German theorist allowed the possibility of achieving this by means of fables which could be utterly remote from the immediate present. Only with *The Vikings in Helgeland*, however, had Ibsen ap-proached success in reconciling the two requirements, Hettner's and the Norske Theater's.

The first thing for which *Love's Comedy* is remarkable is the abrupt rejection of the nationalistic programme. It is certainly a completely Norwegian play—in fact, it can be called specifi-cally a 'Christiania play'.[4] But it is up-to-date, no Chorus celebrates Norwegian virtue or Norwegian conifers, it makes no allusions to popular custom or belief, its style owes nothing either to ballad or to saga. Only *St John's Eve*, whose characters belong to the same rank of society, whose scene is laid at the present time in almost identical environment (but where there are elves, goblins and magic potions) and in which the satirical element has assumed some prominence, shows the smallest premonition of this. Ibsen's apprenticeship had not, however, proved utterly idle—as, indeed, *The Vikings in Helgeland* had already proved. His daily dealings with the repertory of two

[1] It should be remembered that an independent Norwegian literature at this time had the charm of novelty, having virtually been created within the last quarter of a century by Schwach, Bjerregaard, Wergeland and Welhaven. At most the two theatres could command a native repertory of a dozen plays, none of much account before *Lady Inger* and *The Vikings in Helgeland*.

[2] I.e. Norwegian of the Norwegians and not *Danish* of the Norwegians, as the advocates of the former accused the current drama of being.

[3] Hettner, whose *Moderne Drama* Ibsen began to study in 1852, approved of comedy, provided it had a substantial theme ('bedeutenden Stoff').

[4] This is especially noticeable in the first edition. But the scene remains quite precisely indicated: 'Mrs Halm's villa on the Drammensvejen at Christiania.'

theatres (and with the plays of Scribe in particular) had taught the great master of theatrical effectiveness all he needed to know about that, and his experiments in blank verse and ballad-metres (as well as his copious occasional poetry) had given him a proficiency in verse-craft equally great.

## III

The main plot of *Love's Comedy* is relatively simple: the hero Falk approaches the heroine Svanhild and is rejected; she then approaches the hero and is accepted; they part. This tripartite structure corresponds to the division into three acts, save that part of the second link or part overflows into the beginning of the third act. Apart from the small irregularity just noted, each act is structurally similar; in the manner of opera, it leads up to a great duet between hero and heroine just before the fall of the curtain, the first portion of each act being occupied mainly with the concerns of the other characters, notably the minor hero, Lind, and his heroine, Anna, and it is punctuated by what might be called *arias*, in which the hero makes clear his opinions (this *aria* is distributed over a series of duets and a trio in Act III). The operatic nature of the construction[1] seems to be emphasised by the male choruses[2] at the beginnings of Acts I and II and at the end of Act III,[3] an even larger concession to convention than the verse-vehicle which is employed throughout.[4]

Of the latter it might be rash and unbecoming in a foreigner to speak at length, though C. H. Herford, having the unique experience of a translator, may be quoted as testifying[5] to the

[1] In Ibsen's work parallelled, I think, only in *St John's Eve*; because of their metre and theme, *The Feast at Solhaug* and *Olaf Liljekrans* have much of opera about them too.

[2] Up to and including *Pillars of Society*, all of Ibsen's plays (except *The Warrior's Barrow*) were written for a large stage and a large cast.

[3] The device of music at the end, to accompany, with the resolution of the crisis, the definite departure of one of the important characters, is reproduced in *The Lady from the Sea*.

[4] *Love's Comedy*, like Aristophanes's plays, has much of an operetta about it and perhaps should be performed as one. Aristophanes was lauded by Hettner; an obvious link between him and the author of *Love's Comedy* is Heiberg, on whom see pp. 31 n. and 57 below.

[5] 'A Scene from Ibsen's *Love's Comedy*', in *Fortnightly Review* (n.s.), LXXVII (1900), p. 191.

play's 'valiant vivacity and verve', and to 'a medium charged
with eloquence and imagery'; we are told, too,[1] that once upon
a time the schoolboys of Norway learned parts of it by heart for
their sheer romantic beauty. Ibsen adopted the five-stressed
line, rhyming irregularly, less frequently in couplets than otherwise, but rarely with a long interval between the rhymes. If it
be appropriate to speak in terms of metrical 'feet', then it
would appear that the iambic foot is the norm, as appears in
the more slowly spoken serious passages, such as

> Du friske fritluftsblomst på kirkegården,—
> *der* ser du hvad· de kalder liv i våren!
> Der lugter lig af brudgom og af brud;
> der lugter lig, hvor to går dig forbi
> på gadehjørnet, smilende med læben,
> med løgnens klumre kalkgrav indeni,
> med dødens slaphed over hver en stræben.[2]

But, as even the lines just quoted betray, the large proportion of
'feminine' endings in Norwegian and, especially, the number
of disyllabic words bearing the accent on the first syllable give
to satirical lines spoken at speed a dactylic effect, e.g.

> *Der* skal I få at se, som på parade,
> hvert bånd, som Per og Poul i byen knytter;
> *der* rykkes ind hvert rosenfarvet brev,
> som Vilhelm til sin ømme Laura skrev;
> *der* trykkes blandt ulykkelige hændelser,—
> som ellers mord og krinolinforbrændelser,—
> hvert opslag, som fandt sted i ugens løb![3]

Ibsen had not used this metre in any earlier play. *St John's Eve*,
*Lady Inger* and *The Vikings in Helgeland* are in prose;[4] the verse of
*Catiline* is mostly, and that of *The Warrior's Barrow* entirely,
unrhymed; for *The Feast at Solhaug* and *Olaf Liljekrans* the verse-
passages (interrupted by prose) are adapted from the ballad-
metres, irregular not only in the sequence of rhymes, but also in
the proportion of stressed to unstressed syllables.

---

[1] Bødtker, S., *Kristiania-premierer*, I (1932), p. 199.
[2] I, 346.
[3] I, 329.          [4] Songs apart.

Verse was well established in Danish drama—that is to say in the drama currently acted in Norway too. Hostrup, Ibsen's senior by only ten years, was using irregularly rhymed lines, but, in their comedies of present-day life, both he and Heiberg (1790–1861) commonly mingled prose with their verse.

This sketchily treated subject must be dropped with the observation that Ibsen wrote a good deal of formal poetry: in addition to the plays just mentioned, the very lengthy *Brand* and *Peer Gynt* are written entirely in verse, and a substantial volume is needed to contain all his undramatic pieces, the best of which are pithy bits of satire, very much in the vein and style of Falk's speeches in *Love's Comedy*.

## IV

Structurally, it has been seen, *Love's Comedy* falls into three parts, distinguished by the heroine's changes of mind. First she disdains the hero; then she makes up to him and returns his love with an equal ardour; and ultimately she breaks with him for good—the exact opposite of what usually happens in a comedy. If no more than a missish fickleness underlay these tergiversations, the piece would presumably not demand much critical consideration. But the motives are weightier in themselves, and in them we may find the key to the puzzles set by *Love's Comedy* and its unusual outcome.

To one virtue at least Falk can, by common consent, lay claim: complete openness. Poet though he is, we can always believe what he says. When he first woos Svanhild he makes it quite plain that he looks upon her as his Muse in person; his image is indeed more homely: she is a willow-pipe on which he will play his immortal tunes, and, when she demurs at such a function, he is impudent enough to congratulate her on being selected for it;[1] but her rejection of him, as one may well imagine, is none the less flat. When, on the following afternoon,[2] the couple come together again, much has taken place in the interval: the engagement between Falk's crony, Lind, and

[1] The precariousness of such good fortune is made clear by Falk's killing of the song-bird in an earlier scene (I, 291; Archer-Herford, I, 321).

[2] The action is deemed to begin one evening and to conclude the next. That is a very usual time-scheme in Ibsen's 'modern' plays. *John Gabriel Borkman* is noticeably more, *A Doll's House* less, concentrated.

Svanhild's sister, Anna, has been ratified and celebrated, Lind
has been induced to renounce his missionary ambitions,[1] the
situation of Pastor Straamand and his family has been fully
exposed, Falk has unbosomed himself of his speech on Tea, has
threatened to flutter every amatory dovecot in Norway with his
proposed 'Cupid's Archery Gazette' and has been shown the
door by the indignant *pension*-keeper, Fru Halm, mother to
Svanhild and Anna. Falk, previously no more than the bright
boy of his class, has shown himself a man of independence and
courage, contrasting sharply enough with the other frequenters
of Fru Halm's tea-parties, and, moreover, he has declared with
unmistakable energy his intention to oppose their hypocrisy,
lukewarmness and sentimentality, not merely by a few shafts of
satire, but with the zeal appropriate to a moral crusade; he has
even begun to suffer for his cause. To such a man Svanhild feels
that she can devote herself; she approaches him again:

> If you make war on lies, I stand
> A trusty armour-bearer by your side,[2]

and they plight their troth to one another.

The exaltation that threw Svanhild into Falk's arms does not
last. The shortness of its duration may indeed be reckoned
a blemish. Yet no mere reaction of mood brings about the final
*dénouement*, but a consideration of the future, to which Falk,
the despiser of 'the next thing',[3] is naturally averse and which
the intervention of Svanhild's other suitor, Guldstad, renders
urgent. When the point is put to him, Falk, open as he is, avows
that the passion which he feels for his *fiancée* and the genuineness
of which no one doubts may continue for a long while, but
cannot be relied upon to endure eternally; and Svanhild, unable
to contemplate the decay of their rapture, prefers to accept the
unimpassioned, but equally authentic, affection of the wise,
middle-aged and wealthy merchant, which the tooth of time
will hardly gnaw away. That done, nothing will remove, nothing
can tarnish, the glory of her golden hour, even though she and
Falk will never meet again.

---

[1] Lind evidently intends to accompany one of the many parties of Norwegians
then emigrating to the U.S.A.; that is why 'He has an English sermon on the brain'
(Archer-Herford, I, 363).

[2] I, 332; Archer-Herford, I, 404.     [3] I, 279; Archer-Herford, I, 295.

The construction that may be placed upon this factual foundation has, from the very first, formed a subject of acute controversy. Some, it would seem,[1] saw in the whole a puritanical revulsion from passion as such. Ibsen, to be sure, often[2] disclosed an antipathy to erotic passion verging upon the prudish, yet nothing indicates here that he either disbelieved or depreciated or wished to punish the devouring love felt by Falk and Svanhild for one another during this great climax in their lives. That is taken for granted and stays untouched, uncriticised.

The brilliant English translator of the play not dissimilarly interpreted it[3] as a paradoxical defence of *mariage de convenance* against the Romantic clamour for idealised passion as the foundation of conjugal life. Without completely rejecting the argument of Herford, we may agree with Mr Ellis Roberts[4] that, in view of the much older and well-established Romantic convention of *amour courtois*, which excluded the legitimate spouse from all claim to love, such a defence is hardly more paradoxical than it is novel. For its clarification, all depends on a proper appreciation of the chief personalities concerned, to which we shall presently proceed, contenting ourselves at this juncture with observing that Guldstad is not at all the typical *bourgeois satisfait* who, at his time of life, feels that his house needs just one more article of furniture and that a young mistress to whom he is married is cheaper and less nerve-racking than one to whom he is not married; he not merely exhibits prudence and solidity, he has philosophy and genuine affection too, so that one observer has styled[5] him the true poet of the play. Since Svanhild, on the other side, is a very honest, gifted and attractive young woman, enjoying in her mother's house the opportunities

---

[1] I have not come across the argument myself; but the disclaimer of Boyesen, H. H. (*A Commentary on the Works of Henrik Ibsen*, 1894, p. 71): 'It would be a mistake, I fancy, to interpret this as an act of religious asceticism', suggests that it was put forward.

[2] Especially in *Rosmersholm*, *Little Eyolf* and *When We Dead Awaken*.

[3] Herford, C. H., 'A Scene from Ibsen's *Love's Comedy*', in *Fortnightly Review* (n.s.), LXXVII, February 1900, p. 191.

[4] Roberts, R. E., *Henrik Ibsen* (London, 1912), p. 58.

[5] Reich, E., *Henrik Ibsens Dramen* (Dresden, 1903), p. 52. In the admirable revival at the Royal Theatre, Copenhagen, in 1928, Mr Poul Reymert made Guldstad the centre of the play (Elster, K., *Teater 1929–1939*, 1941, p. 181).

9

that have married off seven of her cousins already, and since she deliberately prefers Guldstad whèn she has unfettered freedom of choice,[1] it is more than doubtful whether *mariage de convenance* is the appropriate term to employ in this case.

To arrive at the true import of the play, there are, it seems to me, four sets of considerations about which to become clear beforehand—some complex and some simple. We have (i) to examine the personalities with whom we are put into contact; we must (ii) forbid any prejudice about Ibsen's saturnine disposition to obscure the word 'Comedy' as part of the title of his play; we must (iii) look at it in the light of Camilla Collett's novel, *The Sheriff's Daughters*, and (iv) of certain doctrines of Kierkegaard, which have left equally obvious traces. Point (ii) calls for no more than the remark that, in Danish and Norwegian, 'Komedie' means what it does in English, not what it does in French; *prima facie* we deal not merely with a play about love, but with a play about love *that has a happy ending*.[2] Point (i) depending for its elucidation on the remaining two, it will be convenient to proceed to them now.

Even if it were a great exaggeration to say that Norwegian literature starts with *The Sheriff's Daughters (Amtmandens Døtre,* 1854–5), it certainly does inaugurate that phase of it which is made illustrious by the name of Ibsen, being definitely modern and dealing with urgent moral problems. Fru Collett[3] took for her subject the marrying of young women in unfavourable conditions of solitude and parental neglect, in order to insist on the likelihood of marital shipwreck where the bride has no choice of her spouse, either because convention forbids or opportunity is lacking. The chief heroine of her book, Louise, is unable to marry the man of her choice, a grandiloquent tutor; instead, she resigns herself to a marriage, loveless on her side at least, with a fine-

---

[1] Economic considerations do not enter in, as Guldstad, intent above all things to secure a happy future for Svanhild, promises (1, 355; Archer-Herford, 1, 445) to treat her and Falk as his children if they marry. His sentiments towards Falk, whose energy and unconventionality he appreciates, are thoroughly benevolent except when Svanhild's felicity is threatened.

[2] Ibsen seems to rub in the point on his title-page: 'Kjærlighedens Komedie. Komedie i tre Akter.'

[3] Camilla Collett (1813–95) was the younger sister of the poet Wergeland and devoted herself to literature after the death of her husband in 1851. She was a friend of Ibsen and his wife.

feeling, middle-aged, clerical widower. The author made no secret of her conviction that this was a disaster.

Ibsen goes out of his way to show that in *Love's Comedy* he has *The Sheriff's Daughters* in mind. The speech about Tea,[1] which he puts into Falk's mouth as a parable of Love, has direct reference to the same similitude proffered in the novel.[2] If Ibsen were alluding to Fru Collett's book for no reason but to say 'ditto' to everything in it, a substantial part of *Love's Comedy* would be a waste of time and ingenuity; and the very resemblance should warn us to pay particular heed to differences. To give point to the latter, the parallels must be pretty close, of course, and this argument, I think, applies with particular force to the main characters. At first sight we should expect to find them practically identical, and a closer examination does not belie the expectation. Over Svanhild and Guldstad, there can be no great dispute; the former, like Louise, incarnates feminine vigour, independence and unstaled affection; and Guldstad, like Rein, will be as satisfactory a husband in every way as a man in middle life can be expected to be.[3] The third parallel, however, is not usually drawn as far as perhaps it should be. The hero of *The Sheriff's Daughters* has the brilliance, ardour and vivacity generally conceded to the hero of *Love's Comedy*; but he is also Byronic (even in personal appearance), moody, unreliable and deficient in moral ballast; a reader who goes all the way with Fru Collett may indeed go farther, to lament (as Fru Collett evidently does not) that Louise's case is indeed a very hard one if the only alternative to Rein is Georg Kold. I think it by no means fanciful to suggest that Ibsen did pursue this line of thought, that he had his doubts about that young man and, if he had, that he had his doubts about his *alter ego*, Falk, as well.

Falk's speech on Tea has a triple significance: it deliberately links *Love's Comedy* to *The Sheriff's Daughters*; it constitutes a turning-point in the dramatic action, since the challenge which Falk throws down with it results in his expulsion from Fru Halm's *pension* and in the new esteem which her daughter

[1] I, 322; Archer-Herford, I, 385.
[2] *Amtmandens Døtre*, I (3rd ed., Kristiania, 1879), p. 197.
[3] Bing, J., 'Kjærlighedens Komedie', in *Festskrift til William Nygaard*, places (p. 117) Guldstad below Rein.

conceives of him; and it indicates the general sentiment on which he acts. It is therefore not amiss to give it some further consideration.

Fru Collett's similitude of love and tea does not go very far: a girl's first love, she conveys in her book, resembles the best tea of China, reserved for the Emperor's drinking alone, decocted from the tenderest shoots which hands washed four-and-twenty times and then encased in gloves have reverently culled. With the help of *Chambers's Journal*[1] Falk adds a profuse embroidery. Though he ignores the Emperor, he begins, following up a cue of Anna's, on the 'green spring shoots', to apply the metaphor quite in Fru Collett's spirit:

> every mortal has a small
> Private celestial empire[2] in his heart.
> There bud such shoots in thousands, kept apart
> By Shyness's soon shatter'd Chinese Wall.

He inclines, however, to the notion that the China of this exquisite tea is the land of the blue flower, the far-off hills, the land of Romance, whereas

> we get an after crop
> They kick the tree for, dust and stalk and stem—
> As hemp to silk beside what goes to them,

on which the knowledgeable Guldstad asserts:

> That is the black tea,

evoking the concurrence of Falk:

> That's what fills the shop.

One of the guests then brings Holberg's beef-tea on to the carpet, and Falk takes it up,

> And a *beef love* has equally been heard of
> Wont—in romances—to brow-beat its mate,
> And still they say its trace may be detected
> Among the henpecked of the married state,

to prove his thesis that, as there is tea and tea, always going by the same name, so there is love and love (which may be brute

---

[1] The Norwegian *Skillings-magazinet* (nos. v and vi for 1862) printed a translation of the article 'Tea' from the issue of 9 November 1861 (xvi (London, 1862), p. 253).

[2] Perhaps it is necessary to remind readers of to-day that until recently China was generally called 'the celestial empire'.

lust, with no affection in it at all), still called invariably by that name, and not, as Frøken Skjære[1] romantically protests, only one thing, unique and indistinguishable. That is one point, a logical distinction. But Falk goes on to protract the parallel; tea, as *Chambers's Journal* averred, must come from its native land, not by way of the sea, by 'Freedom's ocean wave', but, if its bouquet (or at least the reputation of possessing it) is to linger, it must be genuine caravan tea, attested by the stamp of all the custom-houses through which it has passed. So

> to pass current here, Love must have cross'd
> The great Siberian waste of regulations,...
> It must produce official attestations
> From friend and kindred, devils of relations,
> From church curators, organist and clerk,
> And other fine folks—over and above
> The primal licence which God gave to Love.[2]

But, worse than that, the source of the tea is in danger of being cut off; China is not what it was, 'the last true Mandarin's strangled'; similarly, 'Love also is departed hence', the Love (that is to say) of the land of romance, of the exquisite bouquet; the modern world is upon us.[3]

The three limbs of the argument are not perhaps perfectly articulated; but they make clear Falk's conviction that what any tepid soul may baptise with the fiery words of Romantic love need not be anything of the sort, that it acquires its brand in (to say the least of it) an extremely odd fashion, and that the Romantic love itself, in which all copulatives, as Touchstone calls them, lay claim to share, may in fact itself be moribund.

Let us now take up point (iv), the bearings of Kierkegaardian[4]

[1] Miss Jay in Herford's version.

[2] A prosaic echo of this is voiced in Oswald Alving's reminiscences of the *Quartier Latin* in *Ghosts* (IV, 212; Archer, VII, 197).

[3] Camilla Collett herself had suggested (*Fortællinger*, 1861, p. 233 *auct.* Ording F., *Henrik Ibsen's 'Kærlighedens Komedie'* (Kristiania, 1914), p. 15) that the moral atmosphere had changed and that the new world of common sense affected sentiments and emotions.

[4] When *Love's Comedy* appeared, Søren Aabye Kierkegaard (1813–55), the Danish philosopher, was an object of the liveliest interest throughout the North, both because of his personality and because of his doctrines. For a further discussion of the relation of his ideas and Ibsen's see the chapter on *Brand* below and my study, *Ibsen: The Intellectual Background* (Cambridge, 1946), p. 79.

doctrine. A difficulty arises at the outset which cannot just be brushed aside. Ibsen indignantly scouted[1] all close acquaintance with Kierkegaard, and an author's disclaimer of such a kind demands respectful attention. But, first, Ibsen habitually minimised resemblances between himself and others; secondly, without any direct borrowing from Kierkegaard, he may have been affected by ideas that had originated with the Danish moralist, but which had been put into more general circulation by others with whom he was in more direct contact;[2] and, thirdly, he admitted[3] that, as regards moral content, *Love's Comedy* stands close to *Brand*, his next work but one, in which it is quite impossible to ignore important Kierkegaardian elements. Even if *la recherche de la paternité est interdite*,[4] it is lawful to point out considerable identity between ideas promulgated by Kierkegaard[5] and ideas to be found in *Love's Comedy*. Some is of no great moment;[6] but some affects the inner structure of the whole play.

The doctrine of Kierkegaard which has the most obvious bearing on the present argument is one of his best known: the sharpest of distinctions which he drew between what he designated the aesthetic, the ethical and the religious 'stadium' in human development. According to his psychology and ethics, the aesthete, the moralist or moral man and the devotee answer to radically different principles, they view the world and their own place in it from incompatible points of view, and the conduct of each is amenable only to his own laws.[7]

It is of paramount importance to grasp that Falk belongs to the first of these 'stadia', that he is an aesthete within the meaning of

---

[1] *Breve*, 1 (København, 1904), p. 149.

[2] Ording (*op. cit.* p. 59 n.) conjectures that Ibsen had read Nielsen's *Paa Kierkegaard'ske 'Stadier'*. It is impossible that the circle revolving about Botten Hansen, to which Ibsen belonged, should not have debated Kierkegaard's notions.

[3] *Breve*, 1 (København, 1904), p. 254.

[4] Bishop Christen Møller observes that 'too great to be called a disciple...what Kierkegaard is in the ethico-religious, Ibsen is in the ethico-aesthetic domain' (*Henrik Ibsen som Skald for Nordens Folk* (1900), p. 4).

[5] Bull, F., in the Introduction to the Centenary Edition (p. 131) calls *Love's Comedy* 'the most Kierkegaardian of all Ibsen's works'.

[6] E.g. the distinction which Falk makes between two kinds of memory ('erindre' and 'huske') (1, 362). It is Samuel Butler's paradox that the things that are truly remembered are things that are forgotten.

[7] There is nothing of this in *The Sheriff's Daughters*.

those distinctions and that he remains so with the fixity which I believe Kierkegaard to have considered almost inescapable. He begins by introducing himself among 'us poets'[1]—and the end sees him striding off into the hills[2] as the tenor of a students' glee-party. It is in complete accord with the standards of the aesthete at his most blatant that he proposes Svanhild for his penny-whistle. When, in his fastidious indignation at the scenes and sentiments to which his friend Lind's betrothal and the arrival of the Straamand[3] family have given rise, he assumes a novel behaviour impressive even to Svanhild, that represents a change of front rather than a change of heart. He certainly makes a holocaust of his manuscripts, he certainly contemplates a life of action, but the terms in which he conceives it are illuminating: 'my poems', he says,[4] 'shall be "lived"'; his actions (that is to say) are to be 'poems', amenable in the first place to aesthetic valuation— just as, Hedda Gabler was later to insist, Løvborg's suicide should be 'beautiful'. Put another way, Falk intends to fight the battle of life, not for the good that shall result from it, but *for the fun of the thing*, a motive that would never occur to the moral man according to the Kierkegaardian discrimination. That he really has nothing in common with such an one is shown by his naïve application to Guldstad[5] to give him a 'mission'; he just can't think of such a thing for himself.

A clear understanding of this bottom to Falk's character simplifies the consideration of his attitude towards marriage in general and, reciprocally, of Svanhild's attitude towards marriage with him in particular. Marriage, Kierkegaard holds, is nothing for the aesthete; for him the flirtation, the *liaison*, the life of Don Juan;[6] since in heaven there is neither marrying nor

---

[1] I, 280; Archer-Herford, I, 298.

[2] It is just possible that there is a special significance in this, which would approximate *Love's Comedy* to Ibsen's poem 'On the Moors' ('Paa Vidderne', 1859), in which a man becomes conscious of being an out-and-out aesthete (so that he enjoys even the spectacle of his mother's cottage going up in flames) on taking a prolonged holiday on the moors.

[3] Strawman in Herford's version.

[4] 'Mit digt skal lives.' The English translation (Archer-Herford, I, 405): 'My verse shall live in forest and in field', rather blunts the point.

[5] I, 307; Archer-Herford, I, 354.

[6] One of the works in which he expounded his views in this domain is entitled *A Seducer's Diary*. Falk, it may be remembered, insinuates (I, 285; Archer-Herford,

giving in marriage, that institution clearly belongs altogether to the 'ethical stadium'. The best representative of the 'moral stadium' is Guldstad, the man who does his duty naturally and has all his heart in his duty. If you want a lover, the situation confronts Svanhild, take the aesthetic Falk; if you want a husband, take the moral man Guldstad. So long as the position remains like that, the odds as between them are nearly equal, with something just slightly tipping the balance in Falk's favour, to which we shall shortly revert. But, when it appears that the choice is (so to speak) between a *temporary* lover and a *permanent* husband, a woman of sense and character like Svanhild does not hesitate: the intensest glory of the blossom has been hers; in autumn she asks for a snug fireside and not a faded muslin frock beneath the unleafed apple-trees.[1] Ording well observes[2] that such a 'capitulation of the ideal before life and reality is one of the guiding thoughts in Ibsen's writings',[3] and what the protracted association of a loving woman with a complete aesthete might issue in is shown in *When We Dead Awaken*.[4]

(The antithesis between spring and autumn and Falk's unequivocal belief in *Carpe Diem* are two themes very emphatically enunciated in the song with which he opens the play:

> Sun-glad day in garden shady
> Was but made for thy delight:
> What though promises of May-day
> Be annulled by Autumn's blight?

1, 308) that when he was still a hopeful poet Straamand took his Maren to live with him, unmarried; all the 'marrying type' scout this notion with great indignation.

[1] The scene of Svanhild's choice between her suitors is strikingly paralleled in the last act of Bernard Shaw's *Candida*, when the heroine again stands between a moral man and an aesthete; kindly but firmly Candida dismisses Marchbanks with the comfort that will appeal to an aesthete alone, and his imagination at once kindles at it. There is a similar triangular scene at the end of *The Lady from the Sea*.

[2] Ording, F., *Henrik Ibsen. 'Kærlighedens Komedie'* (Kristiania, 1914), p. 59.

[3] Feilitzen, a severe judge, of whom Ibsen approved, opines, however, that both Svanhild and Anna are guilty of unchastity, at the same time strangling 'the loftiest possibilities of life in woman' (*Ibsen och Äktenskapsfrågan*, Stockholm, 1882, p. 16); and by ingenious sophistry Schack, A. (*Om Udviklingsgangen i Henrik Ibsens Digtning*, Kjøbenhavn, 1896, p. 29) virtually accuses poor Svanhild of bigamy and perjury, but the ambiguities which he allows himself over the verb *elske* (= to love) do not hold water.

[4] This point is made by Løken, H., *Ibsen og Kjærligheten* (1923), p. 52, who holds that *Love's Comedy* is a comedy precisely because Svanhild slips from Falk's clutches in time.

Apple-blossom white and splendid
Drapes thee in its glowing tent,—
Let it, then, when day is ended,
Strew the closes storm-besprent.

Wherefore seek the harvest's guerdon
While the tree is yet in bloom?...[1]

and Svanhild's last speech in the play may be recalled as
echoing the same:

SVANHILD

*Looks after him a moment, then says, softly but firmly*:

Now over is my life, by lea and lawn,
The leaves are falling;—now the world may take me.[2])

The little matter just mentioned as temporarily tipping the
balance slightly in favour of Falk is one again linked with
Kierkegaardian ideas. It is Svanhild's conception of herself as
a valkyrie. We have seen how she rejected this office when it
was about to be forced upon her in very crude terms; it is,
however, one thing to have the mission of valkyrie imposed,
another to undertake it voluntarily; further, it is one thing to
act as valkyrie to a minor poet (there is nothing to suggest that
Falk is anything better in that way), another to a reformer and
public character (as Falk in Act II proposes to make himself).
Svanhild is perfectly prepared to fulfil the latter sort of function,
only to have it speedily dawn upon her mind, not only that Falk
remains the stone-throwing, pipe-playing aesthete he has been
all along, but that by the transformation wrought in him
between the first and the second act she *has* performed, *has*
fulfilled her valkyrie's mission; she has roused the best in him.
She has filled his 'soul with song and sun',[3] but she does not feel,
she never has felt, that it was her task to darn his socks and
suckle his babes—an occupation he expressly stigmatises[4] as

---

[1] I, 275; Archer-Herford, I, 287.
[2] Archer-Herford, I, 462:
> 'Nu er jeg færdig med mit friluftsliv;
> nu falder løvet;—lad nu verden få mig.' (I, 363.)
[3]
> 'Nu har jeg fyldt din sjæl med lys og digt!
> Flyv frit! Nu har du dig til sejer svunget,—
> nu har din Svanhild svanesangen sunget!'
> (I, 358; Archer-Herford, I, 451.)
[4] I, 327; Archer-Herford, I, 395.

aesthetically revolting. So far as Falk is concerned, she has done what on one occasion Kierkegaard declared[1] to be 'the highest a woman can do for a man...to appear to his sight at the right moment and then instantly to leave him'. We may say that, in the middle of the third act, Svanhild finds her occupation gone; the mission she contemplated has been concluded; she is free to follow the ordinary concerns of life.[2]

We have not quite finished with Kierkegaard. It is permissible to pass by significant trifles like the importance which broken engagements assumed both in his own life and in his imaginative writings,[3] but there remains one major matter calling for more extended mention. If Kierkegaard sharply distinguished between the aesthetic, the ethical and the religious, he equally insisted on their order of merit. To him, the religious 'stadium', preoccupied with holiness, was as superior to the ethical stadium, preoccupied with goodness or social beneficence, as the ethical was to the aesthetic, which recks of nought but the pleasurable. Kierkegaard caused great scandal during his last years by a fierce onslaught on the metropolitan of Denmark, Bishop Mynster, who had just died; the gravamen of his charge was precisely that he was a good man, whereas he ought to have been a holy one.

Now this gradation (which of course Kierkegaard is not alone in making) always perturbed Ibsen, once he had begun to speculate on such matters; indeed it may be argued that his perturbation lies at the root of his tragic power. He knew a dramatist, like himself, to be an artist and as such living, of course, on the aesthetic plane; was he therefore condemned to remain an inferior kind of human being? He does not seem to

---

[1] *Auct.* Ording, *op. cit.* p. 60.

[2] The strongest argument for thinking that the end of the play is not what it should be for Svanhild lies in her name. It will be remembered that the legendary Svanhild was trampled to death by horses and a parallelism would imply that Ibsen's heroine is fatally injured too. I admit the difficulty, and suggest that perhaps the prose play of *Svanhild* had a gloomier tinge which on further consideration Ibsen thought unjustifiable.

[3] 'In the two works of Kierkegaard', says Bing (*op. cit.* p. 116), 'which handle the relations between man and woman—*Either—Or* and *Stages on Life's Road*—the main story comprises the account of a betrothal which is broken for the sake of love, so that it shall be raised to the power of the highest passion (*Either—Or*) or of religion (*Stages*).'

have made up his mind on the point until Georg Brandes set it at rest by showing a way of reconciling the artistic with the social or ethical.[1] Brandes's formula, 'That literature is a live thing is shown by its raising problems for discussion', made the creation of a live work of art a social and ethical act. Before Ibsen assimilated this doctrine in the middle 1870's, he had usually felt constrained to subordinate the aesthetic to the ethical as Kierkegaard had done. The fact has a bearing on the dialogues at the beginning of the third act of *Love's Comedy*, when first the worthy Straamand and then the worthy Styver (reinforced by Frøken Skjære's singing and playing within) put their point of view to Falk. They are awkward; they are, if you like, Philistine; but they are meant to be; they prepare also the way for Guldstad, who (as perhaps his name indicates)[2] has in him all their gold without all the thick dross that hides and debases it in them.

## V

These pages have latterly been concerned for the most part with what may be called the positive content of the play. But it is not that which first and most insistently interests the reader or spectator of *Love's Comedy*. He is arrested and entertained before all else by the *negative* content, by the criticism and the satire of it, with which the brilliance of the dialogue and the crackle of the versification so perfectly accord. That it is satirical, Brandes remarked,[3] is the one thing in *Love's Comedy* on which all agree.

[1] Of Ibsen's personal approaches to the 'religious stadium' we know nothing; it may be conjectured that he considered it, if it existed at all, as definitely beyond him. Some speculations in connection therewith are raised by the chief character of *Brand*. A great expert on Kierkegaard-lore, H. Beyer, believes Falk to have ascended to the religious stadium before the end of *Love's Comedy* (*Søren Kierkegaard og Norge*, p. 133); I cannot follow him.

[2] Most of the characters in *Love's Comedy* have surnames deliberately indicative of their natures: the inflated nonentity Straamand (Straw-Man), the meaningless chatterer Frk. Skjære (Magpie), the light-weight flyer Falk (Falcon), etc., Guldstad means Goldtown, implying excellence and *bourgeois* qualities. Straamand has sometimes been taken for a caricature of the worthy Bishop Riddervold, a very eminent Minister of Ecclesiastical Affairs. I do not think that any other personalities have been detected in the play, unless sly digs at Munch and Vinje (1, 283 and 345; Archer-Herford, 1, 304 and 428) be reckoned such.

[3] *Cit.* Schack, A., *Om Udviklingsgangen i Henrik Ibsens Digtning* (Kjøbenhavn, 1896), p. 30.

In fact, the title may in itself be satirical. The 'Farce of Love' would scarcely be even an ambiguous name for a play—and 'Love's Comedy' is just possibly an analogue.

The nature, the aim and the implication of the satire have, however, been very variously interpreted. The disgruntled cleric Schack, who raked the sequence of Ibsen's masterpieces with steady volleys of moral objection, put his finger on the root of the difficulty when he complained[1] that the satirical lash is wielded by so dubious a person as Falk, 'an incurable declaimer and phrase-monger'. Falk *is* the mouthpiece of the satire; he may not be too harshly judged by Feilitzen when he calls him[2] 'nothing but a harum-scarum rascal, even if an intelligent and idealistic rascal'; and, as has just been pointed out, Ibsen did relegate him to a lower 'stadium' than the people whom he criticised. That does not, however, necessarily invalidate his criticism. Thersites has some very pertinent things to say in *Troilus and Cressida*, things with which we may be sure that Shakespeare agreed; we need not on that account believe that Thersites everywhere speaks the last word, let alone identify Thersites with Shakespeare. It is much the same with Falk and Ibsen.

Against what, now, are Falk's satirical shafts directed? They are aimed at the customs of courtship and the conventional view of the married state obtaining in the better[3] middle-class society of Norway and at a more general attitude of mind underlying them; the shafts are sharp, they are well aimed, and they strike home.[4]

It is unnecessary to expatiate at length on the apparition of Straamand, once wit and poet, now greasy priest and M.P., with his pregnant wife and eight little girls (four more at home), on the pedantic civil servant Styver, on the mummified virgin Frøken Skjære, on Fru Halm, who has so successfully managed her business of running a boarding-house as to approximate it to

[1] Schack, *ut supra*, p. 21.

[2] *Ibsen och Äktenskapsfrågan* (Stockholm, 1882), p. 25.

[3] It is that: the stage direction at the head of Act II declares: 'Well dressed ladies and gentlemen are drinking coffee on the verandah'. Fru Halm's *pension* is on a grand scale; she has at least one man-servant and a *clientèle* comprising the flower of Norway's undergraduates.

[4] 'La Comédie de l'Amour était la peinture indulgente et spirituellement philosophique de la situation singulière à laquelle une société maladroite condamne la passion' (Bigeon, M., *Les Révoltés Scandinaves*, 1894, p. 267).

that of a procuress. Such are familiar and perennially amusing figures of light comedy, and Ibsen makes the most of them. What adds the barb of satire to the fun, what is intellectually interesting, is the circumstance that these people and the attitudes they take up are not necessarily to be looked on as comic or contemptible in themselves, in every light, as the duologues between Straamand and Falk and between Styver and Falk at the beginning of Act III are there to warn us; Ibsen does not insinuate—and not even the intelligent and idealistic Falk dares say—that married folk, even married parsons, should have no families, that there should be no formalities of betrothal and wedding, that it is wrong for persons who have plighted their troth to one another to remain faithful to it. No; these persons bare themselves to the satirist's shafts because their professions do not square with their behaviour, because they, all of them, commit a blunder just as egregious as and much more diverting than Falk's, but the *opposite* blunder. Whereas he, the aesthete, in courting Svanhild, is (part of the time at least) contemplating something that belongs to Kierkegaard's ethical stadium and for which he is congenitally unfit—entering upon the interminable obligations of marriage—*they* invest the solid and often homely realities of engagement and family life with the 'aesthetic' flummery of romanticism. The urge to propagate and set up house, to have a comfortable home and a circle of friends, the wish to be quit of dependent, marriageable daughters, the instinct to stick to a mate once secured, dictated by physical and economic needs, they are always treated and mentioned by them as things in their nature both holy and beautiful, and everything which might indicate that they are not so and anyone who points out, for instance, that advancing years make even a lover fat and a mistress ugly, that the breeding of infants encourages squalor, that to be settled in life is detrimental to the wits, to the charm and to the emotional sensibility of man and woman, is rounded upon for mere indecent blasphemy. On the one side there is the attitude embodied in Frøken Skjære with her flat declarations not only that love knows no gradations or shades, but also of the palpable absurdity that

There is no *Want* where Love's the guiding star[1]

[1] I, 286; Archer-Herford, I, 309.

—as if a married couple had never starved to death in a garret. On the other side stands Falk's belief that, with its etiquette and regimentation, society has succeeded, so to speak, in codifying love away,[1] at any rate away from all the relations which it chooses to acknowledge. Says he:

> Love is with us a science and an art;
> It long since ceased to animate the heart.
> Love is with us a trade, a special line
> Of business, with its union, code and sign;
> It is a guild of married folks and plighted
> Past-masters with apprentices united.[2]

Falk is stung to his revolt by the incarnation of this antinomy, the spectacle of Straamand, his draggle-tail family, on whom Want can be no infrequent visitor, his unctuous complacency and complete intellectual and emotional nullity, when he contrasts it with the report of what Straamand once had been, namely, the Falk of his generation; the old Straamand is now stone dead—the corpse stinks, Falk gives plainly to understand;[3] yet all except himself unite in Hosannas at its everlasting vitality, the conspiracy being made no more excusable for being animated by genuine self-deception.

Up to this point, the aspects of betrothal[4] and marriage on which the criticism of *Love's Comedy* fastens are fairly harmless. But in one direction Ibsen goes farther. Though Fru Halm's Anna seems a nice enough young person, with the makings of a good wife and mother, Lind's engagement to her raises a storm

---

[1] Note that the representative of law and rule, Styver, congratulates himself (I, 277; Archer-Herford, I, 291) on being *officially* engaged, something more, he knows, than being in love; his is the type of mind that automatically puts a Companion of Honour above a man of honour.

[2]        'Hos os er kærligheden snart en videnskab;
         forlængst den hørte op at være lidenskab.
         Hos os er kærligheden som et fag;
         det har sit faste laug, sit eget flag;
         den er en stand af kærester og ægtemænd....'

                                        (I, 329; Archer-Herford, I, 398.)

This original, it will be noted, does not actually say anything about love being an *art*.

[3] I, 347; Archer-Herford, I, 430.

[4] The humours of betrothal had been given full scope in Heiberg's comedy, *De Uadskillige*, and the antics of engaged couples had been repellent enough to break a match in Kierkegàard's *Forførerens Dagbog*.

in a teacup; it is, however, a real storm. Lind, the mild, yet earnest student of divinity, urgently desires to administer spiritual consolations to emigrants and, naturally, wants his wife to accompany him into the Lord's vineyard. But the life of a missionary and a missionary's wife is dangerous and unconventional; friends and aunts are at once mobilized against the project, and, in the warmth of recently crowned affection for his bride, Lind consents, instead, to take a post as an assistant-master in a girls' academy.

The immediate clipping of the wings of enterprise by matrimony is not merely unheroic, sad and, perhaps, slightly comic; it can also amount to a crime. For Ibsen was certain (and the certainty complicated his own life by that self-debate on the real value of art and the aesthete's life to which reference was made above) that every man or woman has a sense of vocation, a call (Norwegian *kald*) to some occupation or undertaking, and that under penalty of spiritual death, he or she must follow the call—at whatever sacrifice (Norwegian *offer*). This dual point is driven home in that *qui-pro-quo* (as the French stage technicality has it), where Falk and Straamand hold forth about the two Norwegian words in question:[1] the former understands by *kald* and *offer* what Ibsen meant by them, namely a personal sense of mission or function in life and a willingness to surrender everything else to its demands, while the portly cleric cannot think but that they designate respectively the 'call' which a church-council might sound in the ear of a candidate for ecclesiastical preferment and the 'offerings' at Easter, Pentecost and Christmas with which the faithful substantiate their call. In his use of the terms, Straamand incurs the guilt that Ibsen was so plentifully castigating in the play, giving vague, high-sounding names to what, however necessary, is purely utilitarian.

## VI

Owing to the cleverness of its verse and the grotesquerie of some of the personages—the coincidence that the entire Straamand progeny should be female, for instance, or Styver's inability to express himself except in the style of the chancery—

---

[1] i, 313; Archer-Herford, i, 366.

the satirical tone rings clearer perhaps through *Love's Comedy* than through any other of Ibsen's plays—though there is the delicious, artificial figure of the *norsk-norsk* champion Paulsen in the early *St John's Eve* to bear in mind, who has 'gone all folkly' and shows it not only by wearing a dirk on his thigh, but by his heroic gesture of defiance in spelling nouns without capital letters.

Satire implying humour or wit (or both), one should turn for examples of it rather to an author's comedies than to dramas or tragedies. After his nonage, Ibsen wrote at any rate two plays allowed by general consent to rank as comedies: they are *The League of Youth* (*De Unges Forbund*, 1869) and *An Enemy of the People* (*En Folkefiende*, 1882). The two disclose certain striking resemblances, the plainest being their bold trenching on the domain of politics, the contemporary politics of Norway. A further point at which *The League of Youth* and *An Enemy of the People* approximate and which, moreover, *Love's Comedy* has in common with them is the volubility of the chief character. But here the parallel must not be drawn too far. It is commonly assumed, indeed, that Dr Thomas Stockmann, Public Enemy Number One,[1] because he has his windows broken and his livelihood taken from him, should be looked on as a completely admirable martyr in the causes of individualism and professional integrity. That is going too far. He is a figure of fun; and traits in his character were copied by Ibsen from his great contemporary Bjørnstjerne Bjørnson, of whom he by no means wholly approved, and from the novelist Jonas Lie,[2] a worthy man indeed, but a debater as confused as he was excited and sincere. Nevertheless, Ibsen's satire in *An Enemy of the People* is not mainly centred on Dr Stockmann, as that of *The League of Youth* is on Stensgaard, and, according to one possible view, that of *Love's Comedy* on its protagonist Falk.

Even if Dr Stockmann, unlike Stensgaard and perhaps Falk, is not the chief butt of the play in which he appears, the general considerations suggested by all three figures stress

---

[1] That would be the equivalent of 'Folkefiende' in the English jargon of to-day, rather than 'Enemy of the People'.

[2] The same who was proprietor and editor of *Illustreret Nyhedsblad*, when it printed *Love's Comedy*, and who paid Kr. 400 for the copyright.

a definite and vital resemblance. In *Love's Comedy*, in *The League of Youth* and in *An Enemy of the People*, whoever may be the main target of criticism, Ibsen directs the point of his attack at the discrepancy between word and deed, at slogans, catch-phrases, pet notions and loud-mouthed professions which falsify the reality supposedly represented by them. About this aspect of *Love's Comedy* enough should have been said. The League of Youth is ostensibly to sweep away the stuffiness and jobbery of 'the old gang', but it is actually called into existence to provide an adventurer with a seat in parliament and a rich wife; in *An Enemy of the People* the 'compact Liberal majority' repress disinterested investigation and free speech, while actively conniving at the ill-health of that community whose good is ever on their lips, in so transparently hypocritical a manner as to prove comic as well as sinister.[1]

Thus it comes that Ibsen's satire is so largely directed against those who live by their powers of expression[2]—politicians like Peter Stockmann and the gross of *The League of Youth*, lawyers like Stensgaard, newspaper-men like Billing and Hovstad of *An Enemy of the People* and Mortensgaard of *Rosmersholm*, clergy-men like Pastor Manders of *Ghosts* and Molvik of *The Wild Duck*, poets like Falk,[3] schoolmasters like Rørlund of *The Pillars of Society* and Arnholm of *The Lady from the Sea*, even a chancery-stylist like Styver. The animus moreover which he exhibited against the Liberal party, with whose principles, after all, he was usually in much greater accord than with those of the Conservatives whom Peter Stockmann represents, was due to his believing the Liberals to be *par excellence* the party of gas-bags. As soon as Johan Sverdrup's party stopped carping in opposition and, grasping the reins of government in Norway,[4] showed that they could exercise authority, he toned down his fleers at them.[5]

[1] *Peer Gynt* unrolls too vast a canvas to describe merely in a footnote to another work, but it may here be observed that its hero is another great *Maulheld* or 'jaw-hero' (as the countrymen of Hitler call such), and that the way, so to put it, in which his 'jaw' messes up his life and character furnishes an essential theme.

[2] Ibsen did so himself: irony at his own expense is by no means to be ruled out.

[3] No doubt a little salutary self-chastisement was therewith intended.

[4] In 1884.

[5] Of course Mortensgaard's 'limited liability' radicalism in *Rosmersholm* (1886), for which Sverdrup's government afforded parallels, does not escape scatheless; the advocate of bold measures is as timid as the 'gentlemen's party' is caddish.

## VII

Humour is about the last attribute with which general fame would endow our author.[1] But the common view of Ibsen as a 'gloomy sort of ghoul, bent on groping for horrors by night, and blinking like a stupid old owl when the warm sunlight of the best of life dances into his wrinkled eyes', which *The Gentlewoman* advanced,[2] is altogether beside the mark. *Love's Comedy* fits in uncommonly ill with such a definition. By itself, that piece should dispel any notion that if Ibsen ever produced comic effects it was by inadvertence or incompetence. Many such effects in that play belong of course to the stock-in-trade of light comedy: the cleric whose paunch and large family (possibly, a red nose too) proclaim his carnal proclivities;[3] the young things' aunts, whose unanimity of conventional utterance possesses the mechanical quality of a chorus; the civil servant who cannot speak except in terms of his mystery (and who goes about in the futile endeavour to renew the promissory note so ubiquitous in mid-nineteenth-century literature[4]); the *qui-pro-quo* or the protracted misunderstanding through which at one time Falk thinks Lind has snapped away his Svanhild and at another Lind believes Guldstad to be after his Anna, as well as the verbal confusions concerning *offer* and *kald* already alluded to. But even these hack devices (except perhaps the business of Styver's promissory note) are treated freshly, as things really seen by the author in a live setting, and are given a crispness and variety by the wit of the dialogue and an ingenuity in rhyming which are altogether Ibsen's own. A French critic has even accorded the supreme praise of attributing 'Latin grace' to them.[5]

[1] Saintsbury, G., *The Later Nineteenth Century* (Edinburgh, 1907), p. 321, speaks of his constant 'demand that such a thing as humour shall be banished from his world'.

[2] *Auct.* Shaw, G. B., *Quintessence of Ibsenism* (3rd ed., London, 1922), p. 89.

[3] On the one hand it may be observed that the anomaly would not be so striking in Norway as in some countries, as the Lutheran is the least 'other-worldly' type of Christianity; on the other hand Herford (*Fortnightly Review*, February 1900, p. 193) is probably right in asserting that this was the first time a clergyman had been profaned by the Norwegian boards and the effect of his appearance on them would be extremely startling.

[4] Cf. *Plain or Ringlets?*, *Père Goriot*, *Framley Parsonage*, etc.

[5] Bigeon, M., *Les Révoltés Scandinaves* (1894), p. 267.

In private life, Ibsen possessed a genuine sense of humour. Holberg, the 'Molière of the North', was his favourite author. One who met him about 1880 reports[1] that he liked little jokes, even coarse jokes, and regretted that the latter were inadmissible in literature. He himself certainly neither made capital of his sense of humour nor gave rein to it. Report has it[2] that as a child he was sometimes, in the literal sense, convulsed with laughter, his body heaving and shaking while no sound burst from his lips—and a humour, of course, of which the manifestations are rigorously suppressed may come near to being no humour at all. Again, Ibsen's humour undoubtedly had in general a saturnine quality which, to the tender-hearted, just as effectively nullifies it; he used, it is said, to divert himself with the imagined predicament of a fish that had incurred hydrophobia, and the joke is made no more palatable to some when he likened man, with his passion for ideals, to such a fish. His humour may be thought of as lightning against an angry sky, rather than the sunny, smiling champaign of a Sterne.

Exactly how much humour may be imputed to Ibsen, since it is as little blatant as may be, will depend largely on the interpretation of the plays as well as on the observer's own fondness for the sardonic and ironical. *The Lady from the Sea* may be taken as an illustration of this. To some it is as tragic as *Hedda Gabler*. But according to another explanation, it is a genuine comedy: a lady is radically cured of some half-crazy notions, to which debased romantic ideas have attached a certain reverence, and through that cure a tippling husband and two neglected daughters are saved from going utterly to the bad; the cure is effected partly by moral prescription (by bestowing on an irresponsible, but not otherwise worthless, person responsibility with freedom to act), partly, too, by a disillusionment, which has a definitely comic aspect: a Stranger, who had appeared to a half-grown girl like some monstrous merman, with nameless crimes, temptations and fascination about his personality, magnified in her imagination a thousand times by the intervening years of undistracted day-dreaming, makes his appearance at last as a participant in a Cook's Tour to the

---

[1] Grønwald, M., *Fra Ulrikken til Alperne* (1925), p. 145.
[2] *Auct.* Koht, H., *Henrik Ibsen*, 1 (Oslo, 1928), p. 24.

Midnight Sun, sporting red bushy whiskers, a tam-o'-shanter on his pate and a hold-all attached to his person. The more obviously neglected of the two daughters, moreover, is endowed with a sardonic humour akin to her creator's: a pure aesthete, she lives, like any disciple of Walter Pater, in order to get as many pulsations as possible into her given time and to this end she finds a peculiar fascination in leading on the young sculptor Lyngstrand; she tempts him to expatiate on his callow ambitions, knowing them to be chimerical, since phthisis will have laid him in the grave long before he has any chance of realising them. Even if, in her sister's words, she is dismissed as 'really a horrid child', that does not dispose of Lyngstrand's fatuity, though individual taste will vary in the lengths to which it will go with his sardonic observer in deriving entertainment from it.[1]

It remains true, of course, that Ibsen's serious plays have no deliberately planned 'comic relief' and that, whatever their comic implications, the situations themselves are rarely comic and, when comic, only mildly so. The momentary misunderstanding of Lona Hessel (in *Pillars of Society*), that the respectable sewing party into which, behind drawn blinds, she has intruded, is a bevy of repentant Magdalenes, may be thought typical, or the joy of poor old Foldal (*John Gabriel Borkman*) at his daughter's luck, when he has been all but run down by the sleigh in which she is driving as one of an extremely dubious *partie à trois*. The three courtships of Lawyer Stensgaard with all the shifts and misunderstandings to which their simultaneity gives rise show that Ibsen was capable of planning this sort of thing on a large scale—and *The League of Youth*, which is built up exclusively on broadish satire and complicated dramatic intrigue; has for nearly eighty years been a 'box-office draw' in the North, much as *The Private Secretary* in England.

Of comic characters, however, Ibsen commands a greater plenitude than of comic situations, though their number rather notably declines at the end of his career, after *The Lady from the*

[1] Again, some, seduced by the beauty of Grieg's music, have seen in *Peer Gynt* a kind of second *Faust*, set in hyperborean mists and uncouthness, with a fevered Saharan nightmare taking the place of the Hellenic interlude; but perhaps it is they, with Anitra and Begriffenfeldt and The Lean One before them, who lack a sense of humour and not the author.

*Sea*, so that *The Master Builder*[1] and *When We Dead Awaken* contain none; *John Gabriel Borkman* has only the ghost of a pathetic smile evoked by poor Vilhelm Foldal, and *Little Eyolf* the grotesque and sinister Rat Wife, who can scarcely have been intended to raise even the ghost of a smile. Before these—even as late as *Hedda Gabler*, with the footling scholar Tesman—Ibsen provides sketches for quite a fair-sized gallery of comic character-portrayals. *The Wild Duck* is perhaps richest in them,[2] with the Dickensian Lieutenant Ekdal,[3] mighty hunter of tame rabbits before the Lord, with the 'demoniac' drunkard of a parson, Molvik, and with the incomparable Hjalmar himself, who, while his heart is supposed to be broken, his brain in a whirl and his honour outraged, plaintively gropes about the lunch-table for more butter.[4] Besides these, to name but a few, there is the grandiloquent philosopher of the casual ward, Ulrik Brendel (*Romersholm*); there are the malicious grotesques, Daniel Hejre of *The League of Youth* and Morten Kiil of *An Enemy of the People*, parts well recognised in countries where Ibsen has a place in the theatres' permanent repertory as highly rewarding to the actor; there is Peer Gynt, the Playboy of the Northern World; there is Dr Thomas Stockmann; there is the quite preposterous standard-bearer of the ideal, Hilmar Tønnesen (*Pillars of Society*), whose banner seems to bear the strange device 'Fennimore Cooper'. The proximity of many of these personages to tragedy adds piquancy to their absurdities. The interaction between a potentially comic character[5] and an

[1] Of course there is something grimly comic, not lost on young Brovik and his friends, about the Master Builder himself, who cannot climb his own towers (and breaks his neck trying to do so).

[2] 'I remember', says Bernard Shaw (*Quintessence of Ibsenism*, 3rd ed., London, 1922), 'a performance of *The Wild Duck*, at which the late Clement Scott pointed out triumphantly that the play was so absurd that even the champions of Ibsen could not help laughing at it. It had not occurred to him that Ibsen could laugh like other men.'

[3] Relling, who, I think, must be trusted throughout, declares 'the old lieutenant has been an ass all his days', and the great actor Olaf Paulsen, who so largely secured the success of the piece at Copenhagen, always acted him very broadly, after the style of the chuckle-headed countrymen of Fritz Reuter's novels.

[4] It is to be observed how in all these cases the comic effect is repeatedly obtained by the contrast between profession and conduct.

[5] I can still recall the 'high light' of Eleonora Duse's acting of *Spettri*, on her last visit to London, when she let Helene Alving break into silvery laughter at the 'grande bambino, Pastore Manders'.

incongruous situation is nowhere better exhibited than in the scene in *Ghosts* where the rascally hypocrite Engstrand, by his glib obsequiousness, not merely disarms the Reverend Mr Manders's just indignation against him, but even induces him to serve as patron to the house of ill-fame which he proposes to set up with the extremely double-edged name of 'Chamberlain Alving's Home for Seamen'.

In the above catalogue only one female figured—to be rejected at once—namely the Rat Wife of *Little Eyolf*. Ibsen did not go in much for funny women or for comic situations in which women play an important part, unless we do young Hilde Wangel the honour of ranking her as a woman. No doubt, as with her prototype Aasta Hanstein,[1] there is good fun to be extracted from the appearance and mannerisms of Lona Hessel in *The Pillars of Society*, but the only feminine character a theatrical manager would be moved to 'cast' directly as a comic one is Madam Rundholmen of *The League of Youth*, a much attenuated Mistress Quickly.

## VIII

*Love's Comedy* was not well received. The outstanding young Danish critic of the time, Clemens Petersen, approved of it, because he liked a work of art from which a 'moral' could be drawn for debate, and Ibsen's faithful ally Botten Hansen praised it in *Illustreret Nyhedsblad*, above all for its brilliant (and justified) satire and for its piquant, pithy verse; even he, however, allowed that the tendency of the satire was disputable and that the author lacked ideal faith and conviction, while Petersen was severe on the play's unclearness. The most influential voice in Christiania, that of Professor Monrad, roundly condemned it as untrue, immoral and unpoetic.[2] Though it seems that *Love's*

---

[1] Painter and militant upholder of women's rights (and wrongs) in the Norway of the 1870's.

[2] I have not had the advantage of consulting these critiques in their original form, and my information is based on summaries by Gran, G., *H. Ibsen*, 1 (Kristiania, 1918), p. 153, and Koht, H., *H. Ibsen*, 1 (Oslo, 1928), pp. 237 ff. What Monrad means by 'immoral' is indicated by Ditmar Meidell, who said in the newspaper *Aftenbladet* that Ibsen exhibited love and family-life as the shadow-side of human existence, not to say the root of all misfortune.

*Comedy* was accepted for the Christiania Theatre, to which Ibsen had become loosely attached in the capacity of literary adviser, the production was shelved for ten whole years; no Danish manager touched it until 1898.[1] In spite of capital verse-translations into English and German,[2] it never enjoyed much success abroad.[3] Once produced, however, it gained a permanent footing in the Christiania repertoire and was acted seventy-seven times in the old house before 1899. Laura Gundersen, the great interpreter of Ibsen's early heroines, played Svanhild. For the centenary celebrations in 1928 the play was rather extensively revived.

What would first and most insistently strike an audience about *Love's Comedy*, and which did account for the resentment felt by its earliest readers, was something new in the Norwegian and Danish drama (which, at this period of time, can scarcely be said to have grown apart). The satire of it, both in expression and nature, had so little geniality;[4] there were so few occasions for hearty laughter—or for *any* laughter without disturbing *arrière-pensée*; and the shadows behind the high lights of wit and ridicule involved so much mystery. Satire, of course, there had been abundantly in the theatre which derived from the great Dano-Norwegian master of comedy Ludvig Holberg, satire, too, that had often been brilliant in form (like Wessel's *Love without Stockings*)[5] or else had trenched on everyday life, as in recent plays by Hostrup and Hertz; but it had not cut uncomfortably near the bone.[6]

[1] The dates of production at Christiania Theatre and the Dagmar Theatre, Copenhagen, are 24 November 1873 and 21 May 1898 respectively.

[2] By C. H. Herford (incorporated in vol. 1 of Archer's Collected Translation) and Christian Morgenstern respectively. I have found no record of an English performance. *La Comédie de l'Amour* was presented at the Théâtre de l'Œuvre in Paris on 23 June 1897.

[3] It was presented in H. Molander's Swedish paraphrase *Kärlekens Komedi* at the Swedish Theatre in Helsinki on 28 January 1889.

[4] There is similar mordant satire (in verse too) in Heiberg's 'apocalyptic' comedy, *The Soul after Death* (*Sjælen efter Døden*, 1841), but it was not intended for the stage; on *The Soul after Death* see also p. 57 below; Francis Bull (Introduction to *Kjærlighedens Komedie* in the Centenary Edition of Ibsen's Works, IV, p. 129) notes stylistic resemblances to Hertz's *Cupid's Strokes of Genius* (*Amors Genistreger*).

[5] Wessel, writing in Copenhagen, was, like Holberg, of Norwegian parentage and birth.

[6] In the Preface which he wrote to the second edition Ibsen made the point that his public was quite unused to the exercise of thought required for seeing its own errors.

31

By its satire, disturbing and new-fashioned though it might be, *Love's Comedy* can nevertheless be most easily ranged in the literary tradition. This becomes plainer on comparing *Love's Comedy* with its obvious precursor *St John's Eve*, where fun at the expense of humdrum present-day folk, congeners of Fru Halm and Anna and Lind, is all mixed up with 'elves and fairies and suchlike mummery'. A preposterous juxtaposition of this order, on which Shakespeare had set the seal of his genius in *A Midsummer Night's Dream* and which survives in our Christmas pantomime—with its obligatory fairy-godmother and demon-king as well as its perennial jokes about mothers-in-law and lodgers—had also enjoyed a long and resounding vogue on the continent of Europe, and there likewise been quickly allied to dancing and popular songs. Perhaps the artistically most perfect form of the hybrid[1] was achieved by a Dane, Johan Ludvig Heiberg, in his *vaudevilles*, as he called them.[2] Heiberg had his disciples, Henrik Hertz and Hostrup, who, gradually discarding, as Ibsen did, the fairy element, approximated the *genre* to the middle-class comedy of manners. It is more than probable that Hertz's *Master and Apprentice* (*Mester og Lærling*), which he saw in Copenhagen during its first season (1852), gave Ibsen the impulse to concoct *St John's Eve*, while Heiberg's plays formed a substantial part of the repertory of all Danish and Norwegian acting-troupes and would consequently have repeatedly come to Ibsen's professional notice in Bergen and Christiania.

But although, in the interval between *St John's Eve* and *Love's Comedy*, Ibsen had taken the important step of discarding the supernatural element, he made no attempt at any later date to reproduce the manner of even the latter play, a refusal which it cannot be said that the attitude of the public made difficult for

---

[1] Mozart's *Magic Flute* is one, a variant of the Viennese *Zauberstück*, but must be called a 'sport', whereas Heiberg consistently elaborated his *genre*, which he defended with a formidable array of Hegelian dialect in the treatise *On the Vaudeville* (*Om Vaudevillen*, 1826); his appellation shows that he himself went back to French models.

[2] Heiberg's *The Inseparables* (*De Uadskillige*) had made fun of middle-class courtship. Botten Hansen, already mentioned in this section, had made a partial attempt already to transplant the Heibergian growth to Norwegian soil in *The Fairy Wedding* (*Huldrebrylluppet*, 1851), in which the pedantic character of the lawyer Karlsen foreshadows that of Styver.

him. Before he perfected his medium, fifteen years of varied experiments in dramatic technique still lay before him; yet even in *The League of Youth*, the play which comes nearest to *Love's Comedy* in *milieu*, in range of character and in tone of approach, nothing of the old *vaudeville* tradition remains.

That tradition had by reason of its externalities always a great deal about it suggestive of the 'romantic' in its loosest meaning. A stage-representation of *Love's Comedy*, with its music, the setting in its *jardin anglais* by the sea, the twofold descent of dusk, would confirm the association. At the outset of his career, inveterate enemy as he later showed himself[1] of its more ingrained prepossessions, Ibsen stood under the aegis of that Romantic Revolt which prevailed in the North so powerfully and so long.[2] All his works down to and including *Peer Gynt—Emperor and Galilean* too—furnish unmistakable proof of it. It is not merely a matter of vehicle and the scene-painter's help: in *Love's Comedy*, the exaltation of Falk and Svanhild, the perpetual canvassing of the claims and nature of human love, the internecine feud presented between the ideal and the practical should furnish sufficient proof of this. Even the issue, the separation of the lovers, which they point by the dramatic casting of their rings into the fjord,[3] links it to the 'Entsagungsroman', the novel of renunciation, with which in their day the Rousseau of *La Nouvelle Héloïse* and the Goethe of *Werther* gave so mighty an impulse to the new literature.

---

[1] *Hedda Gabler* shows this most strongly.

[2] Its last great representative in the realm of *belles-lettres* was Frederik Paludan-Müller (1809–75), whose work Ibsen studied and highly admired; it has been remarked how the lines all beginning 'fallit' (I, 352; 'bankrupt', Archer-Herford, I, 441) clearly echo the repeated 'caput' ('smashed') in Canto I of Paludan-Müller's *Dancer* (*Danserinden*, 1833). Kierkegaard's philosophy is another Danish facet of Romanticism.

[3] A similar incident is reported in *The Lady from the Sea*, where it is a clearer reminiscence of the actual occurrence at Bergen, when young Ibsen and a still younger girl, Rikke Holst, plighted their troth (very soon to be broken) by throwing rings into the sea.

# BRAND

## 1866

### I

IMMEDIATELY upon *Love's Comedy* (1862) followed *The Pretenders* (*Kongs-emnerne*, 1863). *Macbeth*-like tragedy though the latter may be, it was conceived during more than a lightening of the gloom which had invested the writing of the comedy, indeed during some of the happiest moments that Ibsen was ever to know. But the clouds quickly gathered again, if possible more lowering than before. Some of the blackest, coming up from the political horizon, will engage a more thorough attention later on; besides these, there was still the lack of regular employment,[1] the failure to achieve recognition and respect, and the steady accumulation of debt. One more dip of Fortune's wheel, and Ibsen would have become a custom-house officer!

In the nick of time, a syndicate of well-wishers on the one hand and the Norwegian state on the other came to the rescue with subscriptions, grants and a pension. But the Ibsen whom these means enabled to leave Norway for Italy in April 1864 was a badly shaken and humiliated man, dreadfully hurt in some of his tenderest susceptibilities. Had not, for one thing, his notions of government employment virtually implied a readiness to commit what in his eyes was the highest of treasons, defection from the individual's *Kald* or mission?

The fact of a suffering bordering on mental illness is perhaps[2] attested by Ibsen's indecision what literary project to undertake next. He carried out some research into the career of Magnus

---

[1] Ibsen's contract as director of the Møllergate Theatre terminated on 1 June 1862. He became aesthetic consultant of the rival house, the Christiania Theatre, on 1 January 1863, but the stipend was small and irregular.

[2] The impression received from Ibsen's papers is that, as a general rule, on completing one play, he immediately set about the meditating and planning of the matter which was worked into the next of the series. Alternative schemes were possibly considered and rejected, but Ibsen's extreme secretiveness about his projects denies us all real evidence of this. It is just good fortune that we have some documents relative to Ibsen's first months in Italy.

Hejnesen, a Norwegio-Faroese pirate of the end of the sixteenth century,[1] with the view of dramatising it; at Genzano, in the summer of 1864, his friend Lorentz Dietrichson interested him in the person of Julian, the 'apostate' emperor, whom eventually he was to make the hero of *Emperor and Galilean* (*Kejser og Galilæer*, 1873).

Simultaneously with these inchoate schemes, Ibsen had begun to ponder over, and was soon to be actively engaged on, the subject of *Brand*. To begin with, however, he treated it 'epically', as continental scholarship has it, in the form (that is to say) of a narrative poem, bearing some resemblance to Paludan-Müller's satirical masterpiece *Adam Homo*[2] and thus, by reflection, to Byron's *Don Juan*. Four cantos, which do not develop story or theme very far, were completed, together with an introductory, more lyrical poem; and the completed third canto was read aloud, evidently a novelty, to Dietrichson in the spring of 1865.

In July 1865 the way to treat dramatically the subject on which he had been engaged for a year burst upon Ibsen in a flash of illumination. He worked then, during his summer retreat at Ariccia, with such vigour, ease and speed at the 'dramatic' version that it was completed in three months, fair-copied[3] in another and, by mid-November, dispatched to Frederik Hegel, the head of the firm of Gyldendal (*Gyldendalske Boghandel*) in Copenhagen, with whom Ibsen had pledged himself to publish his next work. It appeared[4] on 15 March 1866, in a small edition; but so unexpected and great was the demand which it evoked that no less than three further, large editions had to be issued before the end of the calendar year.[5]

---

[1] This remains the only instance on record of Ibsen's taking up a theme which left no apparent trace in his published works or in his papers.

[2] The title is taken after the hero, a Danish burgess. *Adam Homo* was published 1841–8.

[3] This fair copy is lost, but the draft from which, apart from some stage-directions, it was made is now in the Collin collection of manuscripts in the Kongelige Bibliothek, Copenhagen. This draft is not in all places the first draft.

[4] *Brand. Et Dramatisk Digt af Henrik Ibsen* (Kjøbenhavn, 1866).

[5] The fundamental text is that of the first edition; almost all the changes to be found in subsequent editions were made to bring the spelling into conformity with the rules made in 1869.

Soon after Ibsen had read its third canto to Dietrichson, the manuscript of the 'epical' *Brand* seems to have been laid aside. It was long believed by the very few who knew of its existence[1] that the author had destroyed it. But late in Ibsen's lifetime a Danish collector found it in a second-hand dealer's shop in Rome, and in 1907 it was published as *Henrik Ibsens episke Brand*, in a most careful edition, with some interesting facsimiles and an introduction, prepared by the Danish man of letters, Karl Larsen.[2]

It is not to the present purpose to examine the narrative version of *Brand* as such. No more need here be said than that the first canto, a scene between Brand and Einar as boys, has no counterpart in the drama, that cantos II to IV substantially tell the same story as the first act and the beginning of the first scene of the second act, that Gerd appears as a gipsy hussy akin to the wanton dairymaids of *Peer Gynt*, that the hero can be described as much more the parson tinged with pietism than he later became and that the effect of the poem is rather 'tighter', more photographic, more defined as to time and place[3] than the drama.

## II

Ibsen's humour, we observed in the discussion of *Love's Comedy*, fastened and depended upon the discrepancies which he discovered between profession and action. In the forefront of *Brand* he placed a figure about whom there is nothing anomalous of this sort—in and about whom, therefore, there is no humour and whose fate entails nothing of comedy.

[1] Even Fru Ibsen had never heard a line of it, before Karl Larsen read it aloud to her in the spring of 1907, a year after her husband's death.

[2] The MS. on which Karl Larsen worked, the only extant one, is now in the Kongelige Bibliothek, Copenhagen.

[3] Ibsen spent the summer of 1862 investigating folk-lore in the districts from Sogn northwards to the Romsdal and was shocked by the physical and moral squalor which he observed there and to which Eilert Sundt's recent sociological and statistical investigations had drawn general attention. In so far as *Brand* is located at all, Norwegian authorities seem agreed to place it in this neighbourhood, where living is as hard as on the Aran Islands, on a narrow slip of cultivable land between the mountains and a tempestuous ocean, and where deep valleys are sometimes cut out from the sight of the sun for weeks at a time. On Sogne Fjord there is a place called Kong Beles Haug (see next footnote). P. G. La Chesnais claims (*Brand d'Ibsen*, p. 70) that the insistence on the grim aspect of the Norwegian landscape was novel.

The bare theme of *Brand* can be succinctly stated: a man puts impossible moral demands upon others and upon himself and he perishes in consequence. This man, Brand, is a clergyman, whose heroism in rowing out through a tempest to shrive a despairing sinner gains the admiration of an indigent community of crofter-fishermen, so that they invite him to settle among them as their parish-priest. He remains faithful to this call from them, at the cost of his domestic happiness; at his own charges he proceeds to endow the parish with an airy new church in place of the cramped, tumbledown structure that has served since 'King Bele's day'.[1] But, his flock having laid great demands on him, he now proceeds to do the same by them. As men cannot live by bread alone—one of the cardinal principles of his conduct and, presumably, of his teaching[2]—so worship must be in spirit and in truth, not confined to what the rubrics impose in a building of sticks and stones. Brand throws away the keys of his new church and bids the congregated parishioners accompany him to the throne of the heavenly grace out in the open air. Animated by the zeal of a revivalist meeting, they comply, but, as the pilgrimage leads them higher and higher into the mountains, farther and farther away from their cottages and avocations, the spirit evaporates; weary and disappointed, they stone him and drive him from them to continue the journey alone; he wanders on in an unpeopled, rocky waste and is overtaken by an avalanche.

The structure of the 'fable' is thus fairly simple. There is little either of the 'antecedent situation' which Ibsen characteristically favours or of more ordinary dramatic intrigue. Such complications as theme and fable admit come from the women in the play, fitly emphasising the conflict which his 'call' provokes between Brand's public and private duties. In the first place his relations with his mother and his wife are at issue.

[1] King Bele was a monarch in the Old Icelandic *Fridthjof's Saga*; he is mentioned six times in *Brand*; and Svensson, who believes that he was suggested to Ibsen by the Swedish poet, Tegnér, believes also that by means of this figure Ibsen meant to cover *all* the Northern peoples in the purview of the drama ('Brand och den svenska göticismen' in *Edda*, xxx, 1930, p. 356). Since King Bele was a heathen, the old church may in fact be a pre-Christian, pagan fane.

[2] The 'epical' fragment ends with Brand's ascending the pulpit and beginning a sermon on this very text.

Brand comes as no stranger to the community which put in his hands the cure of their souls. His mother lives among them, their wealthiest member (it would seem)—yet no Lady Bountiful to relieve the wants which call for the public assistance officer, a miser, rather, unwilling to relinquish any fraction of her hoard. She is religious however, or, more correctly, superstitious; and a second reason, besides the parishioners' insistence, inducing Brand to accept the benefice of his home-parish is his promise to be with her and give her priestly absolution on her death-bed. But he attaches a condition: to prove the truth of her faith she must give away her whole substance, not haggling about this portion or that, to be retained for eventual private use. This condition she prudently refuses to fulfil either in health or in sickness; and though at the last she sends for her son and confessor, he remains as obdurate as she, and she dies unshriven and uncomforted. (It is her fortune, descending to himself, which Brand applies to the building of the new church.)

The main subsidiary character, however, is Brand's wife, Agnes. She first comes upon the scene as the *fiancée* of his school-friend, the artist Einar. When, some hours after meeting her, Brand calls for volunteers to help steer him through the storm to the dying sinner he has been begged to visit and none of the experienced fisherfolk offers, she comes forward and, Einar failing too, accompanies him alone.[1] Having about her something of the 'valkyrie' Svanhild—though cast in a smaller and softer mould—she elects to stay by his side for the rest of his life, breaks off her engagement to Einar and marries Brand. He and she have a son, who cannot thrive in the poverty of the place and its exclusion from the sun. The medical prognosis is death, unless he is removed to a milder environment. For a while Brand wavers, but one of the parishioners who induced him to accept the incumbency reminds him of the pact between them. He stays. Alf dies. Brand compels Agnes to part with even the last material reminiscence of him to a worthless creature who comes begging for something in which to clothe her bastard; and Agnes dies too.[2]

[1] The scene resembles one in Schiller's *William Tell*, which Ibsen knew.
[2] One may note that a good deal of dramatic variety is imparted to *Brand* by the two other women-characters: Gerd (about whom more will shortly be said) and this Gipsy-Woman of Act IV.

## III

What have been designated the 'complications' of the fable exist, obviously, for the purpose of showing the hero's resolution in sacrificing all to the demands of his (self-imposed) mission. It must be added that Brand's sacrifices cause him great pain; he is no heartless monster; on the contrary, he is devoted not only to his little son and his wife, but also to his unengaging mother,[1] whose supreme welfare (as he sees it) constitutes the sole concern of his dealings with her. The question now arises: what weighs up the excruciating sacrifice of self and others, what intrinsic value attaches to Brand's mission?

To this a conclusive answer cannot be returned; nor is it reasonable to demand it. That a dramatist presents beings and destinies without accurately determining their worth in the sight of God and man is an axiom generally accepted in one form or another. Still, when the dramatist in the course of his aesthetic avocation presents the destiny of a being so utterly intent on right conduct as Brand shows himself, the effect and validity of his principles offer a *prima facie* case for enquiry.

Brand perishes, his mission having manifestly failed; and the failure is all the more abysmal in that the 'line' of the drama is one that steadily goes up and up till the moment of Brand's stoning and abandonment. Since the failure of his life's programme suggests its impracticability and even its objectionableness, it may be as well to begin the enquiry into the 'moral' of the play with the circumstances of his failure and perishing, with an examination (that is to say) of the ultimate catastrophe.[2]

Brand has been forsaken and badly injured by the flying stones of the faithless faithful; nevertheless, he continues on his upward path, his brain occupied with his flock's apostasy and

---

[1] The psychologist will be interested in two points at least (cf. ii, 155; Archer-Herford, iii, 66); old Fru Brand's hardness is attributed to her having been forced to make a loveless marriage with an old man (and he who moralises over *Love's Comedy* has further pabulum in this); and her son received a great shock as a boy on observing unnoticed the impious manner in which his mother dealt with his father's corpse. (Ibsen read in a paper how a purse-proud widow in Guldbrandsdal clothed her husband's dead body in the rags in which he had first come to her farm; Bing, J., *Henrik Ibsens Brand*, Kristiania, n.d., p. 14.)

[2] ii, 265; Archer-Herford, iii, 247.

its implications. The thoughts of a Lutheran clergyman naturally turn to the Christian story:

> Not for us [he meditates] the cup He drank,
> Not for us the thorny wreath
> In His temples drove its teeth,
> Not for us the spear-shaft sank
> In the side whose life was still.
> Not for us the burning thrill
> > Of the nails that clove and tore.[1]

Up to this point, and even to a point about half-a-dozen lines farther on, Brand's long soliloquy proceeds from, or represents, what may be called conscious meditation. Immediately hereupon he lapses, as he realises, into a state of semi-consciousness; and it remains a question of how much in all that follows must be attributed to that state. It is reasonably safe to concede objective reality to Gerd, to her rifle and to what she says, since the discharge of the gun brings down a material avalanche of snow and rock (and the fact, therefore, that she recognises, through the wounds in his temples and hands, a Christ in him is not without significance since, according to the Kierke-gaardian interpretation, they would prove Brand genuinely to be a Christian).

But if Gerd is a reality, Agnes, at this point, is certainly a hallucination, and her Phantom's messages accordingly spring from a part of Brand's own mind. One of the things which the Phantom does is to remind Brand of the dialogue with the physician ('the aged leech') rehearsed earlier in the play;[2] and this fact would seem to constitute a clear finger-post to the enigmatic last words of the play

> Han er *deus caritatis*.
>
> He is the God of Love.[3]

---

[1] II, 268; Archer-Herford, III, 247.     [2] II, 169; Archer-Herford, III, 88.

[3] It is not greatly to the credit of Norwegian scholarship that Ibsen's learned friends heckled him for not knowing 'what every schoolboy knows', namely that the Latin for 'love' is *amor*; Ibsen, who also had 'small Latin and less Greek', very properly retorted that he meant the specific Christian virtue which the English translators have rendered by 'charity'. The Latin tag at the end (which has precedents as far as Marlowe) may be attributable to Goethe's *Faust*; but it may be a way of emphatically linking this end with the passage where the foreign word was used before.

For in that earlier dialogue the doctor had expressly remarked on the deficit in Brand's '*conto caritatis*' (charity account):

BRAND

Beggar or rich,—with all my soul
I *will*; and that one thing's the *whole*.

THE DOCTOR

Yes, in your ledger, truly, Will
Has enough entries and to spare;
But, priest, your *Love*-account is still
A virgin-chapter, blank and bare.[1]

There is good reason, therefore, for believing that the final words, like the words of the Phantom which point to them, are to be accepted, not as a message coming to him from outside, but as something emanating from Brand's own mind.

If this construction is accepted, something is gained, but not perhaps very much. It would, however, dispose of the theory of Lothar,[2] who holds that the last words are the mockery of the Devil (who does not otherwise enter into the scheme of *Brand*—as he does into that of *Peer Gynt*) annihilating, as it were, the whole of Brand's striving and achievement.

The very opposite explanation has more often been proffered, namely that the Voice is that of *deus caritatis* himself.[3]

Whether we take the concluding words for those of God or for a projection of Brand's own (fevered) thoughts, we do not,

[1]
BRAND

'Rig eller tigger;—helt jeg *vil*,—
Og dette ene strækker til!'

DOKTOREN

'Ja, mandeviljens *qvantum satis*
Står bogført som din rigdoms rad;—
Men, prest, din *conto caritatis*
Er bogens hvide jomfrublad!'

(II, 169; Archer-Herford, III, 88.)

[2] 'Die Stimme...*ist die höhnende Stimme des Bösen, des Teufels.* Die Ironie hat das Schlusswort des Gedichtes' (Lothar, R., *Henrik Ibsen*, 2nd edition, 1902, p. 69). Chesnais holds (*Brand d'Ibsen*, p. 238) that the devil speaks through Agnes. The various interpretations of *Brand* are canvassed by Kinck, B. M., 'Dramaet "Brand", Opfatninger og Tolkninger' in *Edda*, xxx (1930), p. 81.

[3] I gather (from Kinck, *ut cit.* p. 85) that at a French presentation of the play, the words were spoken by 'Agnes'; if, by analogy with the Second Part of Goethe's *Faust*, she is, like Gretchen, to be taken as one of the heavenly host, the difference is not very material.

however, thereby solve the problem of the judgement implied in them; for, clearly, they are not intended for a mere statement of fact, but for something more. A tempting interpretation—in effect a variant of Lothar's—is that they imply sheer condemnation: Brand, according to this interpretation, has shown himself completely deficient in *caritas*, he has ignored what is often reckoned the distinguishing characteristic of the Christian God, and the collapse of his mission is the rightful visitation of such blind and criminal neglect; he has failed and God (or his own conscience) tells him it is right that he should have failed. Brand, the conclusion is, has set up for his own and others' service a false god, fashioned in the image of his own proud, harsh spirit, and the true God damns him.[1]

A curious, but again baffling and inconclusive piece of evidence may be admitted at this point. Originally, the drama bore the epigraph: 'So God created Man in his own Image (*Genesis*)'. This epigraph Ibsen struck out of the fair copy. If it had remained and been printed, it would have been unique: for it was not Ibsen's practice, in this way, to quote other authors, however eminent. And aversion from epigraphs, not a sense of their inappropriateness, may have been the sole reason for leaving out the line from *Genesis*. If it is allowed as evidence, it might be used to support the argument that God created Brand[2] in his own image and that Brand is thereby justified. But how about *caritas* in that case? The rejoinder is not altogether fatal. Brand has not completely ignored *caritas* in the sense that he never concerned himself with it. He has, in fact, violently declaimed against that variety of Christian humanitarianism which forgives everything on the plea of Love:

> Never did word so sorely prove
> The smirch of lies, as this word *Love*:
> With devilish craft, where will is frail,
> Men lay *Love* over, as a veil,

[1] An ingenious explanation is that given by Reuth, N. V., in *De Katholieke Gids*, I (1889), p. 453: the Voice is Ibsen's own voice reproaching the Norwegians for allowing him so meagre a pension.

[2] The other construction, that the fickle multitude and not the outstanding individual are God's image, is somewhat invalidated by the circumstance that the proverbial crystallisation of the notion, 'vox populi, vox dei', is put into the mouth of the contemptible Dean (II, 265; Archer-Herford, III, 243) just when a most undivine exhibition has taken place.

And cunningly conceal thereby
That all their life is coquetry.
Whose path's the steep and perilous slope,
*Let him but love,*—and he may shirk it;
If he prefers Sin's easy circuit,
*Let him but love,*—he still may hope;
If God he seeks, but fears the fray,
*Let him but love,*—'tis straight his prey;
If with wide-open eyes he err,
*Let him but love,*—there's safety there![1]

As against such Magdalene morality, the words 'Whom the
Lord loveth, he chasteneth' have been the text which, in considering the attributes of God, has come first into Brand's mind;
the God whom he has worshipped and who inflicts upon him
the supreme mortal chastisement would accordingly not only
be the true God, but at the same time *deus caritatis*, who sees in
him a well-beloved son.

The interpretations so far given in these pages have, however,
all disregarded some most important passages of the last act,
those lying between the apparition of Agnes and the catastrophe
—in other words, the final scene with Gerd. To these, as has
been urged, some objective reality should *prima facie* be conceded, whatever may be thought of the others, and all the more
importance attaches to them for that. I have mentioned the
gipsy girl's quasi-recognition[2] of Brand as Christ ('Thou art
chosen; thou art Lord'), and we shall shortly have something
to say about the falcon she is pursuing. But there is something
of infinitely greater moment for the understanding of the drama
in a third feature, namely, the collapse of Brand, the collapse
of the old, proud, hard Brand, who bursts into tears[3] and then
emerges from the ruin of himself 'radiant, clear, and with an
air of renewed youth' to say:

Through the Law an ice-track led,—
Then broke summer overhead!

[1] Archer-Herford, I, 89. The lines are found in that crucial first scene between
Brand and the doctor.

[2] II, 274; Archer-Herford, III, 259. I say 'quasi-recognition', as I think that
Gerd is to be taken for a heathen.

[3] This is a stage-direction, as are the words in inverted commas immediately
following.

Till to-day I strove alone
To be God's pure tablet-stone;—
From to-day my life shall stream
Lambent, glowing, as a dream.
The ice-fetters break away,
I can weep,—and kneel,—and pray![1]

Brand, in other words, has put on the new man: he recognises
and bows before a God who is nearer akin to the commonly
accepted *deus caritatis* than the bleak object of his previous
veneration,[2] the giver of the Law; with him he intercedes for
forgiveness of what he did with his 'utmost might', and immediately thereupon comes the avalanche with what, I submit,
should not be otherwise interpreted than as absolving and
redeeming words. Grace descends on the earnest devotee who
has erred, but only after he has recognised his error. Brand has
erred, but erred nobly; he has realised and acknowledged his
error; and God forgives him. It might even be maintained that
in killing the redeemed sinner at this point and in thus putting
an end to his earthly torments, the supreme Power, after
declaring it, is proving its mercifulness, its *caritas*.[3]

## IV

We will leave this last scene of *Brand* after a brief consideration
of certain other puzzling features in it, some of which have at
least been touched on: the 'ice-church', the falcon and the
silver bullet that destroys it, Gerd herself. The first two of these

---

[1] It will be noted that in his last moments on earth, Brand's mind comes back
to the business with his mother:

'Blood of children must be spilt
To atone the parent's guilt.'

These words may be looked on as merely winding up neatly a loose end, but they
may imply an acceptance of hereditary guilt (a point on which Kierkegaard's notions
of the tragic had insisted) much more intimate than the recognition of pecuniary
indebtedness to the community, suitably wiped out by the endowment of a church.

[2] We may remember the last words of Brand's mother as reported by the Doctor
(ii, 184; Archer-Herford, iii, 110):

'He
Is no hard dealer, like my son',

a belief that the son immediately stigmatises as 'that lie'.

[3] The argument that Ibsen huddled up his ending with some sentimental scenes
and clap-trap speeches and that no real meaning attaches to them at all is referred
to in the last section of this chapter (p. 68).

do not seem to me to be particularly esoteric. The ice-church, imagined at a still higher altitude than that to which Brand has attained, a physical phenomenon created either by a crevasse in a glacier or by the meeting of two sliding snow-surfaces to form a roof over a narrow gully, is that towards which Brand is climbing the mountain-side; it has some attributes not unlike the strenuous doctrine which he has laboured to realise, in eliminating from worship everything but the stark, the menacing and the sublime qualities of the supreme being. The falcon is actually explained with a directness rare in Ibsen's writings and, perhaps, shockingly bare. It is 'the spirit of compromise' (*akkordens aand*),[1] Brand seems to declare, against which he has been at perpetual feud and which defies all customary methods of destruction, so that a special missile has to be used, as continental sportsmen pretend that a peculiarly elusive quarry could only succumb to a bullet cast of silver:[2] in a similar fashion —perhaps—Brand could not fully achieve his passionately desired mission of doing a work acceptable to God without renouncing the means hitherto deemed the obvious.

Gerd, it may be remembered, was represented in the narrative form of the poem as a luscious young gipsy-wench, and it is permissible to conjecture that, if Ibsen had already conceived some such incident as that of Agnes's parting, at her husband's behest, with her dead baby's cap, it was in order to provide for one of Gerd's misbegotten brats. In the drama she appears as a much more innocent figure; she is introduced in Act I as a girl of fifteen, running along the rocky crest with stones in her apron, endeavouring to kill birds: not merely a wild thing, but one semi-demented or semi-imbecile. It is she who, then and there, puts the images of the falcon[3] and of the ice-church into Brand's head.[4] She and the gipsy-woman of Act III represent,

---

[1] II, 273; Archer-Herford, III, 256; I do not think it matters much whether at this point Brand is raving or not.

[2] It is the *motif* of Weber's *The Free Huntsman* (*Der Freischütz*), an opera extremely popular in the 1860's.

[3] Of course someone like Gerd is incapable of identifying anything with 'the spirit of compromise' and is not made to do so.

[4] She also draws attention (II, 137; Archer-Herford, III, 33) to the narrowness of the wooden church down in the valley, a two-edged remark, as it were: the parish church is cramped and unfit for free creatures, but her alternative, the ice-church, proves no more satisfactory.

I take it, the altogether uncivilised and unredeemed in the human family, whose life is 'nasty, brutish and short', who have only the least knowledge of Christianity, but whose worship, in the last analysis, proves to be that to which Brand, in his ascent to the ice-church, adheres and only at the eleventh hour renounces—a further piece of evidence (if it be admitted) not only in support of Brand's 'conversion', but for the necessity of it, if he is to be saved.

Prozor has an ingenious gloss[1] upon Gerd which goes along for some little way with the explanation just given. According to him, uncivilised and unredeemed as she is, she represents individualism in its violent and uncouthly anarchistical aspect, as Brand does in a more refined; when Gerd's shot brings down, together with the falcon or 'spirit of compromise', the avalanche, the avalanche stands for the levelling forces of the generality which crush not only the undesirable rebel, but also the unique individual, even 'le principe lui-même de l'indépendance individuelle'. Such an interpretation dissociates the Avalanche from the Voice, in accordance with the aphorism from Kierke-gaard[2] which Prozor adduces: 'Levelling is not of God, and every honest man must know moments in which he is tempted to deplore this work of desolation.' It implies an even com-pleter condemnation of Brand's principles than has hitherto been contemplated, since they destroy society as well as himself.

## V

Ibsen himself made two personal pronouncements on *Brand* of great interest: 'Brand is myself in my best moments'[3] and, of the play: 'It came into existence in its day as the result of something I had lived through—not merely experienced:—it was a necessity for me, with the help of poetic form, to free myself of something I had inwardly done with.'[4] We will pass by the former of these observations with the remark—on which the

[1] Prozor, M., 'Un Drame de Henrik Ibsen, *Brand*', in *Revue des Deux Mondes*, 4th period, cxxvi (1894), p. 129; Prozor considers this particular argument self-evident (p. 160).

[2] This is almost the only Kierkegaardian association which Prozor mentions.

[3] *Breve*, I, 214.

[4] 'Den bliv i sin tid til som resultat af noget gjennemlevet—ikke oplevet;—der var mig en nødvendighed gjennem dikteriske former at frigjøre mig for noget, som jeg i mit indre var færdig med.' (*Breve*, I, 207.)

conclusions reached in §III above make it desirable to lay some stress—that, though Brand suffers defeat and, it seems, divine chastisement, he, the representative of the poet *in his best moments*, should not be looked upon as utterly or even predominantly blameworthy; we will now confine our attention to the latter.

'It came into existence in its day as the result of something I had lived through....' We are not, of course, to infer from this that Ibsen had himself been the hero of some missionary enterprise on the west coast of Norway, any more than that he had actually seen some Brand at work there. Nevertheless, the play reflects parabolically a moral crisis through which he had passed and which proved grave enough to call for cathartic treatment of corresponding severity.

The crisis, aggravated by his private irresolution and unhappiness, proceeded from a political event. In the autumn of 1863—that is to say, about the time that *Brand's* predecessor, *The Pretenders*, was in process of publication—Denmark was threatened, for the second time in a generation, by an invasion of Germany's armed forces, having for its object the divorce of the duchies of Lauenburg, Holstein and Slesvig from her crown. There were groups of men, not alone in threatened Denmark, but in Norway and Sweden as well, who believed that this was a danger of common concern to them all and that they should combine in order to avert it; they contemplated, in one form or another, a federation of the three Scandinavian powers, and for that reason their policy was known as Scandinavianism. The most vocal 'Scandinavians' were members of academic institutions. Representatives of the four northern universities of Christiania, Copenhagen, Lund and Upsala had, for nearly twenty years, been accustomed to fraternise on formal as well as informal occasions and to applaud festal speeches proclaiming their solidarity with one another. These *studentermøter* (student-meetings) were attended not merely by undergraduates, but also by professors and other senior members of the universities. Among the latter Ibsen reckoned himself—though his *bona fides* might not strike every investigator as very well substantiated;[1] he was an ardent 'Scandinavian', as were also his

---

[1] On the only occasion at which he presented himself for the matriculation examination, Ibsen failed to pass it outright and did not therefore qualify for the

closest friends in Christiania, and he held himself and the other 'academics' bound by the pledge of mutual assistance which they repeated as late as the autumn of 1863. Not only that (which was legitimate enough), but he believed also the gross of the Northern peoples to be bound by the promises entered into by their 'intellectual superiors' (who of course were often far from sober when they made them).

The peoples at large, when they knew of it, naturally did not share this view and were, in fact, resolutely opposed to 'Scandinavianism'; and that was the attitude of most of their accredited leaders too, in Norway and in Sweden. The practical result of the German threat and the reactions it provoked were that the parliament of Norway promised armed help if Denmark proper[1] should be assailed, in a grudging and conditional manner, and, in fact, they did not give that help, since the conditions attaching to it were not fulfilled.

Ibsen felt the legal action, the action of the Norwegian parliament, as a crushing humiliation—of himself, of his fellow-'academics', of the Scandinavian party, of the populace of Norway at large. The argument is fallacious, but he held—and held passionately—that Norway had been bound by the private promises of co-operation and had failed to co-operate; that the Norwegian nation were perjurers and that in their troth-breach they belied all those vows of heroic behaviour, of perpetuating the bold enterprise of the Viking ancestors which it was customary to formulate and applaud on Independence Day and similar occasions. In this spirit it was that he wrote the poem 'To my Fellow-Culprits' ('Til de Medskyldige'), which in somewhat differing versions he intended to prefix either to the poem or the drama of *Brand*.[2]

The title, 'Til de Medskyldige', implies guilt—a guilt shared, and a twofold guilt, specific and general, which has just been indicated. The Norwegians as a nation had been proved guilty

letter conferring full academic status; nevertheless, he could, by courtesy, call himself (as he did) 'Herr Student Ibsen', join the Union society and attend university lectures.

[1] I.e. the kingdom of Denmark and the duchy of Slesvig, not Holstein and Lauenburg, which for centuries had always been legally ascribed to Germany.

[2] In the end it was not published till the 'Scandinavian' controversy was dead, in the *Poems* (*Digte*) of 1871.

of making promises they would not redeem and of dreaming for themselves, as counterpart to a heroic past, a heroic future, the risks of which they refused to underwrite. Their refusal sprang from an ingrained conviction that lip-service was all that 'the ideal' called for. And in that guilt he was personally implicated in a very high degree, too, not only because he, together with most of his fellow-'academics', had failed to honour the pledge which they or their representatives really had given, but also because the poets had encouraged the glorification of the national past: he himself had indulged in this with *The Warrior's Barrow*, *The Vikings in Helgeland* and, quite recently, *The Pretenders*, in which King Haakon had engendered the 'kingly thought' of uniting Norway into a nation and had triumphed in bringing it to pass—a conception only a degree less ambitious than, but strictly homologous with, that at which the extremer 'Scandinavians' aimed. It was this sense of guilt and frustration in the pursuit of exacting ideals that Ibsen had to work out of his system. The verdict on Brand is the verdict upon himself.

## VI

A substantial part of the opposition to Scandinavianism and to adventures on the Dano-German frontier came from the politically influential peasants. Ibsen had never been on a friendly footing with them and, largely as a consequence of the political crisis of 1863–4, he came to abhor them. They are, however, not directly attacked or ridiculed in *Brand*, though the poem was another consequence of the same crisis; they are not very conspicuous there, and the part which they play is not particularly culpable.[1] This is all the more remarkable in that the play, as well as being universal and formally timeless, is topical, satirical and polemic; the chosen spot for the central scenes of the drama, the narrow, poor shelf of land between crag and glacier on the one hand and the ocean on the other, with its storms and its sunless chill, its sparse, harsh population, is plainly chosen as highly characteristic of Norway.

[1] A. O. Vinje, their champion, thought, however, that *Brand* was unjust towards the peasants; nevertheless, it was 'a faultless poem of its kind' (*Dølen*, IV, 28).

But if the satire and polemic pass by the ordinary yokel, they fasten with all the greater acidity on the designated leaders of his community, those whom in his translation C. H. Herford called the Mayor, the Dean, the Sexton and the Schoolmaster.[1] That the satire is hostile and topical transpires beyond the hazard of a doubt from the dialogue between the last two, in which, in Ibsen's crispest verse, the Sexton asks the School-master—as a man of learning and a former Member of Parliament—for a definition of a national pledge,[2] and it is conveyed to him that in practice it means nothing at all.

The Sexton comes off scot-free, and the Schoolmaster is represented as an ingenious, if not altogether praiseworthy, logician. Much more abundant and biting, however, is the irony bestowed on the Mayor and, especially, on the Dean. The former certainly does his duty.[3] He first comes upon the scene distributing poor-relief, he zealously busies himself about the good of the parish when he urges Brand to endow a community-centre with his late mother's money, and it is reported that, in saving the parish-records from fire at the risk of his life, he acted like a hero. Yet his zeal is pure formalism, his concern is for 'approved plans', for manœuvring the majority on the parish council, for welfare in its material aspect; matters of morals and the spirit concern him only in so far as they affect the rates; he is pedantically scrupulous in limiting his benefits to the area and scope laid down by the Home Secretary, his master.

Even more open to attack on the score of what their adversaries would call 'lack of vision' is the Dean. *Ex officio*, one might say, he ought to possess it—a demand which it would be unreasonably extravagant to put on the Mayor; but the only visions to which he gives expression are that of the ecclesiastical corporal marching a carefully drilled, docile flock to heaven

---

[1] The *Foged* or 'Mayor' is a salaried official appointed by the central government, a kind of paid chairman of the parish and its executive officer; the *Provst* is not as such attached to a cathedral; he occupies, however, a place in the Lutheran hierarchy between a bishop and an ordinary priest.

[2] II, 227; Archer-Herford, III, 182.

[3] Slackness in fulfilling their official tasks, the usual accusation against civil servants in Latin countries, and one made a few years later in the most acrid fashion by Kielland in his *Working Men (Arbeidsfolk)*, is actually a charge never brought by Ibsen; even Peter Stockmann of *An Enemy of the People* offends by *excès de zèle* rather than the reverse.

and, later, that of the chimerical shoal of fishes by which Brand's parishioners are, in the last resort, lured from him.[1] He again is all for routine and the preservation of the *status quo*, with such patching and 'modern improvements' as the march of time may, regrettably enough, bring with it.

Two things can clearly be deduced from these satirical portraits: the impossibility of expecting anything big or heroic from a community whose accredited leaders are the Mayor, the Dean, the Sexton and the Schoolmaster; and the contrast to their pettiness which Brand exhibits. According to taste, one may say in disparagement of Brand what one likes, that he is harsh, that he is cruel, that he is maggot-headed, that he is uncomprehending, that he labours under the deadly sin of spiritual pride,[2] that he worships false gods (or at least a false god), that he puts demands on himself and others so impossibly stiff as inevitably to induce disappointment, failure, and despair.

But one thing ought not to be denied,[3] that he stands head and shoulders over all the men with whom he is brought into contact; even his faults shine against their drabness; if he makes stiff demands it is because he is convinced they can be met and, in his own person, he demonstrates what can be done to meet them, paying others the compliment of believing that they can do what he can; if he worships a false god and commits one of the seven deadly sins, it shows that he is capable of adoration and that he has not tripped into some venial failing by inadvertence; if his conduct involves hardness and cruelty, he does not exempt himself from the effects of such harshness and he is cruel only in order, from the supreme point of view, to be charitable.

The ruling characteristic in him is will. It is not, as sometimes has been thought, piety. 'My sole aim', Ibsen once

---

[1] II, 245 and 261; Archer-Herford, III, 208 and 236; it is true that the invention of the millions of herrings is the Mayor's, and the Dean may be deceived too.

[2] This was evidently the view of the Reverend Olaf Holm, whom Kinck quotes (*Edda*, xxx, p. 83) as saying in *Kristus eller Ibsen* (1893) that Brand is 'satanic', 'he is the puffed-up moral arrogance that says: Do not come near me, even if you are Our Lord himself.'

[3] It was presumably denied by the Swedish lecturer, whom Prozor heard 'surtout admirer le vigoureux bon sens du magistrat libéral'. (*Revue des deux Mondes*, 4th per. cxxvi, 1894, p. 161.)

remarked,[1] 'was to exhibit an energetic personality'; that such a personality should have embraced the clerical profession was, he further said,[2] an accident—though dramatically, one would like to remark, a very useful one[3]—for he could have set up the same 'syllogism', as he called it,[4] for a man in any other occupation. Whatever else may be predicated, one of the propositions of this 'syllogism' certainly must be: 'The hero believes that will can accomplish anything.' To his mother, in her reluctance to part with her property, he lays down the maxim 'All or nothing'; and that forms the rider to his doctrine of will. It may be observed that the rider is not an unavoidable corollary. Brand does not say to himself: 'Decide with all the power of your emotion and intellect what is the golden mean and then resolutely, but flexibly pursue it for the good of all, at the same time losing no opportunity to recommend the same course to others'—which would also be a doctrine of will. Instead he formulates his programme of action in something like these terms: 'Discover what is your divinely purposed mission in life and, having decided on this mission, sacrifice everything and everybody to it'—which, by the way, is uncommonly like Carlyle's message to the world. Brand conceives as his own mission to do and make others do what is righteous in his sight, but that, it seems, is not an essential tenet of the general doctrine, even if it is brought out most prominently in this drama. For, at the outset, Brand adjures Einar that if he is a man of pleasure—i.e. conceives leading the life of pleasure to be his mission—then he should give himself up to it entirely 'from eve to eve'.[5] The essential is to resolve on a thing and then do it; not, as Ibsen thought the Norwegians did, dream of being Vikings and then haggle about terms, or propose to fly to their neighbours' rescue and then think better of it.

But to what end should the will direct itself? When Ibsen told a correspondent that his life had only acquired a profounder

---

[1] *Cit.* Gregersen, N. J., *Verdensfred* (1919), p. 28.

[2] Letter to Georg Brandes of 26 June 1869 (*Breve*, 1, 188).

[3] The black coat continually impresses the character's seriousness of aim on the audience.

[4] *Breve*, 1, 188.

[5] 11, 129: 'Fra Kveld til Kveld' ('from eve to eve') is not reproduced exactly in the Archer-Herford translation (III, 22).

significance after his marriage, he presumably had in mind the progressive realisation of his own 'mission', the task which every fibre in him announced that he was best fitted to accomplish— to be a dramatist,[1] not a stage-director or a customs-house officer or a gatherer of folk-lore who might beguile his spare time with a bit of play-writing. But the difficulties in the way of obeying the inner call became correspondingly minatory: the predestined dramatist had a wife and son, to whose support he was pledged, and *The Vikings in Helgeland*, *Love's Comedy* and *The Pretenders* proved unequal to supplying them with a livelihood; he was a citizen and a patriot, wishful, no doubt, to ascribe to the community of which he was a member a mission no less arduous and peremptory than his own, and his social conscience pricked him to assume duties, as tribune and even as soldier, for which he rightly knew himself to be unfitted to the degree of inefficiency. But worse cause of inner friction lay deeper still. The whole serious thought of the times tended, not platonically to equate all the main endeavours of the human spirit, but to subordinate the true to the good and the beautiful to the true or, in the nomenclature of another scheme, to depreciate the aesthetic stadium as less valuable than the ethical and the ethical as less valuable than the religious. What, according to that scale, was the worth of even the most perfect art? Could a great dramatist really stand higher than an average, decent *paterfamilias* or than the lowliest of devotees? A man must follow his 'call'—but what if that call prompted him to be an inferior human being? If it is his 'call' to be a voluptuary, should he really be a voluptuary from eve to eve, or should his will try to restrain him?

The artistic expression of such questionings begins already in *Love's Comedy*, partly with the scornful dismissal of 'kald' as Pastor Straamand conceives it (viz. an advantageous opening for earning one's bread and butter), and partly with Falk's profounder, but still uncertain gropings, with which Svanhild

[1] According to Bigeon, M., *Les Révoltés scandinaves* (1894), p. 254, Ibsen once (apparently in the early 1890's) defined to him his mission in these terms: 'It is because I have had the very strong impression of the contradiction we have introduced between human destiny and the societies founded by man that I have written what I have written. It was my vocation.' Bigeon's testimony is not perfectly reliable: and if it is to be believed it may represent a retrospective modification and precision.

sympathises but to which she denies him the right to sacrifice herself. *The Pretenders* directly presents the issue in simple and, on the whole, encouraging terms. The antagonism between King Haakon and Earl Skule, on which the play is built, is between the man who has a genuine mission and the man who, for merely practical purposes, has to steal one from somebody else. The gloomy, uncertain man succumbs forthwith to the man radiant in his self-confidence. It is true that since Ibsen would identify himself with the defeated Skule, the outcome might not look particularly tonic, but he set Skule up as a warning to himself, showing that he recognised where the danger lay and was aware that, if he was to escape catastrophe, he must be sure of his mission and determined to fulfil it.

In *Brand*, as has been seen, the author's sympathy lay principally with the man who subordinates everything to his mission and *pro tanto* would be laudable, but a proviso seems to be indicated as it was when Svanhild dissociated herself from Falk: the mission certainly allows you to sacrifice yourself and everything that is really yours to your will, but, in your dealings with others, *caritas* must prevail; they must not be sacrificed willy-nilly. (A recognition of such a limitation seems to be implied by Brand's insistence that Agnes should give up little Alf's possessions *voluntarily*—though, in the circumstances, he cannot be acquitted of moral blackmail.) The rights of the individual, however powerful, and his demands, however justifiable, are limited by the rights of other individuals and by their demands: to destroy the spirit of compromise may immediately call down catastrophe.

The expansive, not the restricted aspect of individual rights it was on which Ibsen showed himself most intent and which he was usually to place in the foreground of his moral delineations —the right of the individuality to maintain itself and to develop unconstrained by other individualities and the collectivity. It accounts for his identification with feminism, for his nonconformity in politics and for his coquetting with anarchism while, on the other hand, his sense of the ultimate limitations to be set to individuality accounts for his revulsion against Nietzschian notions. The sympathy which he plainly shows for Dina Dorf's revolt against the tutelage of the good ladies and of her would-be husband (*Pillars of Society*), for Fru Alving's successful self-education and, most notoriously, for Nora Helmer's abandonment of house and home is to be referred to the fact not that these are all women,[1] but that they are manifestly personalities with latent powers which have been thwarted and crippled. The contempt and dislike which Ibsen evinced for the 'compact Liberal majority' in *An Enemy of the People* sprang from a very keen fear that all organising of opinion, even the best opinion,[2] cramps what is most precious in the individual—his opinions, his moral life.[3] On the other hand, John Gabriel Borkman, who, for all the poetic sentiments to which he gives voice in senile delirium, cares for nothing beyond the aggrandisement of his own influence, is exhibited not only as an utter failure and, ironically enough, as a prisoner in virtually solitary confinement, but, after Ella Rentheim's exposure of him, as a mere monster deserving any punishment. The cold malignity with which Ibsen treats Gregers Werle—who, as has often been noted, has so much in common with himself—is, as the whole catastrophic progress of *The Wild Duck* exists to show, the consequence of his wish to *impose* himself and his ideals, to 'play providence' to the Ekdal family, the part of a providence so deficient in *caritas* that it lacks the merest decency and common sense.[4]

It follows fairly naturally from his concern with assertive personality that Ibsen's plays represent a great gallery of egoists—something, to be sure, not altogether novel among the tragedians.[5] Brand was certainly not the earliest of them; he was preceded by Falk, about whom Svanhild had precisely

[1] A proof of this assertion is to be found in the almost comical scorn Ibsen expressed for John Stuart Mill for having derived some ideas from his wife—the point on which Max Beerbohm seized in *A Christmas Garland*.

[2] Kroll and his friends scarcely recommend the creed of conservatism in *Rosmersholm*.

[3] Oddly enough, he expressed approval of the Czarist *régime* and the independent old Papal State; the repression which they exercised did not, in his opinion, affect the individual's most precious rights, those of leading his own life and thinking his own thoughts, to anything like the extent which more 'enlightened' politics attempted.

[4] It seems to me that it is in the treatment of the indefeasibility of the individual personality that Ibsen approximates most closely to another tragic writer of the nineteenth century, Friedrich Hebbel, who in his two prime exemplifications of it, *Herodes und Marianne* and *Gyges und sein Ring*, also exhibits women as protagonists and victims.

[5] Cf. Œdipus, Phaedra, King Lear, Rodogune, Wallenstein, etc.

the kind of doubt that Ibsen seems to have entertained of the whole genus, and by Hjørdis, in *The Vikings of Helgeland*, whose monomania of disappointment recalls that of Euripides's Medea; Brand, however, is Ibsen's greatest egoist, the egoist raised to heroic stature. Upon him follow almost an army of others, some already mentioned. Bernick has the makings of a first-rate criminal, but, on the whole, he is displayed, like Brand, in a favourable light by comparison with most of the men about him, he represents a civilising force in his community—something that could not be said of the excellent collectivist Aune; Rubek (*When We Dead Awaken*) is a superlative egoist too, but we must believe that he created great art.

Much may be forgiven to such as Bernick or Rubek for what their egoism drives or enables them to do. However, even if the richer individuality may be allowed some privileges over the poorer, it is when the egoist turns tyrant, like Solness in his treatment of the Broviks (which shocks even as fierce an egoist as himself, Hilde Wangel) or like Rebecca West in her treatment of Beate, that he (or she) is detested. The worst sort of egoist, the individualist run to seed, is a Hedda Gabler, who, having no rich individuality of her own, tries to play providence and sway the destinies of those with positive potentialities, Løvborg and Thea Elvsted. For her discomfiture and fall only her like have tears.[1]

## VII

The slogan 'All or Nothing' to which Brand subscribes has sometimes been looked upon as Kierkegaard's, but that is not so. Kierkegaard may have gone so far as to hold that the Christian who was not utterly Christlike was none, but that was a consequence of his definition of the term 'Christian'. Otherwise, he insisted strongly on the relative value of acts, even if he might admit that a whole-hearted aesthete was better than a half-hearted one, a whole-hearted moralist better than a half-hearted one and so forth. The inference from *Brand* which

---

[1] The case of Gregers Werle is a long way less heinous; fuliginous though his lights may be, he acts responsibly according to them, and, with one exception, the individualities on whom he impinges with the best will in the world are even poorer than his own.

it is allowable to make,[1] namely that Ibsen regarded a double-dyed villain or a voluptuary 'from eve to eve' as better than a backsliding man of honour or a time-serving Christian, is not, I think, in accordance with Kierkegaard's teaching. If the notion was suggested to Ibsen from outside, it probably came to him from Heiberg's *Soul After Death* (*Sjæl efter Døden*, 1841), an aristophanic poem which, with its rejection of what Kipling taught the English to call a 'Tomlinson', left its mark on *Peer Gynt*.

*The Soul After Death* would also have encouraged Ibsen to write a work dramatic as well as poetic in form, but not obviously designed for the stage. The *genre* (which may go back beyond Seneca) received a notable impetus in the literary generations just preceding Ibsen's, those that had brought forth *Manfred* and *Prometheus Unbound*. Though Ibsen's general scheme is original to himself and imposes itself rigorously on all its parts, it will not be perfectly otiose to seek in *Brand* traces of other works similar to those of *The Soul After Death*. The study of absolute will-power culminating in self-immolation which Ibsen's favourite, Frederik Paludan-Müller, made in *Kalanus*[2] was doubtless familiar to him, and in a few externalities the example of Goethe's *Faust*—noticeable again in *Peer Gynt*—has been inferred, as, for instance, in the Latin tag of the last scene.

In search for sources and analogues to *Brand*, however, the investigation always tends to come round to Kierkegaard; and the question obtrudes itself: In what degree would it be true to call it also a Kierkegaardian tragedy? The issue was raised from the very first. Almost as soon as it came out, Georg Brandes, then a young critic fresh from the university, declared quite positively that *Brand* stood 'in direct relation' to Kierkegaard, that almost every essential in it 'is to be found in Kierkegaard and its hero's life has its prototype in his. It actually seems as if Ibsen had aspired to the honour of being called Kierkegaard's poet.'[3]

[1] And which is reinforced by *Peer Gynt*.

[2] Koht, H., in his Introduction in the Centenary Edition (v, 169) opines that the metre and the mixture of the serious and the grotesque owe something to the same author's *Ahasverus*.

[3] Reprinted from *Æsthetiske Studier* (1868) in *Samlede Skrifter*, III (1900), p. 257. (*Henrik Ibsen, Bjørnstjerne Bjørnson*, English translation, 1898, p. 21.)

In considering *Brand* as a Kierkegaardian tragedy, two pre-liminary points may be made: (i) A reminder of a relevant passage in the discussion of *Love's Comedy*, where the view was advanced that the Kierkegaardian ideas which certainly abound in that play were, in ways it is not possible fully to trace, to some extent common property: conversely, an ear attuned to Kierke-gaard's preaching would readily hear as an echo of it a drama in which the hero stands for the indefeasibility and omnipotence of the will and in which that will is apparently dedicated to the loftiest ethical and religious ends. (ii) It must be insisted that, in the interpretation of the play proposed, it involves in the last appeal a *condemnation* of will pushed, in its quest of the ideal, to such sterile, inhuman and uncharitable extremes—a condemna-tion which may be mitigated, but is not altogether annulled, by other considerations, so that *Brand* appears much less a recom-mendation of its hero's conduct than, let us say, *Faust* or *Antigone*.

One of the completest alignments of *Brand* to Kierkegaard's philosophy is made in *The Fortnightly Review* for August 1899, when, with 'New Lights on Ibsen's *Brand*', M. A. Stobart incidentally gave the general British public its first introduction to Kierkegaard. He disengaged 'three fundamental chords of the Danish philosopher's melancholy fugue' and argued that in *Brand* Ibsen played his theme on the same, viz.: '(*a*) That Christianity has been annihilated by the false and specious conception of God as a deity of love and mercy. (*b*) That by Subjectivity alone (that is inwardness and will-power) can religious truth be reached. (*c*) That the *willing* sacrifice of "All or nothing" ("Enten Intet—eller Alt") is the essential requisite of salvation.'[1]

In proceeding to a fuller examination of Stobart's thesis, it may be convenient to alter the order of his propositions and to begin with the second or (*b*).

> It is not for a Church I cry,
> It is not dogmas I defend

Brand exclaims;[2] and nobody could maintain that he could be, for instance, looked on as a champion of Lutheran Christianity in any of its forms, even of the pietistic Haugianism of Ibsen's

---

[1] *Fortnightly Review* (n.s.), LXVI, 229.    [2] II, 132; Archer-Herford, III, 26.

Norway (except in so far as it also stands for nonconformity);
Brand does not even know whether he is a Christian,[1] voicing
an agnosticism which, in Kierkegaard's own case, apparently
amounted to denial. In his conception of religion ('That by
Subjectivity alone...can religious truth be reached') Ibsen
was most nearly at one with Kierkegaard. He was completely
reticent about everything that might be construed as his own
religious creed; formally, it is said, he 'lost his faith' at the age
of nineteen and never regained it; he had a certain reverence
for its founder and appreciated its political significance, but
took little interest in the Christian religion as such. On the
other hand, nothing in his writings or utterances belies the
belief that, to him, religion was something purely personal,
reached entirely by introspection and inward conviction and
then applied to conduct, to manifestations of the will. So that,
if Brand is proved wrong, it is not for having neglected these or
those articles of formulated faith, since they are irrelevant.

Turning next to Stobart's proposition (a) ('That Christianity
has been annihilated by the false and specious conception of God
as a divinity of love and mercy'), we may set aside, as having little
interest for Ibsen at this stage in his career,[2] the question whether
or not 'Christianity has been annihilated'. Clearly, however,
Brand's conception of the divinity closely resembles Kierkegaard's:

> As Catholics make of the Redeemer
> A baby at the breast, so ye
> Make God a dotard and a dreamer,
> Verging on second infancy...
> A God who'll through his fingers look,
> Who, like yourselves, is hoary grown,
> And keeps a cap for his bald crown.
> Mine is another kind of God!
> Mine is a storm, where thine's a lull,
> Implacable, where thine's a clod,
> All-loving there, where thine is dull;[3]
> And He is young like Hercules,
> No hoary sipper of life's lees.[4]

[1] II, 129; Archer-Herford, III, 22.

[2] In *Emperor and Galilean* (1873) he came, for the nonce, nearer to tackling it.

[3] There is a mistranslation here, or more probably a misreading of the translator's handwriting; the original runs 'ubøjelig hvor din er sløv', that is 'Un-
bending, where thine is slack'.    [4] Archer-Herford, III, 25; II, 131.

For that reason it is, as the first of the quoted lines show, that Brand condemns all those notions of God consonant with the word 'humane'.[1] But on this point, if our interpretation of the end of the play be accepted, Ibsen disagrees with Kierkegaard; Brand, it has been submitted, reaches the conviction that he has been hitherto worshipping a false god, the real God being 'Deus caritatis'. True religion thus, in Ibsen's view, does not rule out a 'deity of love and mercy'.

As for the third point, (c), in making which Stobart presumably had in mind the scene wherein Brand forces Agnes *voluntarily* to give up the baby's clothes, the condemnation of Brand's past beliefs presumed in the last scene again leads to the conclusion that Ibsen by no means goes all the way with Kierkegaard.

If therefore Georg Brandes censured the argument of *Brand* as inculcating a morality which, like Kierkegaard's, would 'lead half mankind to starve to death from love of the ideal',[2] he must consciously or unthinkingly have dismissed the counter-argument to Brand's absolutism which we hold that the play as a whole irresistibly imposes. The establishment of that counter-argument does not, however, quite dispose of the argument that *Brand* is inimical to principle. Even if the hero is worsted and is shown to be rightly worsted, the contrast between himself and others who are alien to his idealism, while engaging sympathy for him, confers also great dignity and worth on his personality and philosophy of life. It is, it appears, a better or, at least, a grander thing to have principles than not to have them, to fashion ideals of the spiritual kind rather than those of the material kind which raises community centres, to worship Michelangelo's Jehovah rather than a begetter of social security. But, to be defensible in every resort, the ideal must be the very highest, otherwise it will prove as calamitous as the lack of principle or as the substitution of social expediency for true idealism. From this point of view *Brand* might perhaps be called the tragedy of a Kierkegaardian, even a Kierkegaardian tragedy; the word 'tragedy', however, bears the emphasis.

[1] For Brand's diatribe against this word, which culminates in the Kierkegaardian question: 'Was God "humane" when Jesus died?' cf. p. 42 above.

[2] *Hovedstrømninger i det 19de Aarhundredes Litteratur*, I (1872), p. 26.

Kierkegaard was notoriously insistent that the religious not only differs strictly from the ethical,[1] but may conflict with it, indeed that it may be *un*ethical. His favourite illustration of this tenet was the biblical story of the Sacrifice of Isaac, when, at God's command, Abraham prepared deliberately and ceremonially to murder his own child. It is interesting—and proof presumptive that Ibsen was working with Kierkegaard's ideas in his mind—that this 'Isaachs rædsel', the Horror of Isaac, is mentioned by Brand,[2] when the possibility of his own son's death first occurs to him, and that it steels him to persevere in the line of action which eventually brings about little Alf's (humanly speaking) unnecessary death.

This furnishes something of a parallel to the broken engagement *en plein amour* on which *Love's Comedy* is reared and which the sternest critic allows[3] as the only authentic borrowing by Ibsen of something which he is more likely to have derived from Kierkegaard's writings than elsewhere. A distinction may be made, nevertheless. The irrational, anti-social, unethical sacrifice, which was a matter of doctrine for Kierkegaard, has for Ibsen become no more than an artistic *motif* of considerable dramatic significance in *Love's Comedy* and no more than an ornament in *Brand*.

However, the allusion to the Sacrifice of Isaac, 'horror' as it is to Brand, has another aspect, with Kierkegaardian implications once more. Fear, fear for his son, assails Brand's far from impassive heart, even if, in the end, it steels him to his purpose; similarly, fear operates at critical moments to reveal the pure essence of characters as different as those of Peer Gynt (through the appearance of the Strange Passenger[4] and the shipwreck),

---

[1] Gerhard Gran believed that *Brand* signified a passing from the aesthetic to the ethical; Beyer holds that it represents a passing into the religious; Valborg Erichsen contradicts both, thinking that Ibsen stays in the aesthetic. This is the summary of Chesnais, P. G. la, 'Ibsen disciple de Kierkegaard?' (*Edda*, xxxiv, 1934, p. 399), who himself holds that these categories have no application.

[2] II, 174; Archer-Herford, III, 97.

[3] Chesnais, P. G. la, in *Edda*, xxxiv (1934), p. 402.

[4] Here we are confronted with what seems a direct denial by Ibsen, who was furious with Clemens Petersen (*Breve*, I, p. 159) for interpreting the Strange Passenger as the Concept 'Fear'; but to argue that Peer Gynt was overcome by Fear when he met the Strange Passenger is not the same thing as to make the Strange Passenger an allegorical figure, and it was against the latter explanation that Ibsen, always averse from symbolical exegesis, was, I think, protesting.

Bernick, Fru Alving and Hedda Gabler. This was a favourite notion of Kierkegaard,[1] but it cannot be alleged to be a very recondite one for a writer preoccupied with tragic issues ('pity and fear'), and, without depreciating the merit of Beyer's investigations into Ibsen's relations with Kierkegaard, one is constrained to pass the same verdict on the many other parallels accumulated by him.[2]

If the ascription of Kierkegaardianism to *Brand* be only very partially tenable, to see in its hero, as some writers have done,[3] a portrait of Kierkegaard himself is wild error. The Danish thinker was in his appearance and eremitic way of life an eccentric, nothing about him suggested either the philosopher or the apostle, and at the height of his activity he served as an almost unlimited butt for the chief comic paper of his native town, *Corsaren*. It was indeed asserted[4] that Ibsen had drawn his likeness in the hero of *Love's Comedy* and, though that thesis cannot be maintained either, there is more in common between Falk and the mercurial, brilliant, unpredictable author of *A Seducer's Diary* than between Brand and Kierkegaard.

Other models than Kierkegaard have been sought for Brand —and with better justification. For one whom, *reservatis reservandis*, one could call a Norwegian follower of Kierkegaard, the Reverend Gustav Adolf Lammers, Ibsen must have felt a special interest.[5] For this man, exercising his ministry in Ibsen's native town of Skien,[6] counted members of his family among his flock, with the result that they came to disown the wayward son and brother who had sought his fortune in that devil's temple, the playhouse. Lammers, as may be guessed, was a 'hell-fire

---

[1] Cf. his work *Frygt og Bæven* (i.e. *Fear and Trembling*).

[2] Beyer, H., *Søren Kierkegaard og Norge* (1924), especially pp. 114 ff.; Beyer takes the same view of the Strange Passenger as that indicated above; perhaps the most striking of his parallels is that between Nora's expectation of the 'miracle of miracles', *Det Vidunderlige*, and the same thing in Cordelia of *A Seducer's Diary*. On the other side see Chesnais, P. G. la, 'Ibsen disciple de Kierkegaard?' in *Edda*, xxxiv (1934), p. 355.

[3] Beginning with Helvig, F., *Bjørnson og Ibsen i deres to seneste Værker* (1866), p. 26.

[4] By Christian Møller in (Letterstedske) *Nordisk Tidsskrift* for 1888; Møller's opinions are traversed by Chesnais, P. G. la, *ut cit.* pp. 382 ff.

[5] Cf. Larsen, K., *Henrik Ibsens episke Brand*, p. 244.

[6] But after Ibsen had left it (except for two fleeting visits).

preacher' of great fervour and conviction,[1] and the 'All or Nothing' principle seems to inform a pronouncement such as this: 'Rather unbaptised and unconfirmed children, rather honest heathens than to let oneself be driven by social conditions and employ the institutions of the state-church for the continued breeding of a lying and hypocritical generation.'[2] Ibsen apparently[3] made the personal acquaintance of Lammers, and so violent, ruthless and self-righteous a nature could not but interest him. It has, however, been said,[4] with some plausibility, that Lammers is much nearer to Einar, at his last appearance,[5] than he is to Brand.

Ibsen had, however, much more frequent and close relations with another clergyman of rather similar proclivities, and at a time when Brand was uppermost in his thoughts. This was Christopher Arnt Bruun,[6] who arrived in Rome for a protracted stay during September 1864, a few weeks after Ibsen had made Italy his home. Bruun had a special interest for him. He had felt about the Norwegian defection in the Slesvig-Holstein crisis as Ibsen had done; but more than that: he had gone into the Danish army as a volunteer, and it was to his blunt challenge, why Ibsen had not done the same, that the latter gave the celebrated reply: 'We poets have other tasks.'[7] Bruun, an enthusiastic champion of Kierkegaard, put the same extreme demands on all and sundry as he made upon himself, and such a personage, with such a history, must have left a very deep

---

[1] Johan Bojer has observed: 'les songes creux, les maladies de conscience et la recherche des idéals sont une forme spécialement norvégienne de la vie spirituelle' (Chesnais, P. G. la, *Johan Bojer*, 1930, p. 208).

[2] *Cit.* Bing, J., *Henrik Ibsen's Brand* (n.d.), p. 82.

[3] Cf. Kinck, B. M., in *Edda*, xxxv (1935), p. 501.

[4] Chesnais, *Edda*, xxxiv. p. 368, where it is pointed out that a certain H. C. Knudsen, a missionary whom Ibsen must have met at Bergen, met his death in an avalanche.

[5] Wicksteed, P. H., *Four Lectures on Henrik Ibsen* (1892), p. 49, has an excellent passage about Einar after his conversion, showing how well aware Ibsen was of the operation of the 'All or Nothing' principle on an inferior character.

[6] Of whom a full biography is given by Freihow, H. V., *Henrik Ibsen's 'Brand'* (1936), p. 24. In the event it was Bruun who delivered the chief funeral oration at the state-obsequies accorded to Ibsen in 1906.

[7] 'Vi Diktere har andre Opgaver' (*cit.* Koht, H., Introduction to Centenary Edition, v, 165).

impression on Ibsen.[1] Francis Bull suggests[2] that, as a stage figure, Brand had something of a prototype in John Knox, of Bjørnson's recent play, *Mary Stuart in Scotland* (1864).

To conclude this topic. Bruun had a charming sister, Thea, who was with him in Italy and for whom Ibsen had a warm liking, if, as the same critic thinks,[3] she was the occasion of two of his truest lyrics, 'Borte' and 'En Svane'.[4] According to Bull she served as a model for Agnes in *Brand*, though Agnes plainly has many of the 'valkyrie' qualities which informed the heroine of *Love's Comedy* and for which the inspiration was indicated in the discussion of that play. When the 'epical' *Brand* was read aloud to Fru Ibsen she said[5] she recognised in the personage of Einar Ole Schulerud, the young man with whom Ibsen had stood on a friendly footing at Grimstad and who was instrumental in getting his first play, *Catiline*, published in 1850.

# VIII

Uncommonly crusty was the retort usually elicited from Ibsen when the question was mooted in his hearing whether he had written good roles for the players or might be induced to write such: 'I do not write "parts", I portray men and women', he rasped out at what must be one of the most uncomfortable lunch-parties on record.[6] For all such ferocity, however, his plays *are* plays, and, though in a few—a very few—instances serious difficulties would baffle the impresario and stage-presenter of a brick-and-mortar playhouse, none is a poem chopped up dialogue-wise, like Byron's dramas, for instance, but all are eminently *actable* in the theatre of the mind.[7] Every scene, once set, is fraught with dramatic tensity and calls for acting, not declamation. Ibsen may have called *Brand* and *Peer Gynt* 'dramatic poems' (*dramatiske digter*), but the term

[1] Bruun told P. G. la Chesnais (*Brand d'Ibsen*, p. 95) that Brand was fully formed in Ibsen's mind before their meeting took place.

[2] 'Brand, Bruun og Freihow' in Berggrav, E., *Ibsens Sjelelige Krise* (1937), p. 47. I confess to seeing little resemblance.

[3] Bull, *ut supra*, p. 54.

[4] VIII, 325 and 314 respectively.      [5] *Auct.* Bing, *op. cit.* p. 9.

[6] It is reported by Georg Brandes in *Levned*, III (1908), p. 313.

[7] I would not have it inferred that the theatre of the mind does not admit of a fiasco.

implies perhaps the same kind of understatement which made him withhold even from *Rosmersholm* the title of a tragedy,[1] and his efforts to get *Peer Gynt* played prove that to him the adjective had the same importance as the noun in the term 'dramatic poem'. On the other hand, though less diffuse than *Peer Gynt* and *Emperor and Galilean*, *Brand's* slacker, more episodic technique undoubtedly represents a departure from the tensity and economy which even *The Pretenders* preserved and which characterise all his mature works except these three.[2]

The ascent of a mountain[3] and an avalanche are not exactly bagatelles to the scene-painter and stage-machinist; but the modern audience's physical powers of endurance would furnish the chief obstacle to a manager wishful of presenting *Brand*. For that reason, when it was new, only a gingerly attempt at stage-reproduction was made, Act IV alone[4] being given at Christiania Theatre on 27 June 1866. Nineteen years later (24 March 1885), the gifted, enterprising Swede Ludvig Josephsson—the same who had taken the responsibility for first staging *Love's Comedy* at Christiania—put on the whole of *Brand* in his Nya Teatern, Stockholm, and the audience, convoked for 6 p.m., did not hear the enigmatic 'Han är *deus caritatis*' till 2 a.m. But it proved a theatrical success in Stockholm—one may even say, a triumphant success; for, though it was somewhat (but not apparently very much) abridged for subsequent performances, it was then acted no less than sixteen times in a city a good deal less populous than the Leicester or Portsmouth of to-day.

Such powers of endurance and, to be fair, such managerial faith could, however, not be expected everywhere. When, after the lapse of another ten years, all five acts of *Brand* were for the first time presented in its author's native land,[5] they were much more drastically cut, and even so the experiment, it must be

---

[1] Ibsen did not entitle a single one of his plays a tragedy.

[2] I do not think that after an age which had been notably deficient in dramatic forcefulness and concentration it is necessary to seek one formal model for such 'dramatic poems'; in *Peer Gynt* several reminders of Goethe's *Faust* occur.

[3] There is the same thing in *John Gabriel Borkman* and *When We Dead Awaken*.

[4] This act, containing the scenes of Agnes's grief and sacrifice, was also presented by itself in London on 2 June 1893.

[5] At the Eldorado, Christiania, on 21 October 1895, with music by Ole Olesen.

admitted, has rarely been repeated.[1] In Great Britain, for example, I do not think that the five acts of *Brand*, however much curtailed, were ever shown to a theatrical audience before the Amateur Dramatic Society of Cambridge University presented them in the Lent Term of 1946.

## IX

The record of the early editions of *Brand* indicates the magnitude of its effect. As its subject lay on the borderland between religion and ethics on which the attention of almost all thoughtful readers was, at this time, anxiously directed, so its approach, obviously reverential and poetic, was equally congenial. On no more grateful ground could it have fallen than Scandinavia, where the failure to unite against martial aggression with the consequent *débâcle* had given extension to the profundity of heart-searching encouraged by Kierkegaard. The dramatic poem, a Danish commentator said,[2] was 'read over and over again and read in almost every house all over the country'; it was discussed at great length both in private and in public; and although it was usually recognised as no direct contribution to religious debate, it nevertheless afforded matter for sermons[3] and lit a beacon before many a would-be missioner. Of the many imitations and the like which it evoked, only one can be mentioned here—the anonymously published novel *Brand's Daughters* (*Brands Døttre*, 1869), by Laura Petersen, the young Norwegian lady who a few years later became Fru Kieler and whose fate was curiously associated with that of Ibsen.[4]

Some have held that Ibsen's own drama *When We Dead Awaken* (*Naar Vi Døde Vaagner*, 1899) should be counted among

[1] A fuller stage-version than the Norwegian was given, with a prologue specially written by Holger Drachmann, at the Dagmar Theatre, Copenhagen, in connection with the celebration of Ibsen's seventieth birthday. This was the first performance of *Brand* in Denmark. Koht, who evidently saw it, calls an almost simultaneous Berlin production 'sheer parody' (I, 350). It was acted as a whole by the Théâtre de l'Œuvre in Paris on 21 June 1895.

[2] 'Paul Pry', *Henrik Ibsen* (1871), p. 6.

[3] 'A friend now dead told me that at the time he could always hear in the churches of Oslo an echo from *Brand*' (Indrehus, K., in *Edda*, xxxv, 1935, p. 546).

[4] More will be said about Laura Kieler in connection with *The Master Builder* and *A Doll's House* below.

the *sequelae* of *Brand*. When, in the interval between *John Gabriel Borkman* (1896) and that play, he visited Copenhagen for the celebrations of his seventieth birthday, he saw, on 3 April 1898, *Brand* acted at the Dagmar Theatre, and the performance is said[1] to have moved him deeply. The play which he elaborated and perhaps even conceived[2] after that bore the title 'dramatic epilogue', and that appellation gave rise to a very natural speculation about the series which it might be supposed to 'round off'. Was it the whole body of his work,[3] or was it only a portion of it and, if that, what portion?

Fibiger[4] and others[5] who think like him take the view that *When We Dead Awaken* was a self-confession and a palinode provoked specifically by *Brand*, and that it was meant to set a period to the whole body of work lying posterior to *Brand*.[6] Referring to Arnold Rubek and Irene, the two principal personages of *When We Dead Awaken*, and to the former's confession of failure, Fibiger opines: 'In the days of first youthful enthusiasm,[7] Professor Rubek, *alias* Henrik Ibsen, created a glorious masterpiece (*Brand*), inspired by Irene (the Peace of God)....He became, however, unfaithful to the ideal

---

[1] Fibiger (*ut infra*, p. 16), whose conclusions are not very impressive, seems to rely mainly on the evidence, second-hand even then, of a Frk. D. Prior, who dabbled in sculpture and was a zealot on behalf of the Christian Women's Temperance Association, 'Det Hvide Baand'.

[2] It seems as if Ibsen were pottering about the notion of a new play already in 1897, but the first extant note of his relating to *Naar Vi Døde Vaagner* is dated 2 February 1899.

[3] It might be argued that Ibsen was somewhat 'fey' about his own fate. In 1875, twenty-five years after its first publication, he reissued *Catiline* with the remark that he was standing just at the mid-point of his career, and his last work was published a few days before 1 January 1900, twenty-five years later; according to Elias (*cit.* Archer, XI, xxv, when writing *When We Dead Awaken* Ibsen 'seemed to hear the beating of dark pinions over his head'; this would support the view that he looked on it as his last work. But Ibsen wrote to the Norwegian paper *Verdens Gang* (12 December 1899) emphatically denying such an implication and calling the new work the Epilogue 'to the series of my dramatic writings which takes its beginning with *A Doll's House*'. That ought to have settled the question; on another occasion, however, he seems to have begun the 'series' with *The Master Builder* (Centenary Edition, XIII, 197).

[4] Fibiger, A., *Henrik Ibsen. En Studie over Guds-Linien i hans Liv* (København, 1928).

[5] E.g. Kinck, H. M., in *Edda*, XXXV (1935), p. 535.

[6] This can be taken as consonant with Ibsen's own pronouncement, if *Brand*, as well it may be, is taken as the 'type' of a group comprising also *Peer Gynt* and *Emperor and Galilean*.

[7] Ibsen was, after all, thirty-nine when *Brand* appeared.

of his youth. He fell a victim to the radical trend of thought.'[1] Expanded, his argument runs to something like this: led astray by Georg Brandes—the great director of 'the radical trend of thought'—into believing that he only had to write 'modern' plays in order to do his duty by (God and) man, Ibsen, once *Emperor and Galilean* was completed in 1873, abandoned the more direct moral preaching in which he had indulged in *Brand* and of which his radical mentor expressly disapproved; the outcome was that the wonderful instrument which he had fashioned lost, as it were, its magic, and the best that with its help he could produce had, he recognised, been a caricatural delineation of everything base in mankind, just as Rubek found that he could not make the portrait-busts, his speciality, without showing his sitters as disguised dogs, apes and the like; Ibsen and his art had become dead, so that, in the recognition of the fact and the determination to reform, he wrote 'When *We* Dead Awaken'.

A refinement may be added (and was suggested by Schack)[2] to the argument of 'apostasy and repentance' by somewhat antedating the apostasy, by maintaining that Ibsen jettisoned the serious moral theme of *Brand* before he completely worked it out, somewhere in the middle of the last act; the conclusion, accordingly, is to be considered a pure piece of stage-carpentry, which the critics naturally find hard to elucidate in the light of what has gone before. If it is held that the last scenes constitute a logically tenable as well as effective conclusion to the whole, of course, the refinement of Schack's theory falls to the ground. Another powerful objection to the argument which accounts for the difficulties of *Brand* by postulating a deliberate relaxation of moral grip[3] is the existence of the later *Peer Gynt* and *Emperor and Galilean*, amenable throughout to the same moral criteria.

The recollection of these plays, however, would not lessen any compunction which Ibsen may have felt on reviving his memories of *Brand* after thirty years. But the real obstacle to accepting the whole Fibigerian theory lies in the sureness and uniformity of

[1] The two avalanches must strongly suggest a relation between the two plays.
[2] *Om Udviklingsgangen i Henrik Ibsen Digtning* (1896), p. 60.
[3] It does, however, seem as if, like many another artist, Ibsen sometimes lost his sharpest interest in a work before he had finished it, and the fact, if true, may account for his apparent love of an inconclusive ending.

touch evinced by Ibsen throughout the series of plays beginning with *A Doll's House* (or *Pillars of Society*). In them the artist seems so imperturbably *dans son assiette* as to forbid any belief that he was, all these twenty-odd years, suppressing the 'promptings of his better self'; in the frame of mind which Fibiger presupposes, he would surely, when he sent the letter to *Verdens Gang* mentioned above, have dropped some hint of dissatisfaction with the trend of the work now rounded off by his 'Epilogue'? He certainly then looked forward to new work, perhaps in a new style, but made no claim that the manner and product must needs be better. Considerations of this order do not deny that Ibsen may well have felt an overwhelming emotion at seeing *Brand* performed in 1898; what man of seventy would not be stirred to the depths of his being on seeing, in the liveliest form, presented before him what he had experienced, felt and hoped for just when, in the full vigour of his functions, his world was opening out before his feet?

# PEER GYNT
## 1867

### I

WHAT schemes Ibsen was meditating or beginning to elaborate during the first twenty months or so after the completion of *Brand* in November 1865, we do not know.[1] As late as 2 November 1866[2] he was still undecided what to do next. Nine weeks later, however, he could report[3] himself hard at work on what evidently were memoranda and rough drafts of *Peer Gynt*, which then went forward, first in Rome, then on Ischia and at Sorrento, so speedily that the last piece of manuscript could go to the Copenhagen printer on 18 October 1867. It was published by Messrs Gyldendal on 14 November. Like *Brand*, it was called, not a drama, but a 'dramatic poem'.

So certain was Ibsen about the plan of the whole[4] that he could fair-copy and send off (on 8 August 1867) Acts I, II and III before the last two were written, and it would seem that details, too, were largely exempt from second thoughts;[5] for *Peer Gynt* there exist hardly any of the preliminary notes and variants which, in the case of most of the author's mature works, exhibit the method of trial and error; and we know from Vilhelm Bergsøe's reminiscences[6] that that summer Ibsen was ex-

[1] Most likely the projects for *Magnus Hejnesen* and *Julian*, which *Brand* had crowded out.

[2] Letter to F. Hegel (*Breve*, I, 146).

[3] Letter to F. Hegel of 5 January 1867 (*Breve*, I, 148).

[4] At one time during the work on *Peer Gynt*, Ibsen made an elaborate scenario, which survives as far as the fifth scene of Act IV. There is a facsimile of two of the pages in Bull, F., *Henrik Ibsens Peer Gynt* (1947), pp . 65 f. It is said that the African scenes were not in Ibsen's mind from the first (but what that implies precisely is not clear) and that they were added as a form of revenge upon the Egyptologist Lieblein, who had reviewed *Brand* unsympathetically in *Norden* (Koht, I, 346).

[5] There is only the one 'Utkast', a complete draft now in The Royal Library, Copenhagen, as is the revised fair copy.

[6] This Danish man of science and novelist was spending the summer of 1867 on the island of Ischia also and had daily intercourse with Ibsen, of which he gave a lively account in *Henrik Ibsen paa Ischia* (1907).

ceedingly industrious, regular and happy in his work. The only revisions on record are some of trifling importance in the scene in the Old Man of Dovre's Hall, from which Ibsen eventually deleted certain features that might have given offence as too farcical or as too bitter in their satire.[1] But he certainly embroidered extensively on his original conception; all the more interesting 'phantastic' characters, like the Button-Moulder, the Lean One, the Strange Passenger and perhaps the Boyg, seem to have been invented after the work was well under way.[2]

In the beginning it seems that—a song or two apart, perhaps —Ibsen intended to couch his new play in the regular octosyllabic metre, now iambic, now trochaic,[3] which he had employed in *Brand*, with a few scenes in prose. And, indeed, five scenes[4] of the completed *Peer Gynt* are duly composed in four-stressed lines of regular 'feet'. But, as the new work took shape, the poet on the one hand rejected prose altogether and, on the other, broke up the regularity of the verse in the great majority of the scenes: he almost invariably retained four stresses in each line, but interspersed the stressed syllables with various groupings of unaccented syllables after the model of the ballad-poetry (*folkeviserytmer*) which he had already adapted with much success to *The Feast at Solhaug* and *Olaf Liljekrans*; and the coruscating rhymes, with which *Love's Comedy* was adorned, recur in great profusion. The racy, familiar language of *Peer Gynt* is naturally impregnated with Norwegian idioms in a very

[1] The scene, for instance, originally began with an opening chorus in parody of Nordahl Brun's patriotic song 'For Norge, Kæmpers Fødeland', from which the inference would have been that only monsters utter such ridiculous sentiments.

[2] They are omitted from the 'Dramatis Personae' in both the draft and the fair copy. A collation between each of these and the first edition is made in the Centenary Edition, VI, 246. Apart from changes due to the spelling-reform of 1869, a number of mistakes crept into the editions subsequent to the first edition, the *textus receptus*; a full list of all variants is to be found in Logeman, H., *A Commentary on Henrik Ibsen's 'Peer Gynt'* (The Hague, 1917), p. 382.

[3] And, for that reason, varying in fact from seven to nine syllables per line, as 'octosyllabic' metres commonly do.

[4] Namely, the first scenes of Acts I, II and IV, the seventh scene of Act IV and the fifth scene of Act V; the graveside panegyric in the third scene of Act V is in blank verse. For a further discussion of the metres see William Archer's Introduction to the play (Archer, IV, xxxii). It may be observed that the numbering of the scenes in the English version is Archer's, not Ibsen's.

high degree: so much so, in fact, that it is (to the best of my belief) the only one of Ibsen's dramas that eventually, for performance in Denmark, needed a Danish paraphrase.[1]

## II

Although Ibsen did not finally decide to treat it till the late autumn of 1866, matter for *Peer Gynt* had been collecting in his mind for some years. On the walking tour which he undertook in the summer of 1862, in order to collect folk-lore, he came across the name of Peer Gynt, reporting on him in a letter[2] of that time that he was 'a real person who lived in the Gudbrandsdal, probably at the conclusion of the last [i.e. the eighteenth] or at the beginning of this century. His name is still familiar to the people up there, but of his actions they do not know very much more that what can be found in Asbjørnsen's *Norwegian Fairy-Stories*.'

Before passing to Asbjørnsen's comparatively recent accounts,[3] we may find it of interest to pursue this partially 'real' and partially legendary figure back into history. There are two main theories about its identity. One Engebregt Hougen, a schoolmaster, claimed[4] that everything which Asbjørnsen had written about Peer came from his own lips, stories about him being scarcely known outside his family. Hougen's claim is accepted by Hr. H. S. Bakken[5] and, following up the Hougen tradition, he derives the surname Gynt from the aristocratic German family of Günter, which at one time had its seat at Hage or Hågå in Sødorp (which Ibsen visited on his tour in 1862);[6] supported by Ivar Kleivens,[7] he inclines to identify Peer Gynt with a certain Peder Laurisen Günter (of that family and place), who died in 1665; Kleivens discovered the name of a certain Jonn Gynnthe, who was, in 1557/8, living on crown property that may have been Hågå, a fact which points to the possibility that 'Gynnthe' was the original name and that the

---

[1] By Valdemar Rørdam.  [2] *Breve*, I, 151.
[3] *Norske Huldre-Eventyr og Folkesagn* (1845–8).
[4] Halvorsen, J. B., *Norsk Forfatter-Lexikon*, II (1888), p. 770.
[5] 'Per Gynt Replikk til Pål Kluften', in *Edda*, xxx (1930), p. 681.
[6] A few miles south of Vinstra railway-station in the Gudbrandsdal.
[7] Quoted in the preface to the Centenary Edition, p. 53.

affiliation to the Günter family came later. Hr. Pål Kluften, on the other hand, believes[1] that Hougen was not the sole repository of lore relating to Peer Gynt and that Asbjørnsen, while collecting his materials, stayed at Lårgardseter på Høvringen, and there was told legends by Peer Fugleskjelle[2] about a Peer Gynt who was, historically, Peder Olsen Hage of Hågå, nicknamed Gynt (perhaps from the verb *gjyne* = 'to see'), and who died in 1785.[3] For what it is worth (which is not perhaps very much) the latter theory has the advantage of corresponding rather more closely with the chronological indication given by Ibsen himself. The identification does not seem to be of the first importance, and it is clear that, even if Ibsen had, as he suggests, sources besides Asbjørnsen, they did not contribute anything of moment to his recollections. It will become equally certain, however, from what follows that the stories current about the original Peer Gynt have nothing to do with history.[4]

The yarns about Peer Gynt which, whatever their ultimate provenance, Asbjørnsen committed to paper and Ibsen knew are conveniently collected for English readers in the Archer brothers' appendix to their translation of the play.[5] So no more will now be necessary than to mention or, at most, summarise them, in order to show the uses to which they were turned.[6] Of the longest of the episodes which Ibsen took over even such treatment must be postponed a little; it is Peer's darkling

[1] 'Per Gynt', in *Edda*, xxx (1930), p. 120.

[2] Asbjørnsen acknowledges that the story of Peer Gynt and the Boyg came to him from Fugleskjelle.

[3] Koht mentions (II, 30 n.) a certain Peder Gynt, who lived about 1500 at Klingsbo in Dalarne in Sweden.

[4] In his last essay on Ibsen (*Samlede Skrifter*, xviii, 126), Georg Brandes gives an account of an unnamed young Dane, a great boaster, who, he declares, served as a model for the characterisation of Peer Gynt. Bull (*Henrik Ibsens Peer Gynt*, 1947, p. 95) brings rather better evidence for identification with a Captain Thorvald Møller, whom Bjørnson also used as a model for Bothwell in *Maria Stuart i Skotland* and John Kurt in *Det Flager i Byen og på Havnen*. It is not impossible that Ole Bull and the restless and sometimes crack-brained champion of *landsmaal*, Vinje, whom Ibsen knew from his student days, furnished some traits for Peer too.

[5] Archer, IV, 272; the version there is an adaptation from H. L. Brækstad's collection entitled *Round the Yule Log* (1881): Ibsen did not utilise all the stories about Peer Gynt.

[6] For a fuller discussion of Ibsen's use of folk-lore in *Peer Gynt*, cf. Stavnem, P. L., 'Overnaturlige Væsener og Symbolik: Henrik Ibsens *Peer Gynt*', in *Afhandlinger viede Sophus Bugges Minde* (1908), p. 97.

encounter with Bøjgen or 'The Boyg', which must take a prominent place in the discussion, farther on, of the play's general significance.

The Boyg is a 'Troll-Monster', one of the curious beings rife in Norwegian folk-lore, but for which there is no English counterpart, none at any rate in modern, educated or secondary-school usage. Such a 'troll' is somewhat in the nature of what Hamlet calls 'a goblin damned' or one of the hobs about which Canon Atkinson has to report:[1] supernatural and by no means heaven-born creatures, but definitely corporeal both in their acts and what may be called their consistency.[2] They assume forms to which all the human senses react, and they indulge in behaviour which not uncommonly causes grievous bodily harm. Two relevant passages in Asbjørnsen's *Fairy-Tales* (besides that about the Boyg) depend essentially on a troll's corporeality, those in which Peer comes upon dairy-maids, 'sæter-girls',[3] 'carrying on' with trolls in the dark; one, who was 'called Mad Kari', while her two companions were praying in terror against all assaults of the evil ones, 'said...she would like to see what stuff there was in such fellows'. Out of these two scraps Ibsen made the scene of the three dairy-maids who, in default of their young men, call upon trolls to take them and with whom, to their delight, Peer offers to lie, all three at once.

One short passage in Ibsen's primary source, Asbjørnsen, says something about Peer's character as distinct from his adventures: he is a yarn-spinner and boaster, it says, always making out that 'he himself had been mixed up in all the stories that people said had happened in the olden times'. It is quite in accord with this hint that Ibsen lets Peer appropriate to himself[4] an adventure which, in Asbjørnsen's collection, is

[1] E.g. *Forty Years in a Moorland Parish* (1891), p. 65.

[2] As a Dutchman, R. C. Boer has the same difficulties as an English reader; he points out that the conception of 'troll' lies somewhat between 'evil spirit' (which is incorporeal) and fictions corresponding to our elves, pixies and gnomes (whose activities may be beneficent to man). Cf. his 'Peer Gynt' in *De Gids* (4th series, XI, 1893), pp. iv, 65 n.

[3] The *sæter* are the upland meadows, often far from the home-farms (like the Alpen proper in Switzerland), to which the cattle are driven in summer, under the charge of wenches who look after them and their produce.

[4] II, 279; Archer, V, 4.

attributed to a certain Gudbrand Glesne—the story of the
huntsman's marvellous and terrifying ride astride the reindeer-
buck which he thinks he has killed. Garnished in his most
vivacious, headlong verse, Ibsen uses the recital of this incident
by its supposed hero as a most effective introduction to Peer
Gynt himself and his mother and also to the half-real, half-
phantastic spirit of the whole work—and the introduction
would be all the more striking to anyone remembering who the
putative hero of the ride was according to Asbjørnsen.

## III

The intricate, rich blending of the real and the fantastic
elements in *Peer Gynt* tends in itself to enhance the fantastic
air of the whole, such as Ibsen only once before had so boldly
essayed, in that immature comedy, *St John's Eve* (*Sancthansnatten*, 1853), which forms a curious 'outlier', as we have seen,
to the Danish *vaudeville* of Johan Ludvig Heiberg. As is always
prudent in analogous cases we will first, as well as may be,
disentangle what is 'real' or what may plausibly be taken for real.

The solid outlines of *Peer Gynt* portray a man's life from youth
to the brink of the grave. This man is the son of a deceased
rustic magnate and of Aase, whom her husband's extravagance
and her son's idle improvidence have reduced to poverty.
The first act of the play serves principally to indicate Peer's
personality and place in the world. Attracted by the likelihood
of meeting jolly girls, Peer betakes himself to the wedding-
party in honour of an attractive peasant-bride and a poltroon
of a bridegroom. As the scabbed sheep of the fold in that out-
of-the-way corner of Norway,[1] he is cold-shouldered by all the
company except some strangers, pietistic immigrants; one of
the girls in this group, Solveig, hearing of his reputation, breaks
her promise to dance with him and, in his furious disappointment, he elopes with (and presumably has carnal knowledge of)
the bride, only to forsake her the following morning.

This action of Peer's turns the somewhat passive dislike of his

---

[1] The action of Acts I, II, III and most of V is supposed to take place at the upper
end of the Gudbrandsdal where it approaches the wild regions of Dovre and
Rondane (Bull, F., *Henrik Ibsens Peer Gynt*, 1947, p. 22).

neighbours to active persecution; while bailiffs distrain from Aase almost everything but her bed, the hue-and-cry are after her son, who, however, is warned by the pietists and eventually joined in the distant mountain-solitude, where alone he can be safe, by Solveig, loving and penitent. But before he can complete their log-cabin and begin to live with her, he is constrained to leave the neighbourhood, and, after solacing his mother in her dying hour, he goes overseas.

These incidents, which may be held to comprise anything between a few weeks and several years,[1] fill the first three Acts of the play. Act IV is laid in North Africa—Morocco to begin with and Egypt[2] at the end—and must be deemed to take place many years, perhaps a quarter of a century, later. Peer has by now become a middle-aged man, who has amassed wealth as a Charleston trader, dealing in all manner of commodities, and he takes himself and even his culture most seriously. By the end of this series of scenes, however, he has lost all his possessions to unfaithful acquaintances and the Muhammedan baggage Anitra, and the airing of his notions has brought him into a lunatic asylum.

Act V (which in itself covers only a few days, or even hours) must take place about as long after Act IV as Act IV after the rest. Peer, an old man, has made his way home to Norway to die. He seems destitute—in that a shipwreck flings him naked on to his native shore—and the figure which he may cut in the world preoccupies him no more. He finds Solveig still living in the home he designed for them both, but old, of course, and blind, and they enjoy a rapturous reunion.

# IV

Such a recapitulation as has just been given obviously cannot tell even half the story, the 'real' half of it. On turning to the other, the fantastic, half, we must in the first place pay par-

---

[1] It is not unreasonable to hold that Solveig is a little girl at the wedding-party and of marriageable years when she comes on her skis over the waste to throw in her lot with Peer; and, however 'unreal' the scenes with the *trolls* are supposed to be, the fact that Peer has a son by one of them suggests a certain passage of time. On the other hand, the gait of the scenes suggests precipitancy rather than leisureliness.

[2] Ibsen's own visit to Egypt only took place after the completion of *Peer Gynt*.

ticular attention to the more obvious links between it and the real part. Two present themselves at once as such. The one, that comprised by the African scenes, can be rapidly dismissed in this place.[1] The scenes, indeed, seem 'substantial' enough—the marooning of Peer on Afric's strand, the blowing-up of his private steam-yacht, his discomfiture by apes, his stealing of the prophet's steed and his bilking by Anitra, etc.,—but they may well be considered to be all in the nature of a phantasmagoria.

The second link between the 'real' and 'fantastic' portions of the drama is structurally more important and at least as interesting. It is involved in the question: how does Peer come to leave home, just when all seems 'set fair' after long tribulation? He has (we may remember) eluded his persecutors, he has built himself a house where, it seems, some sort of economic future is assured him, he has just been joined by the woman whose image has haunted his mind from the moment he first met her. Why does he, all of a sudden, turn his back on all this? What is it that constrains Peer to forsake Solveig?

Peer's desertion is an outcome of his first unmistakable trafficking with the supernatural, which starts (so it seems) quite on the natural, 'real' plane and becomes more and more fantastical. After coping with the three dairy-wenches and leaving them, Peer falls in with a female, poorly dressed in green,[2] the 'Green-Clad Woman', to whom he is manifestly attracted.[3] Finding that grandiose talk, as well as coming naturally to his lips, meets with her favour, Peer represents himself as a person of consequence, and she in her turn informs him that she is the daughter of King Brose, 'the Old Man of the Dovre'.[4] Accepting him as her lover, she rides off with him on

---

[1] The subject is taken up again in § X of this chapter.

[2] I presume that she is dressed in this colour, because in folk-lore, especially that of the North (I fancy), green is the traditional colour of the elves, pixies and fairies who haunt woods, streams and mountains.

[3] The stage-direction reads: 'Peer Gynt follows her, with all sorts of lover-like antics.' (II, 309; Archer, IV, 65.)

[4] The Dovre is a wild and inaccessible mountain-region of Norway supposedly the haunt of trolls. The Old Man is to be taken both as their King and (in Act V especially) as their typical representative. No other country has trolls like Norway, and in his trolls of Dovre, as he did with Huhu, Ibsen incidentally made fun of the ultra-nationalism of certain Norwegians: the trolls, for instance, believe in autarchy.

a gigantic pig[1] to her father's hall; in due course this female evidently produces a child, and, just after Solveig has taken possession of Peer's hut, 'an *Old-looking Woman*, in a tattered green gown, comes out from the wood; an *Ugly Brat*, with an ale-flagon in his hand, limps after, holding on to her skirt'.[2] Though astonished, Peer does not deny paternity of the Brat, and its mother promises Peer, if he will discard Solveig, to resume her former attractiveness; otherwise,

Be sure I'll return every day of the year.
Through the door, set ajar, I'll peep in at you both...
When you're tender, Peer Gynt,—when you'd pet and caress her,—
I'll seat myself by you, and ask for my share.
She there and I—we will take you by turns.[3]

It is this prospect that, after some self-debate, Peer cannot face, and he starts off on his lifelong wandering rather than

Go in after this...(so) befouled and disgraced.[4]

Whether or not the preceding scenes with the trolls are to be allowed some sort of objective reality, they obviously are not purely episodic; they mean something very real to Peer since the decisive action of his life is guided by them.


## V

If the African scenes be set aside, there are two groups of purely 'fantastic' episodes, those of the second and third acts on the one hand and those of the last act on the other; they are tolerably distinct, even if the Old Man of Dovre figures in both. The former may be summed up as Peer's Adventures with the Trolls, two focal points in them being the scene in the Hall of the Mountain King and Peer's Encounter with the Boyg.

*Peer Gynt* is a piece of crazy high spirits, as Ibsen insisted to Prozor,[5] and to nail him down, as it were, to a particular—and a profound—meaning in every detail may be, perhaps is, a futile business. None the less, a partial attempt may be made.

---

[1] The pig was apparently a favourite mount of witches; that at any rate is implied by Goethe, to whose Brocken-scenes in *Faust, Part I*, Ibsen may here be indebted.
[2] II, 326; Archer, IV, 101.
[3] II, 328; Archer, IV, 104.　　　　[4] II, 329; Archer, IV, 107.
[5] Prozor, M., *Le Peer Gynt d'Ibsen* (1897), p. 32.

For Ibsen, besides being a conscientious artist, was a satirist, one always intent on what lay behind human manifestations; and even if he played the fool, as after the self-purgation of *Brand* he felt disposed to do as at no other time in his life, he was not the man to babble at random and crack jokes for the joke's sake. Who can avoid feeling that the scene with the Withered Leaves and the Thread-Balls must be intended to convey something?

Two preliminary, matter-of-fact observations on the fantastic element should be put forward, for what they may be worth. First, one must bear in mind the Green-Clad One's emphatic statement that the trials which she is inflicting on Peer are 'For nothing but thoughts and desires'.[1] Secondly, just before his earliest encounters with this creature, that is to say before his earliest actual—not deliberately invented—experience of the marvellous, Peer, in an ecstatic feeling of rebirth amid wild nature after his stuffy promiscuous intercourse with the dairy-wenches, 'leaps forward, but runs his head against a rock, falls, and remains stretched on the ground'.[2] In perfect accord with all Ibsen's adductions of the supernatural or of what seems supernatural (like the White Horses of *Rosmersholm*, the Rat-Wife of *Little Eyolf*, Solness's 'helpers and servers') he opens the door to a purely physical explanation, which, if we choose to ignore, we ignore at our peril. Peer's adventures with the trolls *may* be nothing but dreams as he lies stunned by the accident, and on a fantasy-filled, undisciplined mind they have all the effect of an actual physical experience.

To come now to our 'focal points'. Two things stand out in the scene laid in 'The Royal Hall of the King of the Dovre-Trolls' (II, vi): the King's promulgation of the Trolls' philosophy and Peer's final refusal to become one of them. Peer makes a remark to the effect that he can detect no difference at all between the trolls' [i.e. demons' or devils'] principles and those of mankind, to which his exalted interlocutor, the King, replies

True enough....
Yet morning is morning, and even is even,
And there is a difference all the same.—
Now let me tell you wherein it lies:

[1] II, 328; Archer, IV, 105.    [2] II, 309; Archer, IV, 65.

> Out yonder, under the shining vault,
> Among men the saying goes: 'Man be thyself!'
> At home here with us 'mid the tribe of the trolls,
> The saying goes: 'Troll, to thyself be—enough!'[1]

Now, though this (as it may well do) strikes Peer as 'misty', he is not only willing to grave it upon his scutcheon, as the old King enjoins, but, in effect, even after escaping the trolls' power he applies it as his working rule of life.

'To thyself be—enough' is the Archers' translation of this motto, and in the context of the scene in which it is proclaimed, the translation could hardly be bettered. 'Be self-sufficient' or 'Cultivate self-sufficiency' would be a paraphrase picking out or emphasising a peculiar quality which the Teutonic words 'To thyself be enough' gloss over, but which is demanded by the contrast to the other slogan, to the slogan postulated as being that of mankind. 'Man, be thyself' has no hint of self-*sufficiency*. 'Be thyself'—since it may imply going or reaching outside oneself—is not an extension or limitation of 'To thyself be enough', but it is opposed to 'To thyself be enough'. '*Nok*', 'enough', as the Old Man of the Dovre insists, is the 'potent and sundering word'.[2] The distinction is between individualism and egoism. Milton, in *Paradise Lost*,[3] had also, it is instructive to note, devised 'Live to ourselves' as an article in a devilish programme.

As lapidary as Milton is Prozor with his 'Chacun pour soi';[4] but it introduces into the Troll-King's slogan an element of competition, which, though apt, seems unwarranted here. It would be quite natural if Peer, on becoming a big business man in the golden age of *laissez-faire*,[5] should adopt the principle of 'each for himself—and the devil take the hindmost'. In the scenes, however, which exhibit him in his pride—and not in these scenes alone—Peer is shown as supremely indifferent to the hindmost, they do not exist for him.

---

[1] II, 312; Archer, IV, 71. The two slogans, in the original, are 'Mand, vær dig selv!' and 'Trold, vær dig selv—nok!' Bull points out (*Henrik Ibsens Peer Gynt*, 1947, p. 76) that 'være sig selv nok' (or self-sufficiency) was a slogan often heard in Norwegian politics during the 1850's and 1860's.

[2] II, 312; Archer, IV, 72.  [3] II, l. 254.

[4] *Le Peer Gynt d'Ibsen* (1897), p. 40.

[5] He cruises the Mediterranean in a steam-yacht: this puts the time of his maturity well into the nineteenth century.

Nothing exists for him except his own momentary interests. He is convinced of their indefeasibility; a few trumpery vexations apart, his activities and plans fill him with satisfaction, and he can reinforce his sublime conviction of being in the right by quotations of traditional lore: for it is well known that the self-cancelling aggregation of proverbs, slogans or texts can be made to prove and excuse anything. So the mature Peer, in the unprincipled acquisition of his wealth, in his *allures*—now of an earthly potentate who backs the more remunerative side, and now of a man of refinement and learning—in his refusal to commit himself completely to any person, cause or ideal, does in effect act completely up to the trolls' philosophy.

For all that, Peer ultimately refuses to undergo the ocular operation by which the trolls propose to make him one of themselves. He is about to be tortured to death for his recalcitrance; the Old Man of the Dovre goes to bed, leaving him to the mercy of the swarming Troll-Imps, and they are just on the point of sticking out his eyes, when he cries out, collapsing:

Mother, help me, I die!

Then the stage-direction reads

*Church bells sound far away.*[1]

The would-be tormentors exclaim: 'Bells in the mountain! The Black-Frocks' cows' and '*take to flight, amid a confused uproar of yells and shrieks. The palace collapses; everything disappears.*'[2]

## VI

The upshot of the adventure with the Boyg, which follows immediately after, is very similar.[3] In a scene of pitchy darkness Peer finds himself beset by a vast, amorphous body, that obstructs his passage in whatever direction he attempts to move

[1] Aase had promised (II, 305; Archer, IV, 58): 'If he's taken by trolls, we must ring the bells for him.'

[2] II, 317; Archer, IV, 83. The trolls of the Norwegian uplands associated all bell-ringing with cattle-bells; church-bells therefore are the black-frocked clergy's cow-bells.

[3] Logeman believes that, as the scene with the Boyg was written in the first draft on different paper from the rest, it was a later insertion (*Commentary on Peer Gynt*, 1917, p. 133).

forward. It thwarts and worries him, so he sinks down, finally, at the point of inanimation, to gasp:

> Too dear the purchase one pays for life
> In such a heart-wasting hour of strife.[1]

Just before this, however, he has remembered his first glimpse of Solveig, coming to the wedding-party with her hymn-book, and cried out:

> If you'd save me now, lass, you must do it quick!
> Gaze not adown so, lowly and bending.—
> Your clasp-book! Hurl it straight into his eyes!

The call, evidently, is heard; the Boyg gives up: 'He was too strong. There were women behind him.'[2]

The means of Peer's salvation, at this juncture and elsewhere, must engage our attention further on. But something more must here and now be said of the Boyg—which, in addition to a bodily presence, possesses a voice, and an argumentative voice at that. What is the Boyg? What is it doing here? For what, in the poem, do it and the Trolls stand?

The Boyg is a Voice and a Presence. Its substance is enormous and viscous,

> Not dead, not living; all slimy; misty.
> Not so much as a shape.[3]

If one strikes out at it, that proves of no avail:

> It's the Boyg that's unwounded, and the Boyg that was hurt,
> It's the Boyg that is dead, and the Boyg that's alive.

He does not strike back, but whenever a step forward is attempted, he stands in the way:

> He is *there*! And *there*! And he's round the bend!
> No sooner I'm out there I'm back in the ring.

[1] II, 319; Archer, IV, 87:
[2] Beyer, H., *Søren Kierkegaard og Norge*, p. 159, quotes from Kierkegaard's *Enten—Eller*, II: 'Of 100 men who go astray in the world, 99 are redeemed by women' ('Af 100 Mænd, der forvilde sig i Verden, frelses de 99 af Qvinder').
[3] II, 319; Archer, IV, 85.

A good deal of what he is and is not he imparts himself. He delivers himself of one grand precept

Go round about, Peer,

and he makes one further, very brief remark, calling for notice. When Peer challenges him,

Who *are* you?

he replies, 'Myself'. That may be, as Peer thinks, an unhelpful remark. Yet it is by no means impossible to construe it—and, with it, the whole wild, noisy and whirling skirmish in the indistinguishable dark—as implying a self-debate. Peer, left stunned, unconscious at the end of Act II, sc. iv, may be deliriously disputing with part of his own self.

The Great Boyg was not an invention of Ibsen's fancy, any more than the trolls as a race were: he was well known in folklore and on that score comes into Asbjørnsen's account. His name, Bøjg, is, apparently, connected with the English *bow = bend*, and is therefore correctly rendered in the French version as *le Tordu* and in the German as *der grosse Krumme*. Brækstad called him 'Humpy',[1] but that sounds too benign. Primarily the name implies, as defined in Brynildsen's *Norwegian-English Dictionary*,[2] 'a goblin snake coiled up round a man', perhaps a domesticated variety of the *midgardsorm*, the serpent which encircles the world, according to old Scandinavian mythology. Even in general use, however, it seems to signify something more—as does its cousin, 'the worm that never dies': it may be 'a mythical representation of a man's sinful past',[3] laying its boa-constrictor's coils around him. But when in Act IV Peer formally identifies[4] the Boyg with the Sphinx, we may surely conclude that one of the interpretations present to his mind was metaphysical. 'In this aspect, the Boyg would typify the riddle of existence, with which we grapple in vain, and which we have to "get round" as best we can.'[5] Too much importance, I think, should not be attached to the identification, since only Peer makes it, nor to any generalisation based on it.

---

[1] *Round the Yule Log* (1881), p. 146.
[2] *Cit.* Logeman, H., in *Edda*, VI (1916), p. 356. This article, 'Den Store Bøigen', deals fully with all the interpretations.
[3] Logeman, in *Edda*, VI (1916), p. 357.
[4] II, 370; Archer, IV, 174.     [5] Archer, IV, xxvii.

Whatever 'symbolism' be attached to them, the strong probability must never be overlooked that, like much of the end of
*Brand*, all the troll-scenes of Act II (including the scene with the
Great Boyg) are to be taken as purely subjective phenomena,
that they are a phantasmagoria representing not so much any
hair-raising experiences undergone or sinful acts perpetrated by
Peer in actuality as the devices and desires of his own heart,
those which at one time factually drove him into the arms of
the like-minded dairy-maids.

The Boyg may stand for some kind of physical hindrance or
a materialised inhibition, though it is improbable that the conception is valid here, since, as Logeman points out,[1] the hero's
'sinful past' is already represented (if by anyone) by the Green-
Clad One on her last appearance. The Boyg would seem to
stand for something certainly hindering and inhibiting, but of
a vaster, more ineluctable and even less definite sort, the inertia
which prevents one from conforming to the prime motto of man,
'Man, be thyself'. Not only in Norway does this phenomenon
thrive. H. G. Wells's Mr Polly has his Boyg, since he asks himself: 'Why had he submitted to things, blundered into things?
Why had he never insisted on the things he thought beautiful
and the things he desired, never sought them, fought for them,
taken any risk for them, died rather than abandon them?';
and Professor Logeman pertinently observes[2] that Prince Hamlet
of Denmark may have run up against the Great Boyg long before
Peer Gynt did.

Archer favours something even less defined: 'The truth
probably is that the poet vaguely intended this vague monster
to be as elusive in its symbolism as in its physical constitution.'[3]


## VII

The 'fantastic' phenomena of the fifth act are of a rather
different nature—some at least seem to be: for the episode of
the Strange Passenger may be assimilated to those of the Dovre-
King's palace and the Great Boyg as pathologically explicable

---

[1] *Edda*, VI (1916), p. 358.        [2] *Edda*, VI (1916), p. 364.
[3] Archer, IV, XXVII.

hallucinations. When the 'caprices'[1] of *Peer Gynt* are spoken of, the scenes in Act v (plus, perhaps, the madhouse at Cairo) are usually meant. As has been noted, they very probably were all later additions to the original scheme.

For length and significance, the scenes with the Button-Moulder take pride of place. But, as a *process* of some sort is supposedly at work in this last act, it seems desirable to take and discuss its scenes in their order.

Something about Peer's general state at this stage of his career should be premissed. The stage-direction at the head of the act describes him as 'a vigorous old man, with grizzled hair and beard'; 'his clothing is rather the worse for wear';[2] he has come from Panama and, though he may not be the plutocrat he appeared to be at the beginning of Act iv, he has with him a pretty packet, 'more than enough', the Captain opines, 'to make you of weight among people at home here'. His egoism has, by now, eaten deep into him: he revels in the description of the simple sailor-man's homecoming only in order to contemplate spoiling it; he urges on the crew to attempt an impossible rescue (no doubt in the hope that they, too, will perish); and, later, when the ship is wrecked, he feels no compunction at all in sending, cold-bloodedly and consciously, the Cook to his account.

But before this last-named happening, he has had the first of two encounters with the Strange Passenger (noticed, as is expressly marked, by none but himself), who comes on deck when the violence of the storm waxes dangerous. One of his observations to Peer runs:

> Friend,—have you *once* in each half-year
> Felt all the earnestness of dread [*angstens alvor*]?[3]

and it is a strong temptation to identify him with the fear of death;[4] but Ibsen waxed so rabid against Clemens Petersen[5] for saying that he was the concept Fear that such an identification must probably be abandoned. Nevertheless, if he is not *angst*

---

[1] Cf. Logeman, H., 'The "Caprices" in Henrik Ibsen's *Peer Gynt*', in *Edda*, vii (1917), p. 258.

[2] ii, 381; Archer, iv, 193.          [3] ii, 390; Archer, iv, 212.

[4] His second appearance takes place when Peer is struggling in the rough waters.

[5] *Breve*, i, 159.

(fear), he may still be *alvor* (seriousness); he *may*—but in view of Ibsen's wrath and the somewhat humorous character of the Passenger even this is hazardous—he may, appearing at a moment of great peril, represent Peer's first half-hearted (and therefore half-humorous and self-cynical) essay in taking himself with genuine seriousness, Peer beginning to see himself in rather a new light—which is, maybe, the implication of the German critics who conceive him to be Peer's 'Doppelgänger'.[1]

A third possibility is that the Strange Passenger is the earliest appearance of the Button-Moulder, an interpretation which the first stage-producer of the drama may have had at the back of his mind, when he cast the same actor for these two parts (and, much less defensibly,[2] for the Lean One as well).[3] The Button-Moulder, we are repeatedly assured, is only an agent; he is an emissary of 'Master', much as the Messenger in *Everyman* or Merry-Report in *The Play of the Weather* are the direct envoys of God, and the Strange Passenger, too, seems to come from some mysterious realm which lies outside Peer's personality:

*Where I come from*, there smiles are prized
As highly as pathetic style.[4]

Whatever he may or may not stand for, Peer exchanges two disquieting colloquies with the Strange Passenger; meanwhile, his ship has gone to the bottom, he has pushed the only other survivor, the Cook, off the overturned boat to which they are clinging and he has landed on the shore of Norway with nothing but the clothes he stands up in, not expecting to know anyone or to be known by any. His first experience thereafter is an interment—the burial and parsonic panegyric of the man whom,

---

[1] According to a piece of popular superstition especially prized by writers of the Romantic revival, a man or woman was able to witness a kind of projection of himself, with apparently an independent existence of its own; this was the 'Doppelgänger'; Poe worked out the idea very completely in 'William Wilson'. Heine made use of it and from Heine, whom at one time Ibsen read devotedly, the notion might have come. According to an entry in the *New English Dictionary* (s.v. 'double') the 'appearance of a double...has ever been held...to signify approaching death'.

[2] The Lean One has a horse's hoof, while the Button-Moulder indignantly draws attention to the fact that he has not.

[3] The Strange Passenger betrays the opinion that everything in Peer is dead except his body (II, 389; Archer, IV, 211); that seems to be the view of the Button-Moulder and his Master.

[4] II, 390; Archer, IV, 213.

when they were both lads, he saw[1] chop a finger off his own hand in order to unfit himself for military service. The priest's allocution is both lengthy and, apparently, void of satire; so, even though it meets with Peer's approval, it should evidently be taken seriously. In position, though not in endowments, the departed yokel was very like Peer: he lived in the wilds and had a sweetheart and a family to provide for; this, however, he conceived as absolutely the first obligation upon himself, and to discharge it he not alone mutilated himself painfully and suffered the opprobrium of public opinion, but resolutely adhered to his task in the face of the worst that circumstance could offer, even his own generation's ingratitude. The one task was all to him. The cleric sums up:

> No patriot was he. Both for church and state
> A fruitless tree. But there, on the upland ridge,
> In the small circle where he saw his calling
> There he was great, because he was himself.[2]

As has been said, Peer applauds this speech. In a man who 'was himself' through thick and thin, he thinks to recognise a spirit akin to his own, so that the parson's panegyric might equally well have been pronounced upon himself. He conveniently overlooks the different operations of that spirit.

Upon this ensues a somewhat redundant scene, showing Peer to have become a legend in his own lifetime, together with the not over-facetious anecdote of the Devil and the Pig at San Francisco.[3] It is followed in its turn by Peer's monologue over the onion, which deserves the epithet redundant too, in that it conveys all that the Button-Moulder scenes do and vice-versa. Peer picks a wild onion and begins to peel off its layers, likening them to the different episodes through which he has passed and to himself as revealed in these episodes; one layer succeeds another, but at the last nothing is left more substantial than what has been discarded.

> To the innermost centre,
> It's nothing but swathings—each smaller and smaller,

---

[1] II, 322; Archer, IV, 93.

[2] II, 393; Archer, IV, 217; it is to be remarked that the word translated into English as 'calling' is not *kald*, but *virke*, field for activity.

[3] Logeman, following others, notes (*Commentary*, p. 301) that it comes from Phædrus.

with nothing to swathe. But when he has terminated his moralising over the onion, he catches sight of the log-cabin which he built with his own hands long ago—and thereupon something happens to him, to which we shall advert later.

His house scarcely glimpsed again, Peer takes to his heels once more, and the natural objects in his path begin to talk to him: Thread-Balls complain that, instead of being what they look like, they

should have soared up
        Like clangorous voices,

the Withered Leaves that
                a watchword,
        Thou shouldst have proclaimed us

and so forth; even the Voice of Aase supervenes with a complaint that he has deceived her.

Brandes criticised[1] the last-named scene on the score that the natural objects suggest too lofty demands: what watchwords, songs and thoughts could rightly be expected from the 'miserable Peer'? But the Button-Moulder, the most important of these odd apparitions in the last act, now coming upon the scene, evidently disagrees with Brandes's lowly view of the hero.

        You [he asserts] were designed for a shining button
        On the vest of the world;

he adds, however,
                but your loop gave way.[2]

A button, whatever its metal or brilliance, with a defective loop, being no good at all,

                . . . into the waste-box you needs must go
        And there, as they phrase it, be merged in the mass;

Peer must be melted down, with others, to furnish material for a new magazine of buttons. To the extreme individualist, whether he have accepted the motto 'Be thyself' or 'To thyself be enough', this merging, this loss of the individual *ego* constitutes the most painful lot that can come to him:

                With both teeth and claws
        I'll fight against this.

---

[1] *Samlede Skrifter*, III (1900), p. 297. *Henrik Ibsen, Bjørnstjerne Bjørnson* (English translation, 1898), p. 67.           [2] II, 405; Archer, IV, 288.

But the Button-Moulder comfortably remarks

> Bless me, my dear Peer, there is surely no need
> To get so wrought up about trifles like this.
> Yourself you never have been at all;—
> Then what does it matter, your dying right out?

Peer sees the crux of his case and undertakes to prove that he *has* been himself, and on that condition he is respited.

The first witness whom he hopes to subpoena turns out to be the Old Man of the Dovre, the Mountain-King, who accidentally crosses his path, somewhat come down in the world,[1] and who is pleased to meet his almost-son-in-law again, but whose pleasure and admiration prove most inconvenient when he is invited to testify to Peer's heroic refusal to become a troll, since he intends a laudation of him as an exemplification of the great Troll motto 'To thyself be—enough' with all emphasis on 'the potent and sundering word'. So, after a further intimidating talk with the Button-Moulder, Peer has to sheer off on the other tack; if he cannot establish an identity as an almost saintly hero, then at any rate he will capitalise on his trafficking in slaves and idols and the almost literal 'bumping-off' of the Ship's Cook. If he is not fit for heaven, he will be a candidate for hell. But the Devil,[2] who encounters him in clerical dress, The Lean One, is at once put off by Peer's pawky attempt to strike a bargain, and they part without any mutual benefit.

Peer is now resigned to the fate to which the Button-Moulder, applying for the last time, is minded to inflict upon him; but he is not apathetically or hopelessly or even peevishly resigned. He sees that the game is up, but in that recognition he betrays for the first time an appreciation of the fine game it might have been:

> Thou beautiful earth, be not angry with me
> That I trampled thy grasses to no avail.
> Thou beautiful sun, thou hast squandered away
> Thy glory of light in an empty hut.
> There was no one within it to hearten and warm;—
> The owner, they tell me, was never at home.

[1] This perhaps corresponds to the decay of romantic rapture over fairies, goblins and such which had set in in Ibsen's lifetime.

[2] Proclaimed such by his nails and hoof (II, 414; Archer, III, 257).

Some premonition of this change of heart might have been detected in a scene already touched on, that in which Peer, the peeling of the onion completed, discovers his old log-hut. Hardly has he recognised it, when he hears the voice of Solveig within, not merely singing, but singing of himself. Thereupon

PEER

*(Rises, quiet and deadly pale.)*

One that's remembered,—and one that's forgot.[1]
One that has squandered,—and one that has saved.—
Oh, earnest!—and never can the game be played o'er!
Oh, dread!—*here* was my Kaiserdom!

*(Hurries off along the wood path.)* [2]

It is reasonably clear that at least this once Peer had felt a constriction of the heart, *angstens alvor*, recognised not only that he had committed a gross mistake in not doing more or less what the dead yokel had done, but also that, in committing that error, he had (to use a theological phrase) factually imperilled his salvation. All his 'values' and the personal policy erected upon them have been wrong, fatally wrong. Peer may be said to be convicted of sin; at any rate, his self-sufficiency has suffered a fatal wound.

Now comes the last scene, in which Peer passes beyond the recognition of error and the conviction of sin, to mend his ways and to confess his trespasses. He feels terror;[3] when the Button-Moulder summons him yet again, he pushes him aside with

Though your ladle were huge as a coffin
It were too small, I tell you, for me and my sins.

The Boyg's advice recurs to his mind, but

Ah no [he concludes]; this time at least
Right through, though the path may be never so strait.

---

[1] I.e. Peer and Solveig respectively.
[2]     'En, som har husket,—og en, som har glemt.
        En, som har mistet,—og en, som har gemt.—
        O, alvor!—Og aldrig kan det leges om!
        O, angst! *Her* var mit kejserdom!'     (II, 400; Archer, IV, 230.)
[3] 'angst', II, 418; Archer, IV, 266.

*He runs towards the hut; at the same moment Solveig appears in the doorway, dressed for church, with a psalm-book wrapped in a kerchief, and a staff in her hand...* PEER (*Flings himself down on the threshold.*)
Hast thou doom for a sinner, then speak it forth![1]

It may well be that the details of the process do not emerge with perfect clarity,[2] but it can scarcely be doubted that by his terror, contrition and appeal for mercy Peer does obtain absolution, that the wanderer, home at last, is 'saved' by Solveig's answer to the question where he has been, he, 'the whole man, the true man, with God's sigil upon his brow'—

In my faith, in my hope, and in my love.

## VIII

In so far as both are tragedies, *Peer Gynt* and *Brand* are complementary to one another. If *Brand* is the tragedy of blind idealism, devoid of *caritas*, *Peer Gynt* is the tragedy of a man who, however much of *amor* he may have, lacks principle and ignores ideals. But the conclusion of *Peer Gynt*, as has just been seen, bears an obvious resemblance to that of *Brand*. A change of heart, as it may baldly be called, overtakes the hero, who admits his error and is pardoned. Boer, brought up in a good Calvinistical country, sees the problems of the two plays in terms of grace. 'The question on which *Brand* and *Peer Gynt* turn', he says,[3] 'is none other than that which Christian dogmatics formulate thus: "What must a man do to be saved?"' And later: '*Brand* teaches that no man can find his account [*het stellen*] without grace, *Peer Gynt* preaches that none is excluded from it. But just as for the man of will it is necessary for his redemption that he recognise the insufficiency of his powers, so conversely Peer Gynt, who has sinned through weakness and lack of seriousness, cannot be saved except by an *act*. That act is the decision, not to go round about but at least for once to go straight on. As soon as he does that, he meets Solveig.'[4]

The function of Solveig in the process by which Peer may be

[1] II, 419; Archer, IV, 268.
[2] Why should Peer suddenly ask 'Canst thou tell me where Peer Gynt has been since we parted?'? It is not *where* he has been, strictly, that is at issue now, but rather *what* or *who* he has been.
[3] Boer, R. C., 'Peer Gynt' in *De Gids*, XI (4th series), 1893, pp. iv, 61.
[4] *Ibid.* pp. 78 f.

deemed to work out his salvation deserves some attention, in fact the part in the drama taken by the women as a sex. About the Green-Clad One, about the dairy-wenches, about the bride Ingrid no more need be said than already has been noted, unless it be this, relative to Ingrid. Highly admired as Peer is by the other clowns for his strength in climbing a steep acclivity with a full-grown young female on his shoulders, it is clear that, since he is nowhere presented as a second Hercules, the abduction has the girl's consent. Peer *is* different from the others, who, loop or no loop, were certainly never destined to shine as fine buttons on the cosmic waistcoat; in Ingrid's eyes he is as different from the fumbling ineffectiveness of the bridegroom[1] as he is from the gross boozers and hooligans who attend her wedding. It may be vulgarly formulated that he 'has a way with him'. And, amid the natural confusion of her sentiments, Ingrid appears genuinely sorry to part from him after her unconventional wedding-night.

For all the Ingrids, milk-maids and Green Ones, the 'way' that Peer has with him is not just the primrose path of dalliance. It is to demonstrate that fact that, one may suppose, the scenes with his mother were inserted. It falls hard not to sentimentalise over someone who dies placidly, and in indigence, on the stage, especially when she does so to the strains of Grieg's music, and the sentimentalist must beware of thinking too highly of Aase; with all her better qualities, she is a fond and feckless, limited peasant-woman; worse than that—the unsatisfactory bottom of her son's character, no doubt inherited,[2] must have been aggravated by the mixture of ineffectual storming and valueless approval with which she treated him and his doings. Still, any depreciation of Aase's character must tend in a measure to exalt her son's treatment of her, affectionate, comradely, humorous, by no means sentimental, especially in the scene, rich with humour, feeling and beauty, in which he drives her through St Peter's gate to her last rest.[3]

---

[1] He has something in common with the intended bridegroom in Smetana's recent opera, *The Bartered Bride* (1866).

[2] The dead father, Jon Gynt, who kept open house on insufficient means and, himself, was a bit of a legend, is said to have been modelled on Ibsen's bankrupt father.

[3] Act III, sc. iv; the presumption is inescapable that the fine, 'human' scenes between Peer and Aase were planned as direct counter-weights to the 'inhumanity' of Brand and *his* mother and their mutual dealings.

Peer gets on well with women; and they get on well with him.[1] No uneasy gallantry and vapid flirtation, no inhibited holding-back deforms their relations. In coping with Ingrid and the dairy-wenches, Peer betrays not the least disposition to adopt the Great Boyg's policy: he goes straight to his goal, at considerable and obvious personal risk too, that threatening from the whole infuriated neighbourhood in the first instance, and, presumably, that from jealous monsters in the second. In fact, Peer is *himself* in dealing with women; and it is that which ensures his escape from the demon imps and from the Great Boyg, before Solveig comes to play a decisive part in his destiny.

Solveig is little more than a child when she and Peer first meet. A newcomer to the district, she speedily learns of Peer's disreputable attributes and so, to his intense chagrin, lets her maiden nervousness break a promise to dance with him. But her image has been indelibly stamped on his imagination, so that he actually upbraids Ingrid (whom his disappointment incited him to abduct) with not being Solveig. She on her side does not forget him and is sorry she failed him at the dance. Among the many affecting scenes in which she figures, none is more moving than that[2] wherein she makes up for this by voluntarily coming to him on her snow-shoes, through the scrub and rock, away from parents and home, with no regard for law and convention.

It may be thought that in running away from her so soon Peer follows the programme of life ('Go roundabout') advocated by the Great Boyg. But in fact he cuts a knot, painfully, at this juncture: the easy way would have been for him to pass a sponge over his sinful past and lusts of the flesh, pretending they never existed, and to begin life with Solveig on the chance that all will be well. He cannot, however, bring himself, even in the remotest and most 'symbolical' way, to sully her and, at the obvious risk of losing her forever—indeed of worse, of being offensively misunderstood by her—he goes off, with perhaps the only half-meant order to wait, on what proves a long lifetime of

---

[1] We need not, I think, be greatly concerned if we find the trollop Anitra a little hard to fit into the generalisation.

[2] III, iii.

wandering and separation. Solveig waits without a murmur—not, I think, because Peer has ordered her to do so, but because she knows with absolute certainty *where*, even *what*, her place in the world is; and she has been assured of that by something *real* which she has seen and guessed in the ne'er-do-well whom she loves.

Peer's redemption, I submit, is not effected by Solveig—what after all can a poor mortal do for another in that way?—it is something which he works out for himself, though (admittedly) he could scarcely have worked it out *but for* Solveig, and she acts dramatically also as a kind of recorder, to show when and how it was done. There was a real, true man, 'with God's sigil upon his brow', and, much sophisticated, there had been one all the time, even if the only mundane record of him had been in Solveig's faith and hope and love. If this argument is accepted, then Peer must be regarded as 'saved'—'saved' from the Button-Moulder's ladle at the very least—and that end must be taken, no more than that of *Brand*, as an unreal piece of sentimental, operatic clap-trap.

## IX

If *Brand* is staged with some celestial apparatus for its last scene, and especially if the Latin words which terminate it are spoken by the voice of Agnes, a resemblance, though a somewhat remote one, to the second part of Goethe's *Faust* can scarcely be gainsaid. A resemblance of this order needs fewer adventitious aids to recognition when *Peer Gynt* is substituted for *Brand*, and Mr A. le R. Andrews has discussed it at length.[1] From the first, the freshness, loyalty, simplicity of Solveig and her implication in the hero's 'redemption' had been likened to the same things in Gretchen; and Mr Andrews draws a number of further parallels: Solveig first appears with a hymn book, as Gretchen is first seen coming from church; the Great Boyg is a counterpart to the Erdgeist;[2] as Faust gains serenity through his scheme of marsh draining, so Peer toys with the prospect of

[1] 'Ibsen's *Peer Gynt* and Goethe's *Faust*', in *Journal of English and Germanic Philosophy*, xiii (1914), p. 238.

[2] Though Mr Andrews is wrong in declaring (p. 242) that the ringing of church bells follows immediately on the exit of both.

irrigating and colonising the Sahara;[1] there is a parallel between the way the mere sensuality of the three dairy-maids leads up to the greater grossness *plus* supernatural trafficking in the Old Man of Dovre's Hall and the sequence 'Auerbachs Keller', 'Hexenküche' and 'Walpurgisnacht'. Mr Andrews thinks that the *blasé* middle-aged gentleman, Peer's, dalliance with Anitra 'neath southern skies has something in common also with the middle-aged gentleman, Dr Faust's, celebrated *affaire* with Helen of Troy; and he reaches the conclusion that Ibsen had *Faust* well in mind throughout the composition of *Peer Gynt*, at the same time being 'consciously bent upon improving the woman's role'.

Goethe's *Faust* is actually quoted, or rather misquoted, in the text of Ibsen's play, when at the height of his fatuity Peer observes: 'Das Ewig-Weibliche ziehet uns an.'[2] Mr Andrews does not like this and, conveniently forgetting the German master's own lapses from good taste and overlooking the inaccuracy of the quotation,[3] cries out: 'these profound words... quoted by the worthless Peer under such peculiarly vulgar circumstances might seem an affront offered the great German poet.' They raise, at all events, once again questions concerning the value or beauty of 'the woman's role' in *Peer Gynt* and, beyond that, of the drama's place in the history of European romanticism, in which the redemptive power of women and the love of the sexes had become a commonly accepted article of faith.

On a cursory view, *Peer Gynt* is a highly romantic work. It is difficult to distinguish whether it belongs to the category of satire, of drama or of other poetry; its vehicle, now grotesque, now beautiful, now clever, is infinitely varied,[4] both within and without its prosodical patterns, and none of these patterns is classical. The poem takes a vast subject, comparable to that of Goethe's *Faust* or Madách's *Tragedy of Man*, and deals with it

---

[1] Suggested also, perhaps, by the colonial project (Oleana) of the great violinist, Ole Bull, who gave Ibsen his start in life at Bergen in 1851.

[2] II, 358; Archer, IV, 156; observe Archer's footnote.

[3] Archer at one time thought Peer's words to be a lapse of Ibsen's memory, but later recognised the subtlety of the alteration.

[4] As a poem, Gerard Gran declared it to be 'the richest, the wittiest, the most diverse and the most beautiful in Northern literature'. (*Ibsen*, I, 191.)

and a number of minor, episodic themes in a kaleidoscopic series of scenes which range from Norwegian caves to the village of Gizeh and which cover a lifetime. A great number of personages is introduced, some of them not of this earth, as indeed the bounds between actuality and dream are constantly overstepped. There are a talking statue, two sunrises and a storm at sea. The arts of the costumier and scene-painter, the theatre-mechanic, the musician and even the ballet-master[1] have constantly to be invoked. The hero is a grandiloquent personage, with imagination for his prime quality and love-affairs for the serious concern of his life, and one woman, the pure love of his youth, is associated in his 'redemption'.[2] These things in *Peer Gynt* immediately suggest parallels, not only with *Faust* and *The Tragedy of Man*, but also with such works as Schiller's *William Tell*, Byron's *Don Juan*, Œhlenschläger's *Aladdin*, Hugo's *Marion Delorme* and Hans Andersen's *Fairy Tales*,[3] all typical products of the Romantic ages.

The plays and poems just listed have only to be named together with *Peer Gynt* to suggest, however, an obvious distinction. The old story made it necessary, of course, for Faust's salvation to look like a pretty chancy business, but from the very beginning he plainly enjoys the whole-hearted sympathy of Goethe, who could not by any possibility let him finally be damned. And all the other 'heroes', too, enjoy their creators' moral support much more powerfully than Peer, whose career is, at best, followed with good-humoured, half-sardonic amusement, generally with impassibility and never with unmistakable benevolence,[4] so that to the very end the spectators remain in doubt as to his prevailing over the Button-Moulder.

The pundits of Romanticism had exalted imagination, primarily of course as an informing power in literature; but the representation of its force, under the favourable aspect

---

[1] E.g. for Ingrid's wedding and the scene in the Old Man of Dovre's Hall.

[2] A fine example of 'Romantische Ironie' is the Strange Passenger's assuring Peer he won't drown as they haven't reached the end of Act v yet (ii, 390; Archer, iv, 213).

[3] It is possible that Ibsen took the name of his chief troll from 'Trold-Gubben fra Dovre' in Andersen's *Elverhøi* (Moe, M., in *Edda*, xiv, 1921, p. 158).

[4] How much less genial an attitude could be taken up against the rotter who 'dreams greatly' is shown by Synge's *Playboy of the Western World*, where, by contrast with *Peer Gynt*, a *degenerate* society and a *degenerate* hero are presented.

which fictitious personages could lend it, had tended to recommend it also as a rule of life. The dreamer, because he saw visions and lived an intense simulacrum of life in them, became an object of admiration not in poems and romances alone. With this kind of imagination Ibsen had not the least patience, since it blurred the line between the real and the unreal world and offered too ready an escape from the demands of the former. It may very sincerely be doubted whether what has been brought forward as Peer's best defence, namely that at least he 'dreams greatly',[1] did not actually aggravate his malfeasances and negligences in Ibsen's own eyes. As a writer of imaginative works, he must have been acutely aware of the ease with which he could shuffle off this mortal coil by flying to Soria-Moria Castle,[2] and the really appalling dangers which beset expeditions of this sort had recently been made clear in the curious and interesting novel of the Dane, Hans Egede Schack, *The Phantasticks* (*Fantasterne*, 1857),[3] which remained a great favourite with him.

Flights of this nature were, in Ibsen's view, particularly reprehensible, because they baulked a man's prime duty, the conscientious discovery and elaboration of his mission in life, and encouraged derelictions of it. They constitute nothing less than a vice, and in the body of this fantastical work, Ibsen deals the phantasy a savage blow when Aase asserts that she and her son (left alone and miserable, whilst Gynt senior was squandering their substance) took to fairy-tales as others would take to brandy.[4]

The antithesis of 'dream' (*drøm*) and 'deed' (*daad*), canvassed not alone in *The Phantasticks*, but in many other contemporary works from Denmark, where the disaster of 1864 had been so rude an awakening from delusions, remained one of Ibsen's prime preoccupations. It is an urgent problem for the artist who is at the same time concerned with conduct.

[1] 'Ein Kar som i minsto kunde drøyme stort' (Koht, II, 31).

[2] II, 333; Archer, IV, 113.

[3] In this story, over-indulgence in fantasy, besides sending a friend into a lunatic asylum, brings the hero to the brink of insanity, from which, by a sober resolve and intense exertion of the will (a long-protracted affair, much more formidable than anything that Peer undertakes), he successfully drags himself.

[4] II, 304; Archer, IV, 55; there is a distorted autobiographical echo here. After the dissipations and bankruptcy of his father, Ibsen, as a child, took refuge in an inner world of the imagination, it seems.

Ibsen never ceases to scarify the pure dreamer. In our play, not only Peer Gynt, but Aase, too, is reproved: seemingly, in Mistress Quickly's words on Falstaff, 'A' made a finer end and went away an it had been any christom child', but the close reader will find grounds for thinking that this seeming is deceptive and that in fact the Button-Moulder got her, if the Lean One did not.[1] The same condemnation emerges from the later plays. Hilmar Tønnesen of *Pillars of Society*, who is interested in nothing but childish make-believe, and the *sancta simplicitas* of Pastor Manders in *Ghosts*, who deceives himself as much about the world he lives in as that world deceives him, cut equally lamentable figures; Ulrik Brendel in *Rosmersholm* comes to utter grief when the theories he has spun in solitude are put to the touchstone of even a public meeting; the Lady from the Sea is saved from futility and, it is likely, from insanity only by resolutely quitting the tide of dreams on which she has permitted herself to float; Hedda Gabler, upon the discovery that her imaginary world of free living and noble dying lies in shivers about her, no longer has the vitality to continue existence in the real world and chooses self-annihilation.[2] All these are, in the highest degree, the willing addicts of romantic dreaming divorced from all practical activity, and Ibsen's condemnation of them is not only peremptory, but also, more often than not, unmitigated by compassion.

If we look back again at the outstanding products of literary romanticism, as so much in *Peer Gynt* invites us to do, the closest resemblance to the tart tang with which Ibsen accompanies the presentment of his hero is to be found, perhaps, in Paludan-Müller's *Adam Homo*; here, too, was unfolded with abundance of irony and a minimum of compassion the career from cradle to grave (and even beyond it) of a self-important, lecherous careerist, who, it is worth noting, is saved from eternal damnation by the simple devoted girl whom he had once loved.[3]

---

[1] II, 402; Archer, IV, 233.

[2] The very special terms in which the problem is presented in *The Wild Duck* will be fully considered further on.

[3] If, as Koht holds (I, 318), the 'epical' *Brand* was intended as a Norwegian pendant to *Adam Homo*, the parallel in *Peer Gynt*, affords an interesting instance of Ibsen's habit of 'saving up' what has been discarded from one work for use in another.

## X

At the beginning of §V above, the African scenes were expressly set aside for the time being. Something, nevertheless, must be said about them. They stand apart from the other 'caprices' in two ways: except for the scene of Memnon's statue they do not trench on the supernatural—they even possess a sort of ultra-realistic, or at least *surréaliste* quality; and they are not essential to the elucidation of the play's general meaning. I do not think that they have ever roused great enthusiasm. Georg Brandes condemned them from the start,[1] and, in another fashion, Ibsen, too, may be said to have condemned them, in that he abridged them much more drastically than any other section of the play when preparing his acting-version.

Why, then, was this fourth act retained? It subserves, apparently, a threefold purpose. It helps to fill a large gap in Peer's biography; it exhibits the 'Gyntian' characteristics at their least amiable, when the hero can be excused neither by the charm of youth nor the soul-searching of senescence, and it discloses some traits in him scarcely to be suspected elsewhere, while putting Peer's opportunism and sexual promiscuity beyond the hazard of a peradventure. In bestowing his satire on these qualities in Peer, however, Ibsen aimed beyond him, and the outstanding characteristic of the African act is the *general* nature of the satire which it conveys—one of the grounds for which Brandes, intent on the objectivity of drama, condemned it.[2] Ibsen tilts not only at the commercial morality which can some-times lead big business to support an unrighteous cause, if profitable enough,[3] and at the profundity which globe-trotters affect, but also at Anglo-Saxon preoccupation with gain, French attachment to love and glory, the verbiage and bellicose brutishness of the Germans and the *fanfaronnade* of the Swedes.

The act abounds in minor satirical digs that can only suitably be dealt with in notes to the text, such as Logeman so excellently

---

[1] *Henrik Ibsen* (1898), p. 51. *Henrik Ibsen, Bjørnstjerne Bjørnson* (English translation, 1899), p. 35.

[2] Ibid. pp. 52 and 36 respectively.

[3] The Turkish side, which Gynt is willing to support against the Greeks, presumably represents the German *versus* the Danish in 1864.

provides.[1] Two scenes, however, may fitly be touched upon here: the scene with the Sphinx, and that in the lunatic asylum at Cairo. The former merely serves as a prelude to the latter and conveys little in itself beyond the not over-illuminating resemblances, attested by Peer, between the statue of Memnon and the Old Man of Dovre on the one hand and between the Sphinx and the Boyg on the other (which suggest that Ibsen held a low opinion of antiquities as such).

The kernel of the madhouse scene is constituted by Peer's assertion that the Sphinx is 'himself'—that being his modest, but confident solution of the Sphinx's great riddle—and the crazed philosopher-alienist's somewhat forceful proof that the preoccupation with self, the rigid application of 'To thyself be enough', shows at its clearest among the lunatics committed to his charge. Three of these lunatics are individualised: Huhu, the champion of the aboriginal ape-language of the Malabar coast, with whose 'grunts and growls' Ibsen was seen to identify the *landsmaal*[2] of Norway, championed by Vinje and K. Janson;[3] the Fellah, who, by the scatological fallacy of Deukalion, considers himself the descendant of King Apis—a satirical gibe at the Swedes, with their cult of Charles XII; and the Minister Hussein, who imagines himself alternately a pounce-box and a pen, nothing in fact but a writing-machine, as the Swedish foreign minister of that time, Manderström, prided himself on the efficacy of his official notes in 1864, when he achieved nothing beyond the writing of them.[4]

The indignation raised by the reactions of King Charles XV's foreign minister and of his Norwegian and Swedish subjects in general to the events of 1864 had been vented in *Brand*, mainly in the scene between the Sexton and the Schoolmaster, but it clearly continued to burn in Ibsen's bosom. It can be felt more pervasively and more acutely than in the instance just given. Peer, as has been insisted, is no 'sympathetic' character, or at least is a far from admirable one; and in his pseudo-heroism and

---

[1] *A Commentary on Peer Gynt* (The Hague, 1917).

[2] I.e. the language derived from peasant-dialects that was intended to oust the *bymaal* (town-language) or *riksmaal*.

[3] Janson saw himself in Huhu (*Hvad Jeg Har Oplevet*, 1913, p. 80).

[4] Ibsen confessed to having portrayed Manderström in Hussein (Bull, F., Introduction to Centenary Edition, VI, 31).

brag, in his pseudo-profundity and reluctance to do any hard thinking, in his weakness in deed and proficiency in dreaming, in his self-satisfaction,[1] in his incontinence[2] and in his moral and physical cowardice, in his blandly unconscious egoism and in his general subservience to the Boyg, Ibsen evidently wished to pillory what he looked on as typically national, typically Norwegian defects. There are, to be sure, certain subtractions to be made from the sweeping condemnation. Peer is not as bad as can be. He shines by contrast with many who are brought into contact with him, though the contrast cannot give much satisfaction to Norwegian patriots. Faithful to his old prejudices, it is the peasant-population and the peasant-stock[3] on which the poet principally fastens and on the corresponding ambitions of certain cultural leaders to be 'folky' at all costs: not only have we the butchering of the linguistic reformer, but the shaft with which the toothless pantaloon, the Old Man of the Dovre, is finally dismissed: he has heard that 'national' recruits are wanted for the stage and in his doddering imbecility proposes to offer himself.[4] And we must remember as clearly as his previous reprobation the fact that, in the end, Peer is let off cheaply.

## XI

Yet this figure, to which indeed the coltishness of youth and the pathos of advancing years impart some slight tincture of attractiveness, has become something in the nature of a national hero, even a national type. That seems an anomaly until one reflects that John Bull, Dr Faustus or Don Quixote, comparable figures, all exhibit attributes by no means altogether consonant with perfection or palatable to the more discerning among their compatriots.

[1] Dresdner, A., *Ibsen als Norweger und Europäer* (1907), p. 18, thinks self-adulation a typically Norwegian characteristic: it is doubtful to me whether any modern nation is innocent of this.

[2] Camilla Collett had stigmatised this as her countrymen's chief vice, in *Amtmandens Døtre*; but perhaps she was there referring to the educated classes alone.

[3] None the less, the rowdy village wedding and the heroine's pietistical parents may have been suggested by that glorification of peasantry, Bjørnson's tale, *Synnøve Solbakken*.

[4] II, 411; Archer, IV, 250.

The general favour which play and hero came to enjoy was not immediate. The northern public, prepared for another revivalist sermon *à la Brand*, did not know what to make of this first cousin to a Christmas pantomime. *Brand* sold out the first edition of *Peer Gynt* straight away, but the second edition of 2000 copies remained on the publishers' hands for seven years. However, Jonas Lie (who said that at first he almost constituted a minority of one) and Bjørnstjerne Bjørnson were at once convinced of its greatness, and bit by bit it won general acceptance in Norway, especially after it had made its way on to the stage; by the time of the Ibsen centenary in 1928, it had become the most popular of his works in the original, with Bjørnson's peasant-tales as sole competitor for the first place among the Norwegian classics.

Except for some sporadic outbursts elsewhere (particularly in the twentieth century), the enthusiasm has, however, been confined to Norway. Even the Danes, disliking vulgarity and knock-about, remained sceptical. It was noted above that Georg Brandes disapproved of Act IV, but he disliked the drama as a whole only slightly less. Paradoxical as it sounds to-day, he considered that Peer embodied a libel on the human race. 'Contempt for humanity and self-hatred[1] make a bad foundation', he said, 'on which to build a poetic work.' His senior Clemens Petersen took much the same ground.[2] He voiced an opinion, often heard again with application to Ibsen's modern plays, that *Peer Gynt* was one-sided, parading defects and neglecting to indicate something positive and constructive as counterweight; it disregarded 'the Ideal, without which the work of art cannot take rank as poetry'.

This dictum stung Ibsen all the more sharply as he still stood in awe of the Hegelian phraseology, which Georg Brandes was to discredit for him a few years afterwards, and he uttered the famous prophetic retort: 'My book *is* poetry; and if it is not, it will become so. The concept

---

[1] This is a striking piece of imaginative insight (for Brandes had not at this time met Ibsen), since Ibsen's play was, in part, his own wrestling with and conquest over the Great Boyg, whom thereafter he only kept at bay by the most merciless self-discipline.

[2] In the Copenhagen paper *Fædrelandet* for 30 November 1867.

of Poetry in our country, in Norway, will come to adapt itself to the book.'[1]

Even if, quite a long time later, Ibsen declared[2] that *Peer Gynt* was 'never calculated for performance', he soon began reflecting on its theatrical possibilities and finally, early in 1874, wrote to his great compatriot Edvard Grieg[3] with the suggestion that he should compose some incidental music. Grieg felt reluctant, as the theme struck him as quite unsuitable,[4] but, his mind firmly fixed on the honorarium, he finally complied with Ibsen's proposal; and when the Swedish manager Ludvig Josephson (with a Norwegian troop of actors) presented the play for the first time, on 24 February 1876, at the Christiania Theatre, it had the musical accompaniment with which, ever after, it has been associated. There was a notable revival in 1892, at the same house, of Acts I, II and III with Bjørn Bjørnson, Bjørnstjerne Bjørnson's son, as producer and hero and with young Johanne Dybwad as Solveig. The earliest foreign performances were at Copenhagen in 1886, at Göteborg in 1892, and in 1896 in Paris, under the management of Lugné-Poë at the Théâtre de l'Œuvre. The first production in English was Richard Mansfield's at the Grand Opera House in Chicago on 29 October 1906. After a performance in the Queen's Hall, Edinburgh on 14 February 1908, it was taken into the repertory of the 'Old Vic' organisation, Russell Thorndike (1922) and Ralph Richardson (1945) assuming the title-part.

[1] Letter to Bjørnson of 9 December 1867 (*Breve*, I, 159). Petersen's critique, incidentally, had the effect of provoking a tremendous quarrel, almost a feud, between Ibsen and Bjørnson, the exact reason for which still remains obscure (cf. my *Ibsen: the Intellectual Background*, 1946, p. 128).

[2] Letter to Passarge of 17 August 1881 (*Breve*, II, 93).

[3] 1843–1907.

[4] Letter from Grieg to Bjørnson, *cit*. Centenary Edition, VI, 51.

# A DOLL'S HOUSE
### (*Et Dukkehjem*)
## 1879

### I

BETWEEN *Peer Gynt* of 1867 and *A Doll's House* of 1879 a great gulf is fixed. The purely formal difference, of which a superficial glance at the list of the *dramatis personae* in either play and at the typography of the pages gives a premonition, corresponds to an equally far-reaching difference in scope and approach. The actual character and outlook of the author, nearly forty years old when *Peer Gynt* appeared, could scarcely be expected now to undergo any fundamental change. But in many externalities he put on a new man: he took up his abode in the land of the future, Germany, rather than the land of the past, Italy, he adopted the frock-coat, top hat and umbrella for which the caricaturists loved him, he shaved off his full black beard and, more remarkable, he completely altered his handwriting.

October 1873, midway between *Peer Gynt* and *The Doll's House*, had seen the publication of his most ambitious work, the ten-act play on Julian the Apostate's rearguard action against Christianity, *Emperor and Galilean (Kejser og Galilæer)*. Bringing into the world what had been conceived nine years earlier proved a hard and lengthy labour. If it had not been for that ingrained thrift of his, which hated to discard matter once it had been subjected to the artistic process, *Emperor and Galilean* might perhaps never have been finished. The feebleness of the second part, wherein no dramatic excitement or skill offsets the meagreness of the intellectual content, suggests work against the grain, a loss of interest on the author's part.

There are good grounds for such supposition. In his famous inaugural lecture at Copenhagen in the autumn of 1871,[1]

---

[1] Printed in 'Inledning' to *Emigrantliteraturen* (1872), being vol. 1 of *Hovedstrømninger i det 19de Aarhundredes Litteratur* (not in the English translation). Brandes was then twenty-nine years of age, on the point of becoming one of the directors of his country's thought.

Georg Brandes, mentioning him by name, directly challenged his friend Ibsen to make himself resolutely and constructively 'modern' by falling in with his general programme of 'submitting problems to debate'. The exhortation threw Ibsen into a turmoil: a vast abyss seemed to open up between to-day and yesterday.[1] Brandes had solved for him the vital torturing problem of his mission in life. *Love's Comedy, The Pretenders* and *Brand* had thoroughly argued the question of a man's 'call', had insisted that, to be worthy, he must be conscious of its nature and make its realisation his paramount business. Ibsen was clear that literary production, an aesthetic occupation, was what he had been sent into the world for. At the same time, he was strongly imbued with the then generally accepted doctrine that there was a scale of values, aesthetic, ethical and religious, among which the aesthetic ranked lowest; and he could not rest happy in the conclusion that he had been destined for an inferior occupation.

In the letter of 1866 addressed to the King of Sweden and Norway and applying for a pension, Ibsen had defined his task as 'the most important and necessary in Norway, that of rousing the people and bringing it to think nobly'.[2] That was not just the common form of a begging author: the moral debates following upon *Brand* and *Peer Gynt* go to prove that. But now Brandes had demonstrated *ex cathedra* how the man of letters, labouring in his vocation, could at the same time serve his generation, be social or ethical as well as aesthetic, provided he applied his gifts to the elucidation of questions which his public felt to be urgent and actual. A naked 'case', such as might in certain circumstances confront any of his fellow-citizens, thus assumed for the artist an importance greater than a vaster but less immediately applicable theme like the conflict of Christendom and pagandom or the limitations of the 'All or Nothing' principle.

So Ibsen could embark with a completely clear conscience— more, with a sense of duty—upon the handling of subjects and the portrayal of personages to which he had already exhibited a strong temperamental attraction. Hitherto, as a general rule,

---

[1] Letter to Georg Brandes of 4 April 1872 (*Breve*, I, 249).
[2] *Breve*, I, 114.

his imaginative constructions had been cast into a bygone age or else, as in *Brand* or *Peer Gynt*, any topicality they possessed had formed a thinnish crust over romantic timelessness. Yet, almost from the first, the satirical bent that informed the last-named work had impressed on him the advantages of the present-day scene. He had ventured upon it already in his third play, *St John's Eve*, and had made a brilliant conquest of it with *Love's Comedy*. The immediacy of these plays was, however, somewhat impaired by the introduction of supernatural occurrences in the one case, by the use of verse and some other conventions of operetta in the other.

With *The League of Youth*, *Peer Gynt's* prose successor, Ibsen had in fact anticipated Brandes's programme. But at the time it probably seemed to him less the logical development of his genius than a momentary step aside into ephemeral polemics— polemics against Bjørnson and all he stood for in retaliation against the hostility with which Ibsen (erroneously) believed that his great rival had viewed *Peer Gynt*.[1] For, after *The League of Youth* had been fairly launched (1869), *Emperor and Galilean* was taken up again.

Orientated though he was of his own accord towards the desired direction, Brandes's exhortations none the less proved of cardinal moment to Ibsen in setting his feet firmly on the path he was never again to leave and in ridding his mind of the last inhibiting doubts about his mission, its value and the manner of its execution. He resolutely turned his back on the historic past and, two or three years later, even on the composition of verse.[2] At the same time he probably recognised that the scope of *The League of Youth*, with its exposure of Norwegian demagogy, was too parochial, its criticism too negative and also too incidental to be admitted as a contribution to the great debates which his friend in Copenhagen invited 'modern' literature to initiate. It had certainly been 'actual' enough to have a very stormy reception on its first Norwegian presentation. But something deeper and more valuable, more searchingly canvassed and

---

[1] The full story of Ibsen's quarrel with Bjørnson is to be found in Koht, II, 60. Cf. also above, p. 103.

[2] He wrote to Gosse *à propos* of *Emperor and Galilean* (*Breve*, II, 12): 'I wanted to produce on the reader the impression that what he was reading had really happened. Had I used verse, it would have counteracted my own purpose.'

less obscured by adventitious ornament was called for. This something was *Pillars of Society (Samfundets Støtter,* 1877).

*Pillars of Society* has, to be sure, a good deal in common with *The League of Youth* and is usually ranked and compared with it. But that it represented to its author a new departure is attested by the inordinate labour which he put into it before he could rest satisfied. No less than five successive drafts, for instance, were made of the first Act. *Pillars of Society* advances beyond *The League of Youth,* moreover, by discarding some of the stock ingredients of comedy and reducing the artificiality of others. The stage *raisonneur* (represented in *The League of Youth* by Fjeldbo) is replaced by the foolish babbler, Hilmar Tønnesen; the comic malcontent (Hejre), the *père noble* (Chamberlain Bratsberg) and the facile landlady (Madam Rundholmen) have gone; although young Olaf's stowing away on an America-bound ship is a piece of deliberate machination and although there is some dramatically exploited confusion about the two ships that put out to sea, these things do not deserve to be included in the term intrigue. The general atmosphere, however, that of a small Norwegian community, is much the same in both plays, even if in the later one the clouds overhead hang more ominous; and there is a fulness and bustle of the scene such as only *An Enemy of the People* was to furnish again.[1]

The principal objection raised by Brandes against the substance of Ibsen's early plays was that the problems of conduct which they implied had been remote and general, or else that the solutions and the incidental satire had not been obviously helpful to the human race. So that no accusation of this order could be levelled at his new play, the play that was to follow *Emperor and Galilean,* Ibsen safeguarded himself, not alone by providing for present-day attire and furniture, but, more particularly, by handling the most actual and earthbound of themes, commercial morality.

Herewith he was following the example of Bjørnson. Bjørnson had been a pioneer in Norwegian drama, first with *The Newly Wed (De Nygifte,* 1864), a two-act piece in prose about

[1] It is interesting to learn from Ibsen's papers (Centenary Edition, XI, 162) that the other late comedy, *The Lady from the Sea,* was originally to have had animated scenes with a great many characters: there are vestiges of this in the opening of Act II.

a marriage that threatens to go off the rails, and then with *A Bankruptcy* (*En Fallit*, 1874) which, likewise set in a contemporary middle-class environment, revolves about business speculations.[1] His originality cannot be questioned but Bjørnson was always deficient in psychology and technique. The characters which Ibsen proceeded to put upon the stage in *Pillars of Society* cannot compare in depth and observation with those of his later plays, but they are a great deal more like real people than those of *A Bankruptcy* and *The Newly Wed*, and he enriched a story that was arresting enough in itself with the complications of an antecedent mystery, about which more must be said later on. *Pillars of Society* is too solid an achievement to be considered as a mere experiment; nevertheless its main importance consists perhaps in having given its author once and for all the method which he was infinitely to adapt and deepen, but to which he substantially kept for the remainder of his career.[2]

More specifically, *Pillars of Society* has a direct bearing on the genesis of its immediate successor, *A Doll's House*. Originally proposing to himself the treatment of two sets of problems in the former play, Ibsen discovered that a single one of them provided him with almost too much matter. Commercial morality and the anecdote for illustrating its workings completely filled all the five acts; a second subject, woman's place in society, apart from a few general observations and incidental hints, had to be left over for the next composition.

## II

*Pillars of Society* off his hands, Ibsen settled down to *A Doll's House* (*Et Dukkehjem*). From now on, he observed that almost uncanny regularity of output—signal triumph of will over

---

[1] *The Editor* (*Redaktøren*), of the same year as *A Bankruptcy*, exposes the corruptions of the press.

[2] Carrying on a tradition from the later eighteenth century, the Germans Hebbel and Ludwig had, in the generation before Ibsen, made some experiments in modern prose tragedy embodying criticism of society. Ibsen knew and admired Otto Ludwig's *Erbförster*; there is a curious premonition of Ibsen's famous *réplique* (IV, 187; Archer, IV, 15): 'Millions of women have done so', in the remark which Leonhard makes to Klara in Hebbel's *Maria Magdalene*. 'Tausende haben das vor Dir durchgemacht, tausende werden nach Dir in den Fall kommen und sich in ihr Schicksal finden.' I do not think that Ibsen learnt any more from these playwrights than he did from Augier and Dumas *fils*—'what to avoid', as he put it.

fantasy, of 'deed' over 'dream'—to which the rest of his long
literary life allowed only two trifling and explicable exceptions.[1]
Ten months after the publication of *Pillars of Society*, on 2 August
1878, while still at Munich, Ibsen first mentions his 'new work'
to his publisher; on 19 October, having meanwhile settled for
a second time in Rome, he makes, or at least dates, 'Notes to
the Present-Day Tragedy', suggestive of an early stage in the
process of crystallisation. He then attacked the work with
a concentration for which his wife could remember no parallel[2]
and which once almost reached the pitch of hallucination,
when, as he declared, his heroine came into his study wearing
a blue woollen frock.[3] A *scenario*, it seems, was devised for each
act and a full draft of that act written before the *scenario* to the
next was taken up.[4] On 2 May 1879, a full revised version was
begun, to be executed, mostly at the Albergo Luna at Amalfi
near Naples, by 3 August; the fair copy of this included rather
more alterations from the last draft than was usual in Ibsen's
practice, but, even so, was sent off in sufficient time for printing
to be completed by the end of October.[5]

At this point, however, Ibsen called a short halt; the Christmas market, which then, as always, he had in mind, did not
yet press, and he calculated that the Northern playhouses and
the German translator would find it an advantage to have
before them in advance copies the eagerly awaited successor to

[1] On the completion of one work he apparently brooded over possible successors
—a process about which we unfortunately know nothing—for rather more than
a year. Then, in the late winter or early spring, he would make tentative sketches
and drafts for the subject finally selected, work it out, make a fair copy in some
country retreat during the summer and have it ready for publication in the autumn,
twenty-four months after its predecessor. *An Enemy of the People*, written in a fury of
indignation, followed on *Ghosts* after only a year's interval; three years separated
*John Gabriel Borkman* and *When We Dead Awaken*, but in them fell the very elaborate
celebrations of the author's seventieth birthday.

[2] Cf. Centenary Edition, VIII, 255.

[3] Reported by Koht, II, 173.

[4] These first drafts of each act were destroyed and must not be confused with the
revised draft begun on 2 May 1879, which the editors of the Centenary Edition
designate 'the first complete draft'.

[5] A great deal of manuscript matter relative to *A Doll's House* is still extant. The
most important part of it, i.e. the *scenarii*, the first complete draft and a number of
variants not included in the final text, is reproduced in the Centenary Edition,
VIII, 369; translations of some of this material are to be found in Archer,
XII, 91.

*Pillars of Society,* and make their dispositions for the second half of the current theatrical season. The actual publication accordingly was put off until December 1879.

## III

From a talk between Nora Helmer and Kristine Linde[1] early on in *A Doll's House*, two major points emerge: first, that the former's husband, Thorvald Helmer, has just been appointed Director of the local bank;[2] second, that, her circumstances not always having been so thriving as they now look like becoming, she once, unbeknown to her husband when he was very ill, raised a loan of not less than 1200 *spd.* (about £240) and that she has had a hard time of it repaying principal and interest. More about this transaction shortly transpires, when the lender, Krogstad, calls to request that Nora do what she can towards safeguarding for him the small post which he holds in her husband's bank: he applies pressure by revealing the knowledge that the loan was raised on the security of her father's signature which Nora had herself written into a bill, and by suggesting that the forgery might furnish grounds for a criminal action—an aspect of the business which is apparently quite novel to her.

Nora's subsequent intercessions with her husband on Krogstad's behalf prove fruitless, and her alternative project, borrowing enough from the friend of the family, Dr Rank, to settle the debt, fails too. At her wits' end, since Krogstad, having received his dismissal from Helmer, proposes not to have her prosecuted but to use the threat of that as blackmail over her husband, Nora lets Fru Linde fully into the secret of the loan, about which she had only dropped some exulting hints at their first meeting; and Fru Linde, who is also an old friend of

---

[1] Archer calls her Christina Linden, according to the practice generally prevalent at the time of reducing the strangeness of foreign names.

[2] I have assumed throughout that the scene of action is laid in some Norwegian town other than Christiania. But that possibility is not excluded. Helmer was at one time in a government office (IV, 115; Archer, VII, 18), thus probably in the capital, and no subsequent change of domicile is mentioned. If Helmer is actually a director of a joint-stock bank in Christiania, Ibsen has made a definite step away from the provincialism of *The League of Youth* and *Pillars of Society.*

Krogstad, promises to do what she can to dissuade him from the proposal.

In the event, Krogstad destroys the incriminating paper on his own initiative, but before that is done its nature has been betrayed to Thorvald Helmer, whose paroxysm of selfish fear, anger and recrimination subsides the moment the threat of exposure is removed. He resumes his customary attitude towards his wife as if nothing had happened. She, on the other hand, who had believed that he would appreciate the devotion underlying her act and would even be prepared to take the responsibility for it upon himself, feels all the props of her moral existence knocked from under her: declaring that she must think out her position as calmly and comprehensively as she can, she leaves the house.

To the summary of the main plot, a note on the sub-plot should be added. For the catastrophe to be precipitated in the precise form which it takes, Krogstad's destruction of the forged bill is essential. The incentive is a change of heart in the blackmailer, which is no more completely satisfactory than Consul Bernick's full-length confession and promise of betterment at the end of *Pillars of Society*, but has the technical merit of firmly tying to the main story the figure and fortune of Fru Linde, who, otherwise, would be no more than the *confidante* of the old drama and the heroine of an independent sub-plot. She and Krogstad, it has been observed, are friends of old standing. As the principal action proceeds, he, a widower, and she, a widow, decide to join their 'shipwrecked' fortunes in matrimony, and Krogstad's destruction of the incriminating paper proceeds from his wish to begin their new venture on a basis of perfect openness and virtue. (The change of intention has a bearing on what might be called the main moral plot, as exhibiting the good which may accrue from the *tabula rasa* to which at the end Nora also aspires.)

Except for three virtual supernumeraries, all the persons of the play belong to the educated middle class. Even the blackmailer is by origin of the same social standing as the others; indeed, one of Thorvald Helmer's objections to him is that he presumes on their former companionship.[1] Lawyer Krogstad is

[1] By continuing to address with the familiar 'Du' the man about to become his chief.

a man who has come down in the world, against whom there was once an accusation of forgery and who clings all the more tenaciously to the lowest rung on the ladder of prosperity and respectability. Fru Linde, who, as the stage producer should remember, is of about the same age as Nora, has been through a joyless, sterile marriage. It has given her a sober outlook on life and, disposed though she may be to make the best of things, there is, as we shall shortly see, a certain moralistic strain in her. About the last figure on the secondary plane, Dr Rank, more must be said in another connection. He is a melancholy celibate invalid, dying of inherited disease and, by reason of his loneliness and sad fate, more attached to Nora and Thorvald than they are to him.

Of Helmer, one is to assume that he is a competent man of affairs: otherwise he would hardly have received the appointment on which he is about to enter, nor would he wield the new broom with such ruthless vigour. Outside business hours, there is nothing to distinguish him from the run of ordinary professional men,[1] if it were not for a touch of perversity in his amatory constitution; he likes, as he confesses, to indulge in fantasies of his wife in fictitious circumstances that enhance her erotic appeal; he even likes his corporeal eyes to see her in such circumstances, as is shown by his purchase of the Capri fisher girl's costume and his insistence on her dancing a tarantella in public.

His wife, Nora,[2] is presumably by something his junior, and, mother of three children though she may be, she has remained young for her years, as is revealed by her schoolgirl's taste for sweets and the unselfconscious abandon with which she romps among her children. She dances and sings. Her husband calls her 'squirrel' and 'lark'. She is very charming, entirely devoted to her husband; nor must one suppose that she neglects the ordinary duties which her generation expected of a wife, housekeeper and mother.[3] A stage direction expressly indicates

[1] The evidence of the early notes and drafts goes to show that Ibsen progressively 'depressed' the character of Helmer, who was originally conceived as a definitely 'superior' man.

[2] Christened 'Eleanora'.

[3] Her alleged extravagance is more than doubtful. Helmer may have thought that his wife got through a lot of money, but all the while she was amortising the debt to Krogstad.

that her home is tastefully furnished within the modest means that hitherto she and her husband have enjoyed, and, though Christmas always invites a breach of domestic rules, there is nothing to show that the rooms are untidy or neglected.

On the other hand, a giddy pate often going with a light heart, Nora has the defects of her qualities. She has learned too deliberately to exploit the latter in order to gain her ends and she habitually indulges in chicane and deceit. She may well be excused: not only has she never been taught better by an indulgent father or an indulgent husband, but her peccadilloes, when found out, have as often as not proved a subject for merriment. Only one event in her life has put her character to the test. That, of course, was her husband's serious illness and, though forgery is an ugly word and a still uglier thing, Nora resolutely faced a situation unlike any she had yet known; her perseverance in paying off the debt by very distasteful work, amid difficulties which it does not take much imagination to conceive, is altogether praiseworthy. In estimating Nora Helmer's character, we must not overlook the traces of such solid and hopeful elements.

A criticism is pronounced by the mere statement that in the play Fru Linde fulfils a variety of functions. She provides a sub-plot by her relations with Krogstad and she serves as foil and model to Nora, who recognises through her that a woman is entitled to her own judgement and can lead an independent life. Furthermore, she is responsible for the catastrophe. Through her influence over Krogstad, Nora's forgery might have been hushed up for ever. Yet she deliberately refrains from exerting that influence; in fact, she does the reverse. She has seen, she avers,[1] incredible things in the Helmer household—by which she means in the relations of the spouses to one another, which must have been very different from any she remembers in her own case—she disapproves of them and she is convinced that they ought to be ended, not in order to avert an even more resounding catastrophe than the one that actually supervenes but on purely pedagogic grounds. Her last and greatest function, therefore, is to link and vivify the 'moral' drama which runs its course parallel with the drama of events.

[1] iv, 169; Archer, vii, 118.

The drama of outward events is pointed by so many fine theatrical moments—Nora's emerging from a romp under the sitting-room table to be confronted with the blackmailer in his most ruthless mood, her rehearsing the tarantella when her heart is broken and her mind well-nigh distraught, the attempted cajoling of Rank, the desperate game of suppressing the fatal letter and its discovery by Helmer—that only a cold analysis brings out the somewhat clumsy manner[1] in which Fru Linde's act turns the drama to the end desired by the author. Because of its clumsiness, *A Doll's House* represents a step back in Ibsen's art. It is true that the moral content of *Pillars of Society* is rather too crudely brought out by the concluding speeches; but, earlier on, the two dramas, the drama of events and the moral drama, had been satisfactorily integrated; in *The Vikings in Helgeland*, *The Pretenders* and *Love's Comedy*, the amalgam had been perfect;[2] and none of the later plays exhibits a roughness of the kind indicated in *A Doll's House*.

## IV

The debates which *A Doll's House* at once provoked with an intensity up to Brandes's keenest anticipation focused for the most part on one or other of four points: its technique; its use of the living model; the heroine's conduct and character; and the general ethical and social problems which they might be held to illustrate. With these matters we will now deal in the order given.

In *A Doll's House*, for all that play's slight awkwardness, Ibsen had worked out the characteristic dramatic formula of his later plays.[3] The plan of those fully discussed in the first three chapters of this book is relatively straightforward: the

[1] The clumsiness is reflected in an awkwardness of construction. That Fru Linde should sit up past midnight in the Helmers's flat in order to see Nora in all her finery is unlikely enough; that she should appoint that place and time for an assignation with Krogstad is flatly incredible, whatever plausible pretext Ibsen labours to adduce (IV, 165; Archer, VII, 111).

[2] There had been no soliloquies in *The Vikings in Helgeland*, *The League of Youth* and *Emperor and Galilean*. Nora gives way to soliloquy at least four times (IV, 135, 139, 159 and 164; Archer, VII, 55, 61, 93 and 109), so that in this respect, too, *A Doll's House* marks a retrogression.

[3] For a full and stimulating discussion of this cf. Tennant, P. F. D., *Ibsen's Dramatic Technique* (1948).

point of *Peer Gynt* is, in a way, driven home by the way the action now glides, now jumps, from episode to episode with no taut linkage or causation, and the chronicle of Brand's life unfolds in natural and uncomplicated sequence from the moment that he sets foot in his native parish; similarly, the characters once granted, it needs but Lind's engagement to Anna and Falk's declaration to Svanhild to start *Love's Comedy* on the way that it follows unbrokenly and logically. Yet even through these plays there sounds, faintly, an echo of things long past: a glimpse of Peer Gynt's childhood explains his irresponsible fantasy, and there is a similar brief illumination of Brand's psychological 'pre-history'; Pastor Straamand, in *Love's Comedy*, serves not alone for a butt in the present, but he is a portent from the past too, a warning example of the deformation of character and destiny to which Lind and Falk may fall victims.

Elsewhere in his early work Ibsen had made more use of 'pre-history'. The melodramatic complications of *Lady Inger of Østraat* and their tragic outcome proceed from the sin of the heroine's youth and from her efforts to keep it concealed. In *The Vikings in Helgeland* one drama is, as it were, exhumed while the ostensible one is in progress, and it shapes the latter's end, when Hjørdis, fomenting strife with her husband's guests, discovers that she ought rightly to have been the prize and wife of one of them, since it was Sigurd, and not her husband Gunnar, who fulfilled the condition demanded of her suitors, the killing of the polar bear on guard outside her virgin bower. (The utilisation of a gradually disclosed secret in drama is, of course, almost as old as drama itself, and two supreme tragedies, *Œdipus Rex* and *Hamlet*, owe their peculiar force and fascination partly to the manner in which the secret comes to light and partly to its operating as a still active virus. Ibsen certainly knew *Hamlet* and very probably *Œdipus Rex* too, but was probably put in the way of this particular device by the ingenuities of Scribe and by certain authors of the Romantic Revival, such as the Norwegian Mauritz Hansen.[1])

---

[1] It will be remembered that the so-called 'Schicksalsdrama', which frequently hinges on an inconvenient secret, was one of the most popular contributions of Romanticism. Ibsen's indebtedness to Mauritz Hansen was most ably exposed by Collin, C., 'Henrik Ibsens Dramatiske Bygningsstil', in *Tilskueren* (August 1906), pp. 601 ff.

*Pillars of Society*, again, embodied the process of exhumation,[1] as I have called it—though from the purely dramatic point of view perhaps with not quite so great an effect as *The Vikings in Helgeland*. The story moves quite adequately with the motive power supplied (as it were) by the present: that Pillar of Society, Carsten Bernick, sends a coffin-ship to sea; his own son is discovered to be a stowaway on it; and the discovery brings about his change of heart with the *dénouement* of the piece. But Bernick had a particular motive for letting *The Indian Girl* put to sea in her rotten condition: he wished once and for all to lay the ghost of his facinorous past which had arisen before his eyes in the shape of his returned brother-in-law, an intending passenger in *The Indian Girl*; and the reconstruction of that past, with its momentous consequences in thought and deed, takes up, very naturally, a considerable fraction of the play.

In a twofold manner the reconstruction or exhumation has a deep bearing also on the *moral* drama embodied in the outward action of *Pillars of Society*. For it firmly connects the Consul's change of heart with the awakening of his conscience, which the sharer of his brother-in-law's secret, Lona Hessel, has deliberately come to undertake; and the awakening of his conscience forms part of her programme of letting in light and air on the Society of which he is the product, the victim and the exponent as well as the Pillar. (In any technical comparison, the contrast between *Pillars of Society* and *Hamlet* is plain enough; for the occult crime which comes to light in *Hamlet* is one with which the hero himself has had nothing to do. On the other hand, the parallel with *Œdipus Rex* is fairly complete; in Sophocles's play, as in Ibsen's, there is *both* a past offence of the hero's to be disclosed and expiated—the murder of Laius—*and* a present crime to be punished—Œdipus's defiance of the divine.)

The blending of past and present in *A Doll's House* closely resembles that of *Pillars of Society*. The focus throughout is on the present. It is not the expiation of Nora's forgery, let alone

---

[1] There is nothing of the kind in *The League of Youth*—or, rather, what there is is the same as in *Peer Gynt*, a brief plea for the hero by reference (III, 101; Archer, VI, 194) to his upbringing; the financial transactions of the Monsens and the younger Bratsberg hardly come into account.

the perpetration of it years ago, it is her marital *malaise* that is at issue, and the discovery of the crime serves to transform vague *malaise* into acute crisis. Nevertheless, there is in *A Doll's House* more of the past than a scrap of doubtful paper. I do not refer to Krogstad's own crime and to his old sentimental relations with Fru Linde—though these things serve to build up that firm nexus between passing events and their forerunners by means of which Ibsen contrived to give an extraordinary relief and perspective[1] to his mature works; I have in mind the allusions to, and the demonstrable effects of, Nora's upbringing, which heighten the moral drama. Her father, it transpires, an irresponsible spendthrift, brought her up with no sense of social obligation or serious thought for the morrow, while her husband, finding her a delightful companion like this, did nothing to repair the omission and, indeed, continued to treat her with the condescending playfulness less appropriate to a mother of three children than to a girl in her 'teens. Nora's overgrown irresponsibility, on the one hand, permitted the forgery. The way in which it was regarded, on the other hand, only encouraged her in chicane and bred the uneasiness of a stifled, guilty conscience.

*Pillars of Society* ends, as has been said, with a change of heart. As it seeks its coats and umbrellas, the audience understands that henceforward both Bernick and the Society which he upholds will be different from what they have been. A window into the future is thrown open, as Ibsen seems almost always to have done.[2] But what will now happen to the Consul, his family and the little town in which they live is hardly a question on which the home-trudging multitude exercised its imaginative powers, unless it was in the cynical and rhetorical form: How long will Carsten keep it up? In the majority of his plays, however, Ibsen brought down the curtain on a fresh situation, the solution of which immediately and constantly became a matter for intense argument. We have had occasion to join in that argument over

---

[1] Presumably this is what the philosopher Harald Høffding had in mind (*Tilskueren*, 1898, p. 347) when he applauded Ibsen for introducing 'perspective' into dramatic art, though it is odd that he should have forgotten Sophocles.

[2] This again is no personal idiosyncrasy. The Greek plays which concluded with a *deus ex machina*, for instance, do the same thing, and we may well speculate on how Katherine and Petruchio or Millamant and Mirabell settle down in matrimony.

*Love's Comedy*, over the last words in *Brand* and the similar questions raised by the reunion of Peer Gynt and Solveig.

Nowhere before, however, had Ibsen projected the interest— the dramatic, as well as the moral interest—into the future with such vigour and effect as he now did in *A Doll's House*. Even the problem: 'Was Nora justified in leaving home?' was argued with no greater heat than were speculations as to what she and her husband would do after breakfast the next morning. There were cynical prophecies, there were sentimental prophecies, fantastic prophecies of all kinds. Minds straying that way should remind themselves that, if the end of the play is to be taken seriously, then clearly the greatest battle of Nora's life has already been decided and that nothing thereafter is likely to deter her from doing what she is determined to do: and that is to think out, in independence and solitude, her position in a world whose general laws she has begun to apprehend and means to fathom. Some have seen a damaging admission of irresolution in the happy ending which Ibsen himself cobbled together as an alternative.[1] Ibsen's own defence of it is legitimate enough; since it had to be concocted,[2] least damage would be done if he did the concocting himself.

The speculations to which the end of *A Doll's House* gave rise were revived after almost all Ibsen's later tragedies—all the more understandably as they by no means all involved the death of the protagonist. Would Fru Alving kill her son? Does Gregers, babbling about being the thirteenth at table, go out to commit suicide? Is Ellida Wangel really cured? Will Alfred and Rita Allmers succeed in finding a common purpose and a redeeming peace in their slum-school? Of course, when death concludes the play, questions of this order were not likely to present themselves. Rosmer and Rebecca are dead, Halvard Solness is dead, John Gabriel Borkman is dead and 'there is

[1] Nora is induced to look at her sleeping children for the last time, breaks down and decides to stay. This ending was written at the instance of the German actress, Frau Niemann-Raabe, who had declared that in no circumstances could she, Frau Niemann-Raabe, ever think of leaving her precious offspring.

[2] The existing state of the copyright law gave Ibsen no rights over his own work outside Scandinavia. The 'happy ending' was very rarely used; and in the end even Frau Niemann-Raabe swallowed her prejudice and acted the original version (Koht, II, 178).

namore to seyn'. Even into such pieces, nevertheless, as the discussion of *Brand* has shown, Ibsen's favourite question-mark could obtrude. One finds oneself wondering, for instance, whether Tesman and Thea, with Hedda Gabler out of the way, will succeed in reintegrating Løvborg's book, whether they will make a match of it and even whether Tesman will catch a spark or two from the ashes of his dead rival's fire.

In a sense the interest which issues in these questions is adventitious. Some modern exegetists sternly insist that nothing concerns the audience or the reader of a play but what is in the play itself. But the firmly established *past* in Ibsen's plays, as distinct from the problematical future, cannot be set aside so peremptorily; it is too much part of them. As time went on it tended to bulk even more prominently. Bernard Shaw gave to the last group of plays the collective title 'Down Among the Dead Men'—and certainly of Solness, of Borkman, of Rubek (*When We Dead Awaken*) it can truly be said that when the curtain first rises, their effective life is already over; the tensity and the struggle which drama implies are produced mainly by a progressive reconstruction of what happened to them at a crisis long past and by the full realisation of its implications.[1]

In *A Doll's House*, the psychological implications set aside, the reconstructed past is fairly simple: Thorvald Helmer fell seriously ill and needed a long holiday abroad; Nora forged her father's name on a promissory note and raised the funds required for that holiday, then slaved and saved enough behind her husband's back to pay to Krogstad the instalments of the debt as they fell due. Already in *Pillars of Society* this sort of thing had been more complicated: Bernick had had a liaison with the actress Madam Dorf and, to enable him to make a good match with his sister, Johan Tønnesen had taken the opprobrium upon himself and decamped to America: but, more than that, Bernick had, on the one hand, misappropriated funds to save the family business from bankruptcy and had availed himself of the opportunity of Johan's absence to load that guilt upon him too, quite without his knowledge; and, besides, he had jilted Lona Hessel in order to marry rich Betty Tønnesen; lastly, he had carried

[1] This kind of thing goes back a long way too—at least as far as Aeschylus's *Persæ*.

on secret deals in land which had profited by his public
activities in railway promoting.

In *Ghosts*, the relevant matter preceding the actual action is
not so involved, but, as the title might indicate, it has a profounder significance. The character and activities of a man long
dead, Captain Alving, have to be reconstructed to account for
the mentality of his widow, for the presence of his illegitimate
daughter Regina in her household, for the plans of the latter's
putative father, Engstrand, and for the orphanage round the
ceremonial opening of which the material story is grouped; the
relevance of the past to the present is driven in by the incident
when Fru Alving hears her son amorously fooling in the next
room with Regina, precisely as his father had fooled with
Regina's mother.

Except in *An Enemy of the People*, the pre-history of Ibsen's
mature drama is always of the first significance, and the manner
by which it is revealed, the so-called 'analytic technique', is
characterised by the greatest skill and dramatic effectiveness.

However skilful and, in Ibsen's scheme, indispensable the
telescoping of a long action might be, it struck contemporaries
as novel and for that reason gave rise to aesthetic doubts. These
were most ably formulated by the German novelist, Spielhagen,
who combined practical craftsmanship with an interest in the
technicalities of literature not very common with working
authors. He complained[1] that, in *A Doll's House*, Ibsen had
taken a highly complicated story, the salient events in which
had, one way or another, reference to a great span of time, and,
in order to fit it into a dramatic scheme which very nearly
observed the old Unities, he had laboriously and confusingly to
work backwards at the same time as, more legitimately, he was
working forward to its unravelment; he was endeavouring to do
what was more readily achieved by one of the three-decker
novels of the period.[2] *A Doll's House* has not yet (as *Peer Gynt*
has) given rise to 'the novel of the film', but when it does, we
may be in a position to check Spielhagen's claim. Ibsen's

---

[1] 'Drama oder Roman', in *Theorie und Technik des Romans* (1883), p. 295.

[2] That the 'pre-history' of an Ibsen play might furnish a play as well as a novel
was demonstrated by the interesting, if unsuccessful, attempt *Rosmer of Rosmersholm*
of 'Austin Fryers' (1891).

practice meanwhile has dissipated the unfamiliarity of his methods; and, in any event, his analytic technique, as we have seen, was not quite so revolutionary as it seemed to Spielhagen, who was really protesting against what strikes many as one of Ibsen's great virtues—his 'perspective', the fullness of his dramatic world, a fullness which characterises also the world of Shakespeare and Euripides.[1]

Besides exhuming the past, Ibsen, it has been remarked, opened a window into the future. That, too, was made a ground for critical complaint, and more reasonably. He developed his situation in such a way that in the end it was replaced by another, equally clamant for solution; but no solution was offered or suggested. Besides the double-dyed aesthetes who held that Art precisely should *not* submit problems to debate,[2] others were willing to accept the theory of Brandes and his followers, with the proviso that the artist should answer moral questions he raised. 'What is the good', they urged, 'of showing us how Nora, the married woman, coped with her problems, if Nora, as *femme sole*, is left confronting problems of equal magnitude and complexity? Question marks are not like the negative symbols in mathematics: two of them do not cancel one another out. It is unfair to replace one problem by another and leave the solution of the second to us—that is what, in effect, the conclusion of *A Doll's House* comes to.' Ibsen's defence against accusations of this order was peremptory. He denied the proviso. By *submitting* the problems to debate—and, it is fair to add, by presenting them honestly—he had done all that was expected of him: 'I choose to ask: it is not my mission to answer.'[3]

The nineteenth century was a time of great dramatic technicians. In the eyes of a later generation, some of them—a Scribe, a Sardou, a Sudermann, a Pinero—have no merits beyond slick execution. By contrast with such constructors of the well-made play, authors who introduced 'ideas' to the stage

---

[1] It is interesting to observe how Racine, working in a tradition which aimed at the sparest simplicity, produces, at any rate in *Phèdre*, the impression of a similar fullness by his illusions to the past history or the other adventures of his legendary figures.

[2] Spielhagen was not one of these.

[3] 'Jeg spørger helst; mit kald er ej at svare.' (From 'Et Rimbrev', VI, 403.)

and did not wish to draw undue attention to the mere adjustment of events were thought by their contemporaries to fall
short in technical competence. Such a view did less than justice
to Alexandre Dumas the younger and to Augier, for instance.
In general, Ibsen's careful craftmanship was as thoroughly, if
not so vocally, appreciated as the problems which it subserved.
But the surprisingly exciting quality of his analytic method was
less fully realised, and his failure to found a 'school', at once
recognisable as such and truly vital, may largely be attributed
to that circumstance. There were plenty to follow Brandes in
submitting problems to debate on the public stage and clothing
their problems in home-spun and everyday language. But
a Bjørnson, a Brieux or a Shaw, much surer about his message
and more eager to propagate it, failed to charge the intellectual
content of his plays with precisely that intensity which Ibsen
drew largely from a reconstruction of a past importing life and
death for his personages.

A minor matter on which some cavillers fastened was the
completeness and literary style of Ibsen's stage-directions,[1]
especially the minuteness with which he described the place in
which the action was to take place. The beginning of *A Doll's
House* affords a good example of this (though the description is
not so long as, for instance, that prefacing *Pillars of Society*):

A room, comfortably and tastefully, but not expensively, furnished.
In the back, on the right, a door leads to the hall; on the left another
door leads to Helmer's study. Between the two doors a pianoforte.
In the middle of the left wall a door, and nearer the front a window.
Near the window a round table with arm-chairs and a small sofa.
In the right wall, somewhat to the back, a door, and against the same
wall, further forward, a porcelain stove; in front of it a couple of arm-
chairs and a rocking-chair. Between the stove and the side-door
a small table. Engravings on the walls. A what-not with china and
bric-à-brac. A small bookcase filled with handsomely bound books.
Carpet. A fire in the stove. It is a winter day.

---

[1] Previously stage-directions had mainly been confined to a brief register of
requisites and abbreviated notes of where and when entrances and exits should take
place. It is odd that the objection to informative stage-directions should have been
made in the nineteenth century, when the closet drama flourished as never before
or since.

A bell rings in the hall outside. Presently the outer door of the flat is heard to open. Then Nora enters, humming gaily. She is in outdoor dress, and carries several parcels, which she lays on the right-hand table. She leaves the door into the hall open, and a Porter is seen outside, carrying a Christmas-tree and a basket, which he gives to the Maid-servant who has opened the door.

It may be observed that Ibsen's stage-directions by contrast with Mr Shaw's and those of several other modern dramatists, against whom the same complaint was levelled, are truly stage-directions and do not serve to convey to the reader information which would not at once be apparent to the spectator. He was keenly sensitive to feminine dress,[1] but he rarely prescribed what his actresses should wear and never indulged in descriptions which might involve a reverential producer in a dilemma: he does not, for instance, demand that Nora should have a *nez retroussé*, or that Thorvald should pat her with large fleshy hands. He always had the theatre and its limitations well in the forefront of his mind.[2]

In the course of time it has become almost obligatory for every work of fancy, however profound or sublime, to allow for some love-story or other. There must be courtship and wedding-bells or, failing the latter, the 'benediction of nature'. Nowhere has the convention grown stronger than in the drama: even Dr Faustus must have his Peggy. If the hero cannot fit into an idyll, then perhaps 'Charles his friend' obliges.

Not the least of Ibsen's iconoclastic actions was the infringement of this convention. Not for him the romance of the

---

[1] Paulsen, J., *Samliv med Ibsen*, II (1913), p. 58.

[2] In saying this I am of course mainly thinking of the plays of Ibsen's maturity, and one might fitly exclude *Brand* and *Peer Gynt*, definitely entitled 'dramatic poems'. But the theatrical success of *Peer Gynt* in many lands is proof enough that the author had the theatre sufficiently in his blood never to demand impossibilities of it even here. The avalanche of *Brand* may certainly set the stage-manager a hard task; but its repetition in a late play, *When We Dead Awaken*, shows that Ibsen held it to be practicable. I may perhaps take this opportunity for stating my (unsupported) belief that the comparatively long period of a year or more, which Ibsen completely filled with brooding over every new play before even committing preliminary notes on it to paper, was taken up with devising, after repeated discardings, the *theatrically* possible and effective guise which the projected theme and general situation could assume; and that he rejected countless *scenarii* before settling the final one.

devoted bookkeeper and his employer's daughter with which Bjørnson saw fit to alleviate the problem of *A Bankruptcy*. Ibsen did not, however, altogether discard the love-story, but it becomes one less and less satisfactory to the ordinary public. *Love's Comedy* had Lind and Anna, to whom it is allowable to extend the benefit of every doubt, and *Pillars of Society* comprises the thumbnail romance of Dina Dorf and Johan Tønnesen.[1] In this respect, *A Doll's House* is a little old-fashioned. Side by side with the shattering catastrophe of Nora's love runs the story of Kristine Linde. In a fairly well-developed sub-plot she and Krogstad afford some sort of dramatic 'relief'. But what a relief, conservative playgoers thought, the *amours* of a disillusioned, shabby widow who earns her own living and a middle-aged blackmailer with encumbrances!

Only once again did Ibsen allow himself so complete and independent a sub-plot[2]—to achieve an effect equally wry and by no means so fraught with hope—in the wooing of poor Boletta Wangel by her former tutor in *The Lady from the Sea*. Here the love story, though again closely related to the moral action, does not affect the main outward action nor is much affected by it.[3] Elsewhere, however, such a thing, though less prominent, forms either an integral part of the main story or throws a valuable sidelight on its protagonist. An instance of the former is the scabrous *liaison* of Erhart Borkman and Fanny Wilton—which knocks the last prop away from John Gabriel Borkman; of the latter, the curious engagement of young Brovik and Kaja Fosli in *The Master Builder*.

It is notable how the element of bitterness which, to many palates, taints Ibsen's later plays, largely enters them by such channels. On love in its loftier manifestations, as between a Rosmer and a Rebecca West, or of an Ella Rentheim for Borkman, he set the highest price; but for anything less, it

[1] No one can carp at this much. The case would have been different if Ibsen had carried out his original intention of letting Dina go to America with Johan before marriage.

[2] The next stage in the decay of the sub-plot is reached in the private life and ambitions of Engstrand (*Ghosts*), but these are very closely integrated with the moral and physical action.

[3] An invincible optimist might hold that one of Ellida's earliest actions on grasping the reins of her family responsibilities would be to send Dr Arnholm packing: but this is pure speculation.

seems, he had no use. As his *œuvre* comprises no *Romeo and Juliet*, so he never came near to working himself through to Perdita and Florizel. How different is Marina not merely from the Lady from the Sea, but from Hilda Wangel of *The Master Builder*!

## V

Turning now to the question of possible models for his creations, we observe that, as Ibsen did not concoct 'parts' for actors and actresses, so he never considered it part of his mission to present actual personalities on the stage:[1] his discreet and philosophical temperament would have revolted at any such idea. Yet, in the personages of his plays, he could not, from time to time, avoid incorporating a number of traits which immediately brought real individuals to their contemporaries' minds. In Stensgaard (of *The League of Youth*) and Dr Thomas Stockmann (of *An Enemy of the People*) the lineaments of Bjørnson were at once recognised, though they might be overlaid by peculiarities common also in the former case to the politicians Johan Sverdrup and Ole Richter, in the latter to the writers Jonas Lie and Georg Brandes. Emilie Bardach contributed something to the Hilda Wangel of *The Master Builder*, the Swedish poet Snoilsky to Rosmer of *Rosmersholm*, the crapulous scholar Hoffory and Ibsen's own German translator Elias to Løvborg and Tesman of *Hedda Gabler* respectively. He confessed that the same model served him for Hjørdis of *The Vikings in Helgeland* and for Svanhild of *Love's Comedy*, the model being his own wife. But nowhere else (that we know of) did Ibsen work more directly from the life than he appears to have done in *A Doll's House*.

It is by no means easy to disentangle the true history of Laura Kieler and the complicated interrelations of that history with *A Doll's House*.[2] 'Interrelations' is the correct term; for not only did, on this occasion, truth issue in fiction, but the

---

[1] Bjørnson, followed by Gunnar Heiberg, did this repeatedly.

[2] The business is most fully dealt with by Kinck, B. M., 'Henrik Ibsen og Laura Kieler', in *Edda*, xxxv (1935), p. 498; Kinck uses sources otherwise inaccessible. Laura Kieler herself wrote a short essay on Ibsen which she included in her book *Silhouetter* (1887), and which is curiously unenlightening. It shows, however, that at this date she bore Ibsen no ill-will.

fiction in its turn reacted on the life story of the model. The difficulty of the case proceeds partly from Ibsen's customary reticence—from his own utterances[1] one could scarcely guess that Fru Kieler had played any but the smallest part in his life; it lies likewise in the unreliability of the lady's evidence, given very often as an untested plea in her own defence, generally some time after the events which it is meant to illustrate and always under the stress of great emotion.

Laura Petersen (as she then was),[2] the young woman curiously linking two of the seminal books of modern Norwegian literature, Camilla Collett's *Sheriff's Daughters* and Ibsen's *Brand*, had concocted a kind of pendant to the latter in the form of the novel *Brand's Daughters* (*Brands Døttre*), which she published in 1869. She wrote to Ibsen at the time;[3] the following year they met; and in 1876, three years after she had married a Danish schoolmaster called Kieler, he saw a good deal of her and her husband on their journey through Munich. Her vocal cheerfulness earned the young woman Ibsen's *sobriquet* 'the lark',[4] and he conceived so idyllic a notion of her household as to dub it 'A Doll's House'.[5] The two appellations, while proving that in themselves they imply no condemnation on Ibsen's part, also establish the main link between Nora Helmer and Fru Kieler so firmly that the parallel between certain details of their careers is unlikely to have been quite fortuitous.[6]

Behind the *façade* of cheerfulness, however, the Kielers lived no idyll. The *radix malorum*, according to the wife, was *cupiditas*, an almost pathological reluctance in her husband to part with money, which drove her surreptitiously to incur debt, partly for ordinary household expenses, but partly also to pay for a foreign

[1] *Breve*, I, 206; II, 174.

[2] Laura Petersen (1849–1932) was born at Tromsø, one of the northernmost towns in the world. It is notable how some of Ibsen's most glamorous heroines 'descend', as it were, from high latitudes,—Rebecca West, Ellida Wangel and Hilda Wangel.

[3] Cf. her *Silhouetter* (p. 9), where Ibsen's answer is printed.

[4] By which name Helmer also calls Nora (IV, 107; Archer, VII, 4).

[5] *Lærken* and *dukkehjem* in the parties' own idiom.

[6] The fact that Laura Kieler came into Ibsen's orbit as the continuer of his most serious work may add a trifle to the argument that there was from the beginning a substantial substratum of seriousness in Nora.

holiday which Hr. Adjunkt Kieler's health rendered imperative. To clear off her liabilities, Fru Kieler again turned to authorship, in which, indeed, Ibsen had encouraged her. He was fully seized of these circumstances, and on 26 May 1878, when he was presumably passing through the first stage of meditation on a successor to *Pillars of Society*, he wrote a letter[1] to his friend, urging her to make a clean breast of the whole business to her husband. At the same time he condemned as worthless the literary effort she had submitted to him. In her ensuing despair, Fru Kieler applied her pen to another purpose, namely to forgery. That is her own story, but since she adds that she neither gained anything nor deceived anyone by her act, it sounds a little like melodramatic embroidery borrowed from *A Doll's House*. With or without the supererogatory crime, the wife's practices were discovered by the husband, and a terrible domestic upheaval ensued. Fru Kieler did not walk out of the house, but was removed from it, lodged in a lunatic asylum and eventually divorced by due process of law.[2]

Her story was sufficiently well-known in Denmark at the time, and it was openly maintained that Ibsen had turned it to literary account. Naturally all Nora's delinquencies, such as her forgery and her readiness to desert her children, were laid at Fru Kieler's door. That, no doubt, was unjust, but it can hardly be disputed that Ibsen copied from the life the marital deceit, under its dual aspect of praiseworthiness and culpability, and the contrast between the outward and inward aspects of a 'happy marriage', together with many personal traits for his heroine. The unusual warmth of sympathy for his heroine which Ibsen betrayed (and which may in fact account for the play's popularity) is no doubt attributable to the personal contact.

---

[1] Printed by Kinck, *ut cit.* p. 507.

[2] Actually, the spouses came together again. It is an odd circumstance that the decree of the Danish court depriving Fru Kieler of the custody of her children roused the indignation of another dramatist. With *Eva* (1881), Hostrup, now a country parson, returned to the theatre after an interval of some twenty years, to take up the cudgels on behalf of women exposed to such a calamity if they had serious differences with their husbands. Hostrup maintained that he had drafted the full *scenario* of *Eva* before *A Doll's House* was published. More will be found to say about Laura Kieler's relations with Ibsen during the discussion of *The Master Builder* below, p. 184.

## VI

After dealing with Ibsen's technique and his use of the living model,[1] we may now proceed to the issues which provoked the very liveliest of the innumerable debates stirred up by *A Doll's House*. Questions about the dividing line between the novel and the drama were the concern mainly of aesthetes. How far Nora Helmer could be identified with Laura Kieler could not interest anyone outside Denmark. Nearly everyone, however, to whose notice they came, was eager to sit in judgement on her character and her conduct.

The questions at issue can be reduced to something like this dual form: What are precisely the motives that drive Nora Helmer to break up her home; and is it credible that these motives should have presented themselves spontaneously to such a person as the author represents his heroine as being and should so effectively have actuated her?

In elaborating, as is now necessary, the sketchy analysis of Nora's character already attempted above, one may, for a moment, dwell on two negative factors. First, giddy-pated and irresponsible though Nora might be, nothing suggests that she was the woman to consider walking out of the house a trivial matter: the Helmers' front door had not been slammed after every tiff or wifely disappointment: the act is unique and momentous. Second, in delineating Nora's character with an almost supererogatory regard for its formation in the past, Ibsen gave no hint that she was either, in the commonly accepted sense, a *femme méconnue* or even a *femme inconnue*, fundamentally capricious and, like the prophet Habakkuk, capable of anything; there seems to be no pathological or semi-pathological incoherence in her personality, as there is, for instance, in that of Ellida Wangel.

What, then, drove this somewhat feather-headed, but sound and home-loving young woman to the grave act of abandoning home, husband and children? The term 'home-loving', liberally interpreted, may point to the answer. Though apparently un-

[1] It is maintained by Johnsen, P. R., *Om og omkring Henrik Ibsen og Susanne Ibsen* (1928), p. 20, that Ibsen had also a model for Dr Rank, in a certain Dr Andreas Holmboe of Bergen.

stayed by religion, Nora's is a deeply passionate and devoted heart. The keynote is firmly struck before we know anything about her crime, which after all was committed from unreflecting passionate love of her husband: Helmer asks[1] where Nora would be financially if a tile blew off the roof and knocked his brains out, and she replies that she cares not where she would be if he were not with her. It is inconceivable to her that her feelings should not be absolutely reciprocated. Helmer may have his funny ways in pulling her up short when she looked like outrunning the constable; he could, no doubt, on occasions be cross with her; but there was a horror she had never so much as dreamed of, the distorted mask of fury and aversion that he turned upon her after opening Krogstad's fatal letter. It *was* the face of a strange man with whom she had been living.

An equally deadly shaft had already pierced her heart. Krogstad, she learns,[2] once did what she had done, committed forgery and evaded the consequences; and Helmer—the fount of wisdom for Nora—gives it as his opinion that such a man must be the poisoner of his own children. By implication, he adjudges her unworthy to be a mother. It shows the seriousness with which she accepts this judgement that thereafter she keeps her children away from her as much as possible.

These two blows, the conviction of her unworthiness to be a mother[3] and the knowledge that Helmer's love for her was fallible, have completely shattered the vital basis of Nora's life. To leave the hearth on which the fire has gone out can give her no further pangs.

The instinctive grounds of Nora's final act are thus abundantly justified. But that does not constitute a complete defence. It might have been so if, on Helmer's outburst of recrimination, Nora had, in panic horror, thrown a wrap over her fancy dress and fled incontinently into the night. But then the great settling of accounts between husband and wife would have fallen away. And that Nora walks out of her doll's house offends some observers less than that she should dally to argue

[1] IV, 108; Archer, VII, 6.    [2] IV, 137; Archer, VII, 59.
[3] The 'happy ending' which Ibsen himself devised may be partially justified by arguments bearing on those just advanced. Helmer, taking Nora to see the sleeping children, implies that he still holds her worthy to bring them up, and so affords her the best grounds for staying.

about it. An unthinking creature, they feel, takes to rationalising an instinctive impulse and begins talking as if she had swallowed John Stuart Mill's *The Subjection of Women* whole.

In endeavouring to account for the change in Nora's demeanour, besides the double shock, we must not overlook something a trifle febrile and morbid which her manner portrays from the start—her irresistible longing, for instance, to use strong language[1]—which disquiets her friend Fru Linde. The long strain imposed by the repayment of her debt to Krogstad cannot entirely account for it, since it is just about to be removed. There seems to be something more. Nora tells her husband[2] that she has been merry but never happy. That, no doubt, is an exaggeration, which profound disillusionment readily explains. Nora was probably quite happy most of the time. But there has been a small, lurking residuum of dissatisfaction, a waiting for something that does not happen—'Det vidunderlige'.[3] One would probably not go far wrong (since nothing apparently ails the children) in seeking the cause of *malaise* in her marital relations and more precisely in those aspects of her husband's attitude which distress third parties too. To account for the final serious discussion between husband and wife, we must base it on some unsatisfied, if slender sense of seriousness[4] in Nora; if the principle be accepted, it is not altogether surprising that *all* Nora's seriousness should come out at once and, unpractised as she is in giving voice, sound in places forced and priggish.

This does not claim to be a complete apology. The gap between Nora, the solemn defender of individuality, and Nora, the squirrel and the lark, has generally been felt too wide to explain away, though the magic of a great actress's art has on occasion conjured it away.[5] There is, similarly, another flaw at the other end of the career which we are permitted to follow. Frankly incredible it seems that Nora should have failed to

---

[1] IV, 125; Archer, VII, 36.    [2] IV, 183; Archer, VII, 144.

[3] Cf. p. 143 below.

[4] It is given a touching aspect when Nora for a moment (IV, 120; Archer, VII, 27) thinks of a time when her husband will no longer find her beautiful.

[5] Thus Gran (*Henrik Ibsen*, II, 1918, p. 95), speaking of the Finnish actress Ida Ålberg, declares: 'This Nora did not fall apart into two halves and it never occurred to us that it was not the same creature who crept on all fours and barked at her children in the first act, and in the last sat there as a responsible woman.'

recognise her forgery as a crime. 'People like me don't get found out or else bluff their way through', is just a possible attitude for the spoiled and feather-brained, but Nora's very uneasiness *vis-à-vis* Krogstad and her desire to have the dubious IOU returned to her plead against her ignorance of the nature of her act.[1]

One may observe too that in reality a Krogstad must have known his threats to be mainly bluff. But here the dramatic situation needed something 'strong': the dangerous black-mailer confronting the inexperienced woman who committed a crime from ignorance and love[2]—and the position he takes up easily passes muster with theatre-audiences. In the same way the moral situation demands something 'strong' in the third act, and Ibsen opined with less justification that Nora's *volte-face* and last words would just carry conviction.

*Le sérieux* in Nora, such as it is, guarantees *le sérieux* of her last exit, and of the entire drama. But it also, I think, admits a ray of hope. Thorvald is sobered and impressed by it; it is not at all impossible that he has, if dimly, apprehended where the real rift between his wife and himself lies nor that '*det vidunderligste*' of which he whispers as the curtain falls is the same thing as Nora's '*vidunderlige*'.[3] Of course, it cannot be more than a gleam of light. Thorvald may not be the man to take his share in realising the miracle. The summing-up of all this may well be that Nora's character is more consistent, that the tragedy which befalls her is deeper and that, at the same time, the conclusion comes rather nearer a reconciliation than these things are often thought to be.

---

[1] Though he takes a low view of Nora's character, the ingenious Wulffen, E., *Ibsens Nora vor dem Strafrichter und Psychiater* (1907), p. 52, thinks that she might have been acquitted in a court of law. This could, perhaps, happen in Norway or Germany, but scarcely in England. A judgement, printed in the Norwegian paper *Fædrelandet* (no. xvi for 1880) and reported by Halvorsen, J. B., in *Norsk Forfatter-Lexikon*, III (1892), p. 62, acquitted Nora, but mulcted her in the costs of the action.

[2] It is of course strengthened by the appearance of Krogstad for his big scene as Nora is romping with the children; in fact she is hiding under the table. Nowhere after *A Doll's House* (where there are several such) did Ibsen permit himself such approximations to melodrama.

[3] IV, 189; Archer, VII, 155.

## VII

It was a testimony to the sympathetic interest in his heroine which Ibsen had aroused that her particular case should be so hotly disputed. But the arguments at once ranged much further. The bang of the Helmers' front door would not have alarmed so many people had they not been fearful that it might bring down on their heads nothing less than the whole fabric of marriage. The dismay was all the greater, since, in the welter of uncertainties which new scientific discoveries, new cosmic theories and the recent redistribution of political power had caused, domestic institutions and the private virtues alone seemed still to stand unshaken. Paterfamilias, looking at the partner of his joys over a morning newspaper full of the repercussions of Bismarck's policy, the Paris Commune, Papal infallibility, Darwin's Evolutionism and the Higher Criticism, had always been able to say to himself: 'There is still the Home. There is still Marriage. We still have one another.' But could he be so absolutely sure now?[1]

It is always tempting to build up a generalisation from a concrete case, a generalisation not of necessity universally valid, but at any rate embodying a definite doctrine. Soberly considering the point, most people would agree that it is indefensible to hold an artist responsible for an ethical tenet, apparently justified in a single imaginary instance. Because *All's Well That Ends Well* does in fact end well, we must not suppose that Shakespeare approved of jugglery with the marriage-bed, nor that Sophocles cried up matricide because his Orestes so cheerfully sends Clytemnestra to her account. If Ibsen's *œuvre*, viewed as a whole, with its apparent tergiversations, implies anything, it is that circumstances alter cases: Stockmann's claims of the ideal are justified, Gregers Werle's are not. Like his ally Brandes, Ibsen believed that the age of relativity had come in, admitting of no general rules. He would never wish it to be claimed, for instance, on the evidence of *Pillars of Society* and *John Gabriel Borkman* that all big business is barratry, or, on the strength of *An Enemy of the People*, that every man who stands alone is in the right.

[1] An able and sympathetic Swedish critic, writing three years after the appearance of *A Doll's House*, likened its melancholy effect to *Paradise Lost* ('Robinson', *Ibsen och Äktenskapsfrågan*, 1882, p. 74). 'Robinson' was the pseudonym of U. Feilitzen.

His very ingenuity in presenting an individual case so that it should convince logically and be dramatically moving, together with his choice of themes, did none the less lay Ibsen open to the charge that he was playing the advocate and presenting theses, not problems. The impression was particularly strong in *A Doll's House* by reason of the heavy-handedness with which Fru Linde's schoolmarmish proclivities drive Nora to an *éclaircissement*. At all costs, it appeared, the author was intent to stage a debate on matrimonial relations leading to a predetermined conclusion. The improbable argument at the end between the heroine and her husband confirms the impression that the play was largely written for its sake—otherwise it would not have been necessary to wrench probability so ruthlessly. Nora arraigns, not Thorvald only, but every husband; not the Helmer *ménage* is criticised, but marriage as an institution. As R. C. Boer puts it:[1] 'The abnormal case of Helmer and Nora is forced on us as the norm.' Husbands look upon themselves as superior beings, who, holding the economic reins and legally omnipotent, concentrate in themselves all the responsibilities of the household and alone embody its serious aspect: they condescend to their wives, relegating them to the level of concubine, nurse and housekeeper, and thereby encourage all the vices of the harem—deceit and sensuality foremost—from which grave corruption, all manner of dangers may spring.[2] That is what the charge looks like.

Even if the early plays are admitted to the count, Ibsen portrays, to be sure, more unsatisfactory than satisfactory marriages. It would be otiose to give the catalogue. Yet he does allow of happy marriages; that of Dr. Thomas Stockmann provides an excellent case in point: so the institution is not condemned root and branch. And what Ibsen does *not* hold up is equally important to remember. His works contain no

---

[1] Boer, R. C., *Ibsen's Dramas* (1928), p. 187. Others, besides Ibsen, believed that all was not well in every Norwegian home. Defending him in a letter to Fru Heiberg, Ibsen's wife's step-mother, Magdalene Thoresen, the authoress, refers to 'the dirt which is concealed behind the shutters of the so-called *Home*' (*Breve fra Magdalene Thoresen*, 1919, p. 202).

[2] We bear in mind Meredith's almost contemporary epigram on husbands in *Diana of the Crossways*: 'They have rounded Seraglio Point; they still have to double Cape Turk.'

defence of celibacy direct or implied. Nor is there any glorification of unlawful or transitory unions. The notorious picture
which Oswald Alving[1] draws of happy liaisons on the left bank
of the Seine is coupled with the hint that only lack of means
forbids the consecration by Monsieur le Maire or Monsieur le
Curé; and if any union is thoroughly rotten, it is that in
which Fanny Wilton and Erhard Borkman have involved
themselves.

Ibsen's sense of relativity again comes into play. Talking
à propos of *Love's Comedy* to Brandes about betrothals, he
remarked[2] that there were good potatoes and that there were
bad potatoes, and that it was his misfortune only to have met
with the latter. As far as marriages go, he appears to have been
luckier. All depends on conditions. After affection between the
contracting parties, he clearly sees candour to be one of the most
important of these conditions, implying a frank and thorough
exploration of themselves and one another.[3] This gives knowledge while the affection gives understanding. Such conditions
once fulfilled, it is almost remarkable how many potentially
satisfactory unions Ibsen can envisage. In the present play, for
instance, we have that of Kristine Linde and Krogstad, who
harbour no illusions about the degree in which life has battered
themselves and the hardness of the road before them. There are
the Bernicks and the Allmerses as well as the Stockmanns.[4] The
most striking one is that in *The Wild Duck* between the old rake,
Werle senior, and his far from maidenly housekeeper, Fru Sørby,
who look like enjoying a pretty happy old age together, having
as a matter of common sense and friendliness told one another
all about themselves and the vicissitudes of their past lives.

The absence of candour and mutual knowledge, the failure to
face common problems jointly and seriously, are seen to be the

[1] IV, 212; Archer, VII, 196.
[2] Brandes, G. C. M., *Henrik Ibsen* (1898), p. 110; English translation, *Henrik Ibsen, Bjørnstjerne Bjørnson* (1899), p. 76.
[3] An examination of *The Wild Duck* will show that, as with all principles, Ibsen did not wish this one to be universally and rigidly applied.
[4] I do not share the doubts sometimes expressed for the future of Dr and Mrs Wangel (*Lady from the Sea*), in large part because the conditions of affection and candour have been firmly established. I have indicated my belief that in so far as *Love's Comedy* implies a criticism of *The Sheriff's Daughters*, the marriage of Svan-hild and Guldstad should be considered as beginning under favourable auspices.

root defects in the Helmers's marriage, the main fault lying with the husband and his 'superior' attitude. The diagnosis closely resembles that made in *The Subjection of Women*, where Mill traces the 'slave mentality' of women back to the legal privileges reserved to the husband and the male, a point not directly made in *A Doll's House* itself, though it is implied in *Pillars of Society*[1] and made one of the guiding notes for *A Doll's House*,[2] in which Ibsen remarked that women are judged and condemned according to laws which they have had no hand in making. To this aspect we shall return shortly.

In his criticism of marriage, Ibsen was seen to be joining in that disturbing modern movement of looking in general upon man and his social arrangements from the factual, scientific, unsentimental and antitraditional point of view which was turning *belles lettres* into a branch of natural history. *A Doll's House* afforded support for this apprehension outside the treatment of the Helmer marriage.

Nora is irresponsible and frivolous, not only because the serious elements in her nature have never received encouragement, but also because she has inherited from her father a disposition towards frivolity and irresponsibility. In *Peer Gynt* and *Brand*, as was pointed out, Ibsen invoked childish memories as formative elements in the characters of his heroes, who, moreover, have a great deal in common with their respective mothers, the formidable Fru Brand and the feckless Aase. But the insistence on inherited characteristics in Nora's case is something novel.

The most striking instance of inherited disabilities is presented, however, not by Nora herself but by Dr Rank. In the play's economy, he fills a part analogous to Fru Linde's. He is partly 'functional', his timid declaration of love depriving Nora of her last chance to placate Krogstad and avoid the *éclaircissement* with her husband, and his loneliness (savoured as such by the epicure Helmer) and sad fate affording a theatrical contrast with the snugness and supposed happiness of his friends' fireside; partly

---

[1] IV, 44; Archer VI, 304.
[2] 'Optegnelser til nutids-tragedien' (Centenary Edition, VIII, 368): 'There are two sorts of spiritual laws... but in practical life woman is judged according to man's law, as if she were not a woman but a man.'

he serves to point a moral. As in his body he suffers for the excesses of his father, so Nora's weakness of character derives from *her* father, and, together with her criminality, can be transmitted to her children.

The *motif* of heredity—then much discussed in Norway as part of the Darwinian hypothesis and with particular reference to the combating of leprosy[1]—is not adduced by Ibsen with very great frequency. Rosmer has all the traditions of his old family to contend against, but his inheritance seems to lie entirely in the moral realm,[2] though we cannot perhaps say as much for Rebecca West, and it is overwhelmingly reinforced by his environment. In accounting for the character of Hedda Gabler, Ibsen makes less play with the taint derived from her ancestry than would have been warranted by Strindberg's short story[3] from which he took a hint for his theme. Erhard Borkman seems to have nothing of his father or of his mother in him. Such deformation of character as may be reproved in Hilda Wangel is apparently due to nurture, not nature. *The Wild Duck*, however, has two strands of heredity woven into its fabric, as we shall see. But the most notorious instance, of course, of Ibsen's utilising this idea is that which, as one might say, springs directly from Dr Rank: *Ghosts*, with the 'worm-eaten' constitution which Oswald Alving derived from his father and its whole sermon on 'the sins of the fathers are visited on the children'.[4]

As *The Doll's House* resumed half of the original theme of its predecessor—'It is you women who are the pillars of society'[5]—so, in its turn, its action projects after a fashion into that of its successor, *Ghosts*. The repetition of Dr Rank's fate in Oswald provides only one instance. The larger theme which the Oswald theme subserves may very probably have been suggested by the

[1] Cf. my *Ibsen: the Intellectual Background*, pp. 163 f.
[2] However, children never laughed at Rosmersholm!
[3] 'Mot Betalning', in *Giftas*, II (1886).
[4] Before parting from Dr Rank, there is one more observation to be made with regard to him. The scene of his advances to Nora, which could be very variously received, may not be strictly necessary, but in inserting it, Ibsen parried from the start the objection: Was the catastrophe unavoidable; could not the kind and wealthy friend of the family, Dr Rank, have been made chivalrously to oblige? The necessity of the rest was guaranteed by this superfluous scene.
[5] IV, 104; Archer, VI, 409.

criticisms of *A Doll's House*. Mrs Alving, it has been remarked,[1] may be looked upon as Nora Helmer twenty years on—a two-faced observation, since it throws as much light on the latter as on the former, confirming the postulate of an underlying seriousness in her character and a capacity for social effectiveness. More obviously, however, *Ghosts* constitutes a retort to the Pastor Manderses of criticism, who had vociferated about the unconditional immorality inherent in a wife's leaving her home. For does not *Ghosts* rehearse the fate of a woman who, driven to the same desperate extreme as the condemned heroine of *A Doll's House*, consented, for all practical purposes, not to leave husband and home?[2] The consequences of her orthodoxy are shown as far more dire than the worst predictable for Nora's unorthodoxy. After demonstrating in *A Doll's House* that marriage, instead of being the conventional heaven, might be purgatory, in *Ghosts* Ibsen exhibited it as hell.

# VIII

Nora Helmer, the bank manager's wife, and Medea of Colchis have almost as little in common as any two women could have.[3] But just as Euripides had done, to the great discomfiture of Athenian audiences, so Ibsen, in another play which is not quite a tragedy, presented his heroine revolting against her husband and against the society in which she lives and upon which, in the end, she defiantly turns her back: the revolt is carefully motivated and to that extent justified, even more than justified. Nora turns against her husband and against convention not only as Medea rounds on Jason when he discards her in favour of Creusa, for a particular act, but also because she has become aware of something more general that oppresses and constricts —Helmer's sultanic attitude towards her and the menace of a code she barely comprehends. Her leaving home is to be

---

[1] Bull, F., Introduction in Centenary Edition, ix, 19.

[2] Mrs Alving, of course, did actually run away like Nora, but was induced by Pastor Manders and other friends to go back at once.

[3] An elaborate parallel between Ibsen and Euripides is drawn by Steiger, H., *Euripides* (1912), p. 5.

construed perhaps more accurately as an act of liberation than as one of revolt.[1]

Fundamentally, that is the great problem in all the works of Ibsen's maturity—the liberation of the personality from restrictions and inhibitions. The probing began seriously with *Brand*. There the problem comes nearest to assuming a religious form: how can the soul free itself from self-imposed dogma? is one way of formulating it. In *Peer Gynt*, it is more thickly complicated with other issues and is seen under a mainly negative aspect; but the spiritual frustration of the hero by his adoption of the Boyg's slogan, 'Go round about', is never lost from sight for long. *The League of Youth* and *Emperor and Galilean* may not yield very much to this particular investigation, though the former may be held to inculcate, after a somewhat roundabout fashion, the semi-Carlylian doctrine that freedom cannot be obtained through tinkering with political machinery.

*Pillars of Society*, however, tackles the hindrances of freedom in the modern world more directly and more precisely. In that play, they take the form of a hypocritical society and a corrupt competitive commercialism: to keep himself afloat as a business man, Consul Bernick has to throw his soul overboard. In *A Doll's House*, the restrictive agency is, in the main, family tutelage formidably abetted by one-sided laws; in *Ghosts*, conventions in the domestic sphere are reinforced by the operations of heredity; in *An Enemy of the People*, as the title may indicate, the struggle resembles that of *Pillars of Society*, variety being obtained by substituting an 'untainted' hero in the one for the 'tainted' hero of the other. From 1877 to 1882, thus, Society, represented by the Rørlunds and Rummels, the Thorvald Helmers and Pastor Manderses, Peter Stockmann, Aslaksen and Company, furnishes the villains for Ibsen's pieces.

After 1882, the quarry changes: Society as such is no longer pursued. In *The Wild Duck*—to put the matter very briefly in this place—the hostile agent is idealism, but still, as it were, invading the individual personality from outside. In the last

---

[1] Her case is foreshadowed in that of Margit of *The Feast at Solhaug* and that of Selma Bratsberg of *The League of Youth*, whose husband had kept her out of all the serious concerns of life, also in that of Dina Dorf in *Pillars of Society*, whose *fiancé* evidently intended to do much the same. On a vaster scale, Hjørdis of *The Vikings in Helgeland* had cut herself away from every tie.

plays, the foe, the Boyg of the constricting coils, lies within: distrust of life in *Rosmersholm*,[1] romantic dreams in *The Lady from the Sea*, *ennui* proliferating like a cancer in Hedda Gabler, Master Builder Solness's sickly conscience, Alfred Almers's stifling of practice by theory, John Gabriel Borkman's megalomania, Rubek's sense of guilt.

Nora and her problem fall naturally into their place in the general scheme. It must, however, have been noticed that, in the catalogue of victims to the Boyg, women form the minority,[2] Ibsen clearly seeing the male sex as being no more exempt than they from the need of emancipation. From the time of Furia (*Catiline*), Blanka (*The Warrior's Barrow*), the Lady Inger of Østraat onwards, Ibsen had as spontaneously as invariably approached the women of his plays on exactly the same terms as his men; their common humanity and not their special sexual characteristics were always uppermost in his mind.[3] Nevertheless, the fact that in *A Doll's House* it is a woman who stands opposed to Society and that the issue here is joined with such perspicuousness and dramatic effectiveness, raised a particular interest at a time when the 'woman question' first attained general prominence.

All over Europe and North America feminists abounded in the 1870's. They were of all sorts, between those who dumbly felt that Miss Nightingale had had a case for getting female nurses to tend sick soldiers, and those who stridently announced the vast superiority, certainly in morals and probably in everything else except brute strength, of women over the self-styled lords of creation. Scandinavia had its fair share of them, and no less scandal than hilarity had been caused by the painter Aasta Hanstein, who had championed the cause of a frail and disappointed Swedish Countess against her youthful Norwegian seducer, and who herself always strode about with a riding whip

[1] *Rosmersholm* shows itself to be a work of transition, in that Rosmer's internal enemy is strongly aided by the environmental pressure of an inherited family tradition and of fierce political strife.

[2] Leaving the holocaust of *The Wild Duck* out of the calculation and allowing Mrs Alving and her son equal shares in *Ghosts*, I make the count $2\frac{1}{2}$ to $6\frac{1}{2}$ points.

[3] Certain special disabilities of women in their struggle for spiritual enfranchisement did not escape Ibsen's notice: the rather mysterious business of Hedda Gabler's pregnancy and the increase in Ellida Wangel's malady on the loss of her child immediately after its birth are cases in point.

to prevent anything of a similar nature befalling herself. Some traits from her have probably found their way into the delineation of Lona Hessel in *Pillars of Society*, with her unceremonious manners and queer appearance. Camilla Collett had not ceased, after *The Sheriff's Daughters*, to voice the sentimental woe of her sisters.

The Ibsens saw a good deal of Camilla Collett during their first Munich sojourn, and, escorting her home in the evening, at a time when *Pillars of Society* and *A Doll's House* were uppermost in his preoccupations, Henrik Ibsen, it seems, was not above drawing her out into expressing her most extravagant opinions. Paulsen[1] would have her and Fru Ibsen the prime sources of his feminism, while another friend of his declares,[2] on the strength of a most reliable authority, that these plays were written from a sentiment induced by hearing his wife's talk about Stuart Mill's book *The Subjection of Women*, which Georg Brandes had translated. Ibsen, by the way, professed detestation of *The Subjection of Women* and, especially, of Mill's tribute to the help his wife had given him: 'Fancy', he said to Brandes,[3] 'if one had to read Hegel or Krause without any certainty whether one had Mr or Mrs Hegel, Mr or Mrs Krause before one.'

Ibsen would have nothing directly to do with the 'woman question' under any of its triter or more general guises. Even when the Northern Association for the Woman's Cause[4] entertained him at a ceremonial dinner in 1898, he bluntly told them that he did not quite know what the 'woman's cause' was, whereupon he proceeded to deliver himself of a homily which some of the organisers of the party must have thought distressingly old-fashioned. It was as wives and mothers, he insisted, that women were most fruitfully active, the perpetuators and educators of the human race.[5] To that principle, of course, there are numerous corollaries with which, though he did not make them then, he presumably would have concurred, such

[1] He minimises Mill's share (*Samliv med Ibsen*, i, 1906, p. 164).

[2] Johnsen, P. R., *Om og omkring Henrik Ibsen og Susanna Ibsen* (1928), p. 29.

[3] Brandes, G. C. M., *Henrik Ibsen* (1898), p. 112; English translation *Henrik Ibsen, Bjørnstjerne Bjørnson* (1899), p. 76.

[4] Kvindesagsforening.

[5] The interesting study, Boettcher, F., *La Femme dans le Théâtre d'Ibsen* (1912), p. 204, holds that this doctrine is seriously advanced throughout the plays, though the critic admits that her theory breaks down in *John Gabriel Borkman* and *When We Dead Awaken*. I must confess to finding little evidence for the plea.

as the necessary consequence that as long as the educators remain servile, ignorant and cowardly, they can ensure only an inferior breed. In themselves, the particular objects of the feminist agitators did not apparently much interest him—the opening of the professions to women, the grant of the municipal and parliamentary vote, equal pay and the like. He did, however, break his almost invariable rule of abstention from political action when he joined in signing a petition in support of the Norwegian equivalent of the Married Women's Property Act; he suggested a female librarian for the Scandinavian Club in Rome, and he so vehemently supported the proposal that, in the Club, women members should have the same voting rights as men, that he nearly involved himself in a duel with a naval captain.[1]

Euripides, the presenter of a criminal Medea, an infinitely unpleasant Electra and an almost equally repulsive Iphigenia, was curiously enough looked upon by the Athens of Pericles as the equivalent of a feminist. A better argument for thus designating Ibsen, too, may rest on the circumstance—which his follower, Bernard Shaw, has erected almost into a dogma— that his plays represent the women as more purposeful and energetic than the men: the poor seducer Niels Lykke, in *Lady Inger*, is run off his feet by Eline, just as Catiline does not stand the ghost of a chance against Furia; Lona Hessel hustles Carsten Bernick, as young Hilda Wangel later was to hustle Halvard Solness; Mrs Alving and Regina act in *Ghosts*, while Manders, Oswald and Engstrand mainly do what they have been told; Rebecca West's is a much stronger personality than Johannes Rosmer's; the hard metal of Borkman does not prove so tough as that of Ella Rentheim. In proportion as their powers and potentialities are greater, so the restrictions put upon them are more obvious, more galling and more deplorable; hence the 'victims' in Ibsen's works belonging to the feminine sex evoke the more immediate sympathy, and for that reason, more than any other, he might be set down a 'feminist'. His interest in women (such as it was)[2] was certainly no satyr's itch to explore

[1] Gran, G., *Henrik Ibsen*, II (1917), p. 58.
[2] There is no evidence that in his private life he had more to do with women than with men. His not very illuminating Boswell, J. Paulsen, says he infinitely preferred the company of the latter (*Samliv med Ibsen*, I, 1906, p. 158).

*les dessous*, from which the younger Dumas is not always exempt, nor the wish to provide 'fat' parts for tear-compelling actresses.[1]

The further argument (as in Euripides's case) remains that he idealised women.[2] True, in making them more purposeful and energetic than the men against whom they are matched, he did in a certain sense give them *le beau rôle*; and without any of the gallantry that characterises, for instance, his contemporary Meredith, he inherited some of the romantic respect for women as such and faith in their powers: Rebecca West and even Hedda Gabler are not, in Johnson's phrase about Lady Macbeth, 'merely detested', as they would have become under most seventeenth-century or eighteenth-century playwrights' hands. Yet these two personages, responsible for the deaths of finer personalities than their own, should caution against too facile an assumption of idealism. In a fine dramatic piece of criticism, Herman Bang describes[3] how on Rebecca's drawing the curtain in Act II of *Rosmersholm* and coolly confessing to having played the eavesdropper, Ibsen's confidence in women apparently evaporated as utterly as Rosmer's faith in Rebecca: on her follow Ellida Wangel, who neglects her duties towards husband, home and step-children for the sake of a morbid dream and perpetual sea-bathing, Hedda Gabler, who not only lays everything waste about her, but does so of set purpose, and Hilda Wangel, who well and truly kills her Master Builder. But perhaps that was not such a complete revulsion as Bang would have us believe. Furia had already hounded Catiline to death, Hjørdis of *The Vikings in Helgeland* is notoriously an early study for Hedda Gabler, and while he had done justice—perhaps more than justice—to the concealed powers for good in Nora Helmer, Ibsen had made no attempt to throw a veil over her defects, her deceit, the way she speculates upon her physical attractiveness, her egoism and her crime.

[1] I cannot help thinking that the success of Johanne Dybwad as Hilda Wangel in *The Lady from the Sea* ensured the revival of the character in *The Master Builder*; nor should I wonder if the physical contrast between her and Fru Wetter-Gren was responsible for the antagonism of Rita and Asta in *Little Eyolf*.

[2] Brandes, for instance, thought this aspect of *Peer Gynt* 'offensively doctrinaire' (*Henrik Ibsen*, 1898, p. 110; English translation, 1899, p. 76).

[3] 'Hedda Gabler' in *Tilskueren*, IX (1892), p. 829; Bang believed (p. 830) that Ibsen, far from idealising women, always painted them as morally undeveloped; if the thesis is valid, it would enhance their dramatic effectiveness, since, for instance, a perfectly moral Othello or a perfectly moral Coriolanus is inconceivable.

## IX

It is unfortunate, if unavoidable, that so much of the discussion of *A Doll's House* revolves round 'problems'. For Ibsen justly maintained that his first aim was the presentation of human beings and their destinies. But rightly or wrongly, the piece has always given rise to further speculations, and a commentator could scarcely avoid touching upon them.

A last one has still to be discussed: the meaning of *det vidunderlige*, the 'miracle', which Nora first mentions in Act II,[1] but which is not then defined. Is it the same thing as *det vidunderligste*, the 'miracle of miracles',[2] on which her last words to Helmer turn and which she does define as 'that communion between us shall be a marriage'? In her fine-feeling study of Nora's character, Lou Andréas-Salomé[3] seems to assume that what all along Nora has desired is—shall we so call it?—a spiritual consummation of her union with Helmer, analogous to the physical. She has been a bride too long, now she wants to be a wife. With the early hint at depth and seriousness in her character, that interpretation has the desirable advantage of linking the 'old Nora' of Acts I and II firmly with the 'new woman' of the close. But there are great objections to it. For when Fru Linde in Act II asks what the 'miracle' is, Nora replies: 'But it is so terrible, Kristine; it mustn't happen for all the world.' Surely Nora could not wish *this* particular miracle not to 'happen for all the world'? The obvious alternative, however, is not much more satisfactory. If Nora is contemplating in Act II (clearly as something that has been in her mind before) what she formulates in Act III, namely, Thorvald's full recognition of the motive underlying her crime and assumption of all the blame for it, she must at that time have been well aware of the seriousness of her act, while one is forced to think that much of the plot and of the moral theme depends precisely on her lack

---

[1] IV, 160; Archer, VII, 100. The word was given, it seems, an additionally mysterious annotation by being obsolete in Denmark and 'old-world' in Norwegian. Otherwise the language is the contemporary current Danish (Paulsen, J., *Samliv med Ibsen*, I, 1906, p. 26).

[2] IV, 189; Archer, VII, 155.

[3] *Henrik Ibsen's Frauengestalten* (1892), p. 39.

of this awareness. Perhaps the alternative need not be accepted in whole, but only part. In Act II Nora may have dreamt only of Thorvald's discovering and appreciating the act of devotion by which she saved his life, while his taking her guilt upon himself may have been an afterthought, added when the full seriousness of that act of devotion had been brought home to her.

Some have thought that by the 'miracle of miracles' which Thorvald whispers as the final curtain drops, he means something different from Nora, that he is thinking merely of a restoration of his domestic felicity on much the old basis with an added appreciation of the joys of calm after a storm—something rather parallel to his reactions on hearing of Rank's final departure. Thorvald certainly is *l'homme moyen sensuel*, but at such a moment this little note of acerbity seems not only jarring, but improbable. In every sense of the word, Thorvald is sobered, and can indeed see himself as a new man living with a new Nora.

## X

Some, like Philip Wicksteed,[1] have considered it a misfortune, both for the general public and for Ibsen's reputation, that his early, poetic works became known as a general rule tardily and inadequately. The fact is undoubted. The fame of *Brand*, as has been seen, permeated the North very speedily after publication, and ensured there at least a *succès d'estime* for its successors and some of its predecessors. Outside Scandinavia, however, only rare rumours of the great new author permeated before *Pillars of Society*. This play, with its upper-middle-class *milieu*, its broad effects, large cast and obvious moral, seemed like a development of the *Volksstück*, such as writers like Anzengruber and L'Arronge[2] were attempting, and for that, among other reasons, met with a great reception in Germany. Within a few days, it was acted at no less than five different theatres in Berlin, and thereafter, its author was never a stranger on the German stage. Simultaneously, his reputation began to spread in Britain.[3]

*A Doll's House* harvested where *Pillars of Society* had already

*Four Lectures on Henrik Ibsen* (1892), p. 15.

[2] Henry Arthur Jones was doing something like them in Britain during the 1880's.

[3] *Quicksands*, an adaptation of *Pillars of Society*, was produced at the Gaiety Theatre, London, on 15 December 1880.

prepared the soil, and became in course of time the most popular of Ibsen's plays generally, and the agent by which more often than not his fame was propagated to parts of the world previously in ignorance of it. The earliest performance was given at the Royal Theatre, Copenhagen, where Betty Hennings, a gentle slender figure who had previously played Selma Bratsberg, enacted the chief role. A former *prima ballerina* as she was, she may possibly have been in Ibsen's mind when he gave Nora the dramatically most exciting scene of dancing a tarantella, and certainly Fru Hennings seized this, the greatest opportunity in her career, with both hands: henceforth, throughout Northern Europe, Betty Hennings was Nora and Nora was Betty Hennings.[1] The child-wife, heroine and martyr, who had already ensured the success of *Froufrou*,[2] was bound to prove a strong attraction: and the masterly unfolding of her crime and agony, the uncommon skill with which the great scenes were introduced and the dramatic tension was varied, accorded altogether with the taste of the times. Even the arch-conservative, technique-adoring Sarcey, while disallowing the *donnée* and *dénouement*, could not withhold his admiration[3] for all that lay between. Nora became a favourite part both for *comédiennes* who wished to show that there was 'something more in them' and of the emotional actresses who saw their opportunities in the passions they were called upon to express in Acts II and III, in the cold triumphant debate which they had to lead in Act III. Nor were the parts of Helmer, Rank and Krogstad to be despised as mere 'feeders'.

After the original production at Copenhagen on 21 December 1879, *A Doll's House* was presented in Swedish at Göteborg eighteen days later,[4] in the original at Christiania and Bergen on 20 and 30 January 1880 respectively, in Finnish at Helsinki during the next month and in German at the Munich Residenz-theater on 3 March of the same year.[5] Madam Helene

---

[1] And to only a less extent the 'Ibsen woman' was Betty Hennings.

[2] By Meilhac and Halévy (1869).

[3] *Quarante Ans de Théâtre*, VIII (1902), p. 362.

[4] Its success in Sweden was, by reaction, one of the effective causes in establishing Strindberg's misogynistic mania.

[5] There had been a performance within the German Empire, but in Danish, at Slesvig on 20 January.

Modrzejewska (or Modjeska) acted Nora in Polish at St Petersburg (November 1881) and Warsaw (February 1882) and in English at Louisville, Kentucky (in 1883). A version by Henry Arthur Jones and Henry Herman under the title *Breaking a Butterfly* was presented at the Princess Theatre, London, on 3 March 1884.[1] Belgium, Hungary, Italy and Serbia followed suit before the end of the decade; and *A Doll's House*, with Gabrielle Réjane as Nora, was the first play by Ibsen to be done in a commercial theatre in Paris.[2] By the end of the century it had been acted in nearly every country which had a theatre susceptible to European influence.[3]

No other play by the author enjoyed quite the same international success. Favoured for rather similar reasons, *Hedda Gabler* is probably the runner-up, and in the twentieth century the infinite variety of *Peer Gynt* has gained for it fairly widespread acceptance in the theatre as well as in printed form, while *The Wild Duck* and *The Master Builder* have always enjoyed a steady, if less spectacular fame wherever a serious interest in their author has been aroused. Because of the severity and hesitations of the censorship in various countries, *Ghosts* has never failed of at least a *succès de scandale*, but probably for four playgoers out of five, Ibsen remains above all the author of *A Doll's House*.[4]

---

[1] There was a curious translation into English made by the Dane, T. Weber, and published in Copenhagen in 1880.

[2] At the Théâtre du Vaudeville, 20 April 1894.

[3] According to Gran, G., *Henrik Ibsen*, II (1917), p. 82 it proved a failure in Australia and South America.

[4] It is interesting that *The League of Youth* and *Pillars of Society* have consistently been the favourites of the Norwegian public; they are clearly (with *St John's Eve*) the most local in their appeal of Ibsen's prose plays.

# THE WILD DUCK
(*Vildanden*)
## 1884

### I

THE two plays by Ibsen which lie between *A Doll's House* (1879) and *The Wild Duck* (1884) are *Ghosts* (*Gengangere*, 1881) and *An Enemy of the People* (*En Folkefiende*, 1882). About *Ghosts* and the manner with which it links up to, and supplements, *A Doll's House*, everything needful for present purposes has already been touched upon, except the great scandal which it provoked. Ibsen's staunch defender, Jonas Lie, said that *Ghosts* was 'a major operation with the knife plunged straight into the un-mentionable'[1]—rotten marriages, sexual misconduct, venereal disease, elimination of the unfit, etc. Small wonder that the public exposure of such things, particularly in a form commonly associated with social entertainment, was fiercely and widely resented. Ibsen had invited the public to a party for which they had had to pay, and then thrown a stink-bomb into their midst.

The reception of *Ghosts* gave its author the theme of his next play without any of the outward and inward searching and sifting he found necessary at other times. If he was to be accused of malodorous practices he would examine more fully than his critics the justification for indulging in them. So he invented Dr Thomas Stockmann, the large-hearted medical officer to a Spa Committee, who publicly discloses the grave scandal that the Spa's water supply is tainted, and is ignominiously deprived of his livelihood as an Enemy of the People: at the same time, Ibsen made it clear that, to all but those who are 'to Themselves—Enough' and in fact in the eyes of everybody outside the Spa, Thomas Stockmann was doing his duty and that in principles and personality, he was, for all his precipitancy and tactlessness, much to be preferred to those who hounded him out of office.

---

[1] *Cit.* Centenary Edition, IX, 32.

No play by Ibsen has greater concreteness than *An Enemy of the People* with its small seaside town struggling to raise itself in the world as a health resort, its Rate-Payers' Association and mean local newspaper, its municipal panjandrum and the effluvium from the wealthy citizen's tannery which causes all the mischief. The scale of things may be petty—and Ibsen was not above rubbing in his disdain of Scandinavian conditions by deliberately making it so—but the implication is not utterly provincial: Bath[1] or Aix-les-Bains might find itself in a similar quandary. The story, lacking all 'pre-history', suggestions of abstruse symbolism or unnecessary question marks, is straightforward; yet at the same time it constitutes an answer to the critics of *Ghosts*, and, to that extent at least, is a parable. Never were Ibsen's theme and methods to be so simple again; and one way and another, the parabolic gained ground.

Never again, it may be added, did Ibsen attack specific abuses as he had done in the four plays published between 1877 and 1882; a partial explanation for this may be found in the termination of the great struggle between prerogative and the will of the Norwegian people (which, however, still fills the background of *Rosmersholm*, 1886) and the inauguration of a new political era by the rise to power of Sverdrup and the 'Left' in 1884.

## II

The title for *The Wild Duck* was certainly suggested to Ibsen by one of the finest poems of his compatriot Welhaven, '*Søfuglen*' (*The Sea-bird*). Welhaven's Sea-bird is not only a wild duck, but the fate also that overtakes it is clearly reproduced in the play. Injured by a sportsman, prevented from reaching its nest and unwilling to make moan, it dives into the deeps to where the weed grows broad and fresh and the mute fish dwells.[2] It is just possible that from the mouth of his friend Jens Peter Jacobsen, the Danish translator of Darwin, or otherwise, Ibsen learnt of Darwin's observation: 'We have seen how soon the wild duck, when domesticated, loses its true character, from the

---

[1] The novelist-physician Smollett did in fact try to play the part of a Stockmann in the Bath of the eighteenth century.

[2] Welhaven, J. S., *Digterverker* II (1921), pp. 35 f.; cf. v, 38; Archer, VIII, 263.

effects of abundant or changed feeding, or from taking little exercise.'[1] For the wild duck of the play is certainly becoming acclimatised in its unfamiliar surroundings; and in so far as this acclimatisation represents a kind of degeneration and Ibsen was intent in his play to show the effects of degeneration through a parable—two debatable propositions—he may have chosen precisely this exemplification, to which Darwin introduced him, with the poetic associations which Welhaven had imparted to it.

The original conception must have differed considerably from the play which ultimately became *The Wild Duck*. The earliest notes on it[2] we have make, for instance, no mention at all either of the duck herself or of the menagerie in which she queens it. We find there, however, the idea of the family that has come down in the world, even if it comprises a somewhat larger number of persons, one of whom, the son, is a photographer;[3] the family probably played fatuously with the idea of their eventual rehabilitation. They were in contact, too, with another family, that of a merchant. Here again there is a notable difference. For the son of this last-named family, for Halfdan Walle, Ibsen apparently took for his model the author Alexander Kielland.[4] Kielland, after Ibsen himself, Bjørnson and Jonas Lie the greatest Norwegian writer of the time, was a scion of a famous patrician mercantile family of Stavanger: his grand-father had been reputed the richest man in Norway. In a very short space of time Kielland had made a considerable name for himself both with short stories (e.g. *Novelletter* of 1878 and 1880) and with novels which not only described faithfully and warmly his own social environment, but very plainly revealed also an unmistakable radical outlook. Like others, Ibsen was fascinated by the contrast between the man who had all the appearance and manner of a great merchant prince and the understanding, if unsentimental, sympathy which he bestowed on the humble

[1] Darwin, C., *Variation of Animals and Plants under Domestication*, II (1868), p. 278. It would indeed be possible to argue that this sentence re-echoes also in *The Lady from the Sea*.

[2] Now in the University Library, Oslo. Cf. Centenary Edition, x, 163. In a letter to Georg Brandes of 12 June 1883 Ibsen speaks of his next play being in four acts (*Breve*, II, 122).

[3] Rather perplexingly called Gregers at this stage, his *vis-à-vis* having the name Halfdan.

[4] Referred to as 'A.K.' or 'A.K-d' in the notes.

of spirit and estate. He was inclined to think of him as a 'sybarite' —this is the word he used—the complete Kierkegaardian aesthete, who derived an additional pleasure in his luxurious life by the contemplation of others' misery. One of Ibsen's notes sketches him lying cosily tucked up in bed after a good supper, revelling in the thought of tired, cold wayfarers plunging through the splashing rain outside. We may conjecture—but it is no more than a conjecture—that in the original conception of *The Wild Duck* this sybarite was to amuse himself by contemplating the misfortunes of his former school friend, the photographer, and probably playing Providence to him and his squalid family (somewhat after the manner in which old Werle does so in the finished play), and that the disaster was caused by this purely aesthetical, quite unidealistic activity. That scheme, however, would not work and had to be abandoned; but the names Walle or Werle, Ekdahl or Ekdal, Gina, Hedvig, Graaberg and Pettersen were perpetuated; the two groups of personages, the contrast between the opulent group and the down-at-heel, persisted and, oddly enough, the elder Walle or Werle probably took over many of his son's characteristics just as the latter took over the photographer's Christian name; and the matter-of-fact physician was presumably developed out of the schoolmaster Nanne, who may originally have combined the functions of Relling and Molvik.

The changes in conception just indicated took place mostly between the early days of 1883 and April 1884, when, at Rome and on the 20th of that month, Ibsen began the first complete draft (subsequently much altered) of Act I. The drafts of all five acts were completed by 13 June: Ibsen then took up his quarters at Gossensass in the Austrian Alps, where *An Enemy of the People* had been finished off, and in July and August made the fair copy, which was sent off to Messrs Gyldendal of Copenhagen on 2 September. Publication in a slightly smaller edition (8000 copies instead of 10,000) than the first edition of *Ghosts* and *An Enemy of the People* took place on 11 November; a second edition was called for three weeks later, but remained on the publisher's hands for thirty years.[1]

Competition for the *première* was very keen. In the event

[1] In the interval, however, there were some collected editions of the works, the first in 1898.

the prize fell to the Christiania Theatre, which presented it on 9 January 1885, with Ibsen's old friends Gundersen, Brun and Fru Wolf as Old Werle, Old Ekdal and Gina respectively, Hammer as Gregers, Reimers as Hjalmar, Isachsen as Relling, Frøken Krohn as Hedvig.[1] The earliest performances in Finland, Denmark (at Aalborg) and Sweden were given the following January 16, 25 and 30 respectively. The theatre's 'censor', Erik Bøgh, though as a rule well disposed towards Ibsen, had reported adversely on *The Wild Duck*,[2] yet on 22 February 1885 the Royal Theatre at Copenhagen gave it most successfully with great realism of staging and a magnificent cast: the brothers Emil and Olaf Paulsen played Hjalmar and his father respectively, Betty Hennings was the Hedvig,[3] and young Karl Mantzius Dr Relling. Emil Paulsen, it may be observed, was a fine comedian, and so much prominence was given to the ludicrous elements in *The Wild Duck* that, for all the brilliance of the presentation, Ibsen felt constrained to protest mildly that he had written a 'tragi-comedy' in which word the 'tragi' was as important as the 'comedy'—otherwise Hedvig's death, as he said, would become 'incomprehensible'.[4] Olaf Paulsen excelled in parts like Falstaff, and this should be borne in mind by those theatrical producers who take the opposite view to that reprobated by the author and who seek to sink the play in gloom.[5] At its first presentation, *The Wild Duck* produced in the more discerning little more than puzzlement. Its superficial formlessness and the mixture of the tragic and farcical had, in the long run, a pervasive effect on dramatic technique, to which, in their different ways, Hauptmann's *Ratten*, Shaw's *The Doctor's Dilemma*, Chekhov's dramas and many plays of the Dublin Abbey Theatre[6] bear witness. It has never been *widely* popular,

[1] Johanne Dybwad (then still Frøken Juell) did not take up the part of Hedvig till 1889.
[2] In particular he insisted that the drunken parson, Molvik, must be omitted; that was not done. Wherever (as in Denmark) he was in a position legally to enforce his wishes, Ibsen refused all tampering with his texts.
[3] Ibsen said of this production 'Fru Hennings *is* Hedvig but the others fall short'.
[4] *Cit.* Centenary Edition, x, 38.
[5] *The Wild Duck* was first acted in Germany in 1887, in France in 1891 and in Britain in 1894.
[6] It is amusing to find that a blowzy old woman in Walter Macken's *Galway Handicap* (1947) is called 'Winnie the Wild-Duck'.

but general consensus of the best opinion to-day would probably consider it 'the Master's masterpiece'[1]—at any rate if the dramatic poems were set aside.

## III

In a letter sent to his publisher, Frederik Hegel of Gyldendal's, at the same time as the manuscript of *The Wild Duck*, Ibsen had written: 'In some ways this new piece occupies a place apart in my dramatic production; the method of procedure differs in certain respects from the previous.'[2] The novel method of procedure reveals itself at once when the attempt is made to summarise the extremely elaborate antecedent data which, though they are fraught with the weightiest consequences, exhibit little of the precision of Nora Helmer's forged bill or Consul Bernick's successful use of Johan Tønnesen as his scapegoat.[3] The facts in themselves are nowhere really established; they sink into virtual irrelevance; what matters is the construction which the personages of the play with or without warranty put upon them. For convenience they may be arranged in three groups which, however, are closely related: (i) Old Ekdal's disgrace, (ii) the home life of Haaken Werle during his wife's lifetime, and (iii) Hjalmar Ekdal's marriage to Gina Hansen. A fourth group of data concerned with the earlier relations of Gregers Werle, Dr Relling and Berta Sørby has only subsidiary importance.

(i) Twenty years or so before the action of *The Wild Duck* begins, Lieutenant Ekdal and Haaken Werle, then comparatively young men, were in partnership together in Højdal, a remote part of Northern Norway where the latter still owns certain 'works'. Ekdal was convicted and condemned to imprisonment and loss of military rank for having unlawfully felled (and presumably appropriated) timber on Crown property, availing himself of an unreliable map which he himself had drawn. His partner was involved in the prosecution but

---

[1] Bødtker, S., *Kristiania-Premierer gjennem 30 Aar*, I (1923), p. 162.
[2] *Breve*, II, 137; 2 September 1884.
[3] In *Ghosts*, it may be noted, the true nature and origin of Oswald's illness are left somewhat uncertain.

acquitted. So much seems certain. But about Werle's complicity there is a difference of opinion. His servant Pettersen, who seems to be no respecter of persons, harbours no suspicions of it nor seems to have heard of discreditable rumours: 'They say that he [Ekdal] once played Mr Werle a very nasty trick.'[1] But Werle's son, Gregers, who, it may be borne in mind, has spent sixteen or seventeen years in the district where the criminal transactions took place, is persuaded that his father was an accomplice and construes his later acts of charity to the Ekdal family as the expiations of a bad conscience. Hjalmar Ekdal looks upon his father as a martyr, but at first bears Haaken Werle no grudge; Relling, who apparently knows something about this old story, remarks that Lieutenant Ekdal was always 'an ass'.[2]

(ii) Haaken Werle's marriage, of which Gregers was the fruit, was an unhappy one. The spouses were at odds, and Gregers always took his mother's side. She had weaknesses and according to the testimony of a former maid (on whom she laid violent hands) occasionally had 'crazy fits';[3] if she was an alcoholic addict, that would fit the descriptions. Her husband, on the other hand, exposed to unending domestic scenes, ran after the said maid with dishonourable intentions, but whether he was actually unfaithful to his wife is not made explicit.

(iii) When Fru Werle died, the widower continued his pursuit of Gina Hansen—through the comparatively decent intermediacy, it may be noted, of her mother—and 'had his will of her'. Soon after this she married Hjalmar Ekdal, who also had enjoyed extra-marital relations with her and who, his university career broken off by his father's disgrace, had recently been trained as a photographer and installed in his own studio at Haaken Werle's expense. That the latter furthered the marriage of Hjalmar and Gina in any other way is not stated. Gina's child, Hedvig, born in wedlock, had been conceived before, but the paternity is left uncertain; Gregers unquestionably assumes that she is his half-sister, and the assumption is supported by

[1] v, 4; Archer, VIII, 194.
[2] v, 90; Archer, VIII, 368.
[3] 'fysiske raptusser' (v, 65; Archer, VIII, 317).

the fact that both she and Haaken Werle suffer from a serious affliction of the eyes.[1]

This then is the complex relationship to one another of most of the principals at the beginning of Act 1, when old Werle, a highly prosperous merchant, is giving a sumptuous dinner in honour of his son Gregers and his return home after a long absence. Gregers has insisted on the inclusion of Hjalmar Ekdal among the guests (though this brings the number at dinner up to thirteen); they had been friends in the old days of their fathers' partnership, but had maintained no correspondence: so Gregers is quite unfamiliar with the Ekdals' circumstances and even with the identity of Hjalmar's wife. He learns something about all this during an after-dinner talk interrupted by a painful episode when the shabby, shambling figure of Old Ekdal has to make its way through the reception rooms from Werle's office where he has been fetching the copying work—grossly overpaid—on which he subsists. Gregers is indignant at what he considers Hjalmar's tame, not to say cowardly, acceptance of the situation and further outraged at the offer of a partnership in the firm which his father then makes to him. Gregers looks upon the offer and the festive celebration of his return as a mere *façade* which he is to embellish and by which his father wishes to cover up any suspicion of family disunion, as well as the marriage on which he now proposes to enter with the present housekeeper, Berta Sørby.

Not all the reasons transpire on account of which, at the outset of *The Wild Duck*, Gregers has travelled up from the Højdal works to the capital.[2] His father's invitation does not by itself exhaust them; for the offer of a partnership comes, apparently, as a surprise to him, while, at the same time, he has made no plans to return. His talks with Hjalmar Ekdal and his father in the first act, however, furnish him with a definite

---

[1] On the other hand, Lou Andréas-Salomé argued with some ingenuity that, if Hedvig's artistic leanings which make her wish to be an engraver are inherited, they are more likely to have come from Hjalmar Ekdal than from Haaken Werle (Andréas-Salomé, L., *Henrik Ibsen's Frauengestalten*, 1892, p. 88).

[2] The general stage-direction of the finished play says no more than that 'The first act passes in Werle's house, the remaining acts at Hjalmar Ekdal's'; but the original draft declared that the action took place in Christiania, and I think that this should be assumed.

purpose: to open Hjalmar's eyes to his true position and thus induce him radically and immediately to change it: for, having as high an opinion of his friend's character as of his abilities, he cannot but believe that only sheer ignorance can account for his continuing to put up with something that he, Gregers, looks on as dishonourable.

The second, third, fourth and fifth acts are laid in an environment strikingly different from the opulent—not to say the ostentatious—luxury[1] of Haaken Werle's study; they play in Hjalmar Ekdal's third-rate photographic *atelier*, which commonly serves also as his family's living-room. Some necessary professional apparatus and litter apart, it is snug, if cheap and shabby, and not greatly in demand for its ostensible purpose. A remarkable feature is the extension of this room—which is at the top of the building and has a convenient sky-light—into a large, derelict attic, harbouring not only more usual lumber, but in addition, a small forest of decaying Christmas-trees and a quantity of livestock.

Owing to his neglect of it, Hjalmar Ekdal's business scarcely thrives, and an additional source of income accrues from the sub-letting of rooms in his house. One of these Gregers Werle, calling shortly after Hjalmar has returned from the dinner-party, proposes to take, and Hjalmar's wife, Gina, who knows Gregers of old,[2] reluctantly consents to the arrangement. The following act, the third, takes place next morning and is largely taken up with the lunch-party which Hjalmar gives for Gregers and to which he invites also his other lodgers, the doctor Relling and the parson Molvik. His indignation exacerbated both by fuller appreciation of Hjalmar's environment—not least, by the make-believe wild life in the attic—and by a last friendly overture which his father calls to make, Gregers invites his old friend for a long walk and, in the course of it, reveals to him Gina's

[1] 'A richly and comfortably furnished study: bookcases and upholstered furniture. ...At the back, open folding-doors.... Within is seen a large and handsome room, brilliantly lighted with lamps and branching candlesticks' (v, 3; Archer, VIII, 191).

[2] Gina was Haaken Werle's housekeeper and mistress after Gregers had left home, it seems; but she was a servant girl in the house before. From the first, her aversion to Gregers is very marked and significant, though different interpretations may be put upon it. Perhaps, like Relling, she knew him as an inveterate mischief-maker.

intrigue with Werle senior and the dubious nature of the latter's benefits to the Ekdal family. Gregers purposed thereby, no doubt, to perform 'the miracle of miracles', whereby a true marriage should come about between Hjalmar and his lowly, but loyal wife; the effect of his interference, however, is only to rouse in Hjalmar a sullen resentment at the disturbance in his mental habits—a resentment which is heated to a warmer glow by the receipt, in Act IV, of a deed of gift from Old Werle for the benefit of Ekdal senior and, after his death, for that of Hedvig. Firmly convinced now that the little girl is not his, but Haaken Werle's, child, Hjalmar repulses her and joins Relling and Molvik on a drunken tour through the town. In the course of the following morning (Act v) he returns home to arrange for the final removal of himself and his old father. But the project is shattered by the death of Hedvig, who, urged by Gregers to sacrifice to her father's love what she holds dearest in the world, has gone into the attic to shoot the wild duck and has turned the pistol against her own breast.

As four of *The Wild Duck's* five acts play amid a physical confusion and squalor for which the author's earlier plays scarcely show a parallel,[1] so the level of the characters shows in almost every respect a marked degradation. Thomas Stockmann was an uncommon doctor to find in a small provincial town, and much of the point of *Pillars of Society* would be missed if Consul Bernick were not conceived as an *entrepreneur* of great energy and initiative; Fru Alving was a remarkable woman, and it may not be irrelevant to remember that, in some ways, Nora Helmer was something of a study of her in her youth. No one quite of their calibre—unless a partial exception be made in favour of Dr Relling—takes a chair round the lunch-table in Hjalmar Ekdal's studio, nor is there even an indication that Haaken Werle, for all his wealth, is a commercial *matador* like Carsten Bernick.

The diminished scale of the figures becomes even more obvious when we compare the two most fully portrayed characters, Hjalmar Ekdal and Gregers Werle, with their fore-

---

[1] In some ways *An Enemy of the People*, culminating in the disorderly public meeting, anticipates this: but the squalor of Aslaksen's printing office is largely professional untidiness.

runners Peer Gynt and Brand. Hjalmar is the complete egocentric who cloaks his lack of principle and purpose, not (as Peer Gynt did) with scraps of proverbial wisdom, but with the kind of sentimental rhetoric he had learned in post-prandial orations, and who always finds himself in positions into which more purposeful individualities and the drift of circumstances have pushed him. He could never have seized the opportunities that would make him master of an ocean-going steam-yacht; his utterly fatuous working at a great invention (which from first to last has been a suggestion foisted upon him from outside) lacks the grandeur both of Peer Gynt's dizzy ride on the reindeer and of his project of a super-Faustian 'Gyntiana'; his affection for his father and for Hedvig is mainly self-dramatising patronage of the grey- (or white-) haired veteran maimed in the battle of life and of the trustful child on whom eternal darkness is about to descend: he lets the former fuddle himself whenever others furnish the necessary liquor, and has no scruples in allowing the latter to strain her eyesight when it suits his convenience. The genuineness of Peer's devotion to Solveig becomes plain when it is contrasted with Hjalmar's using of Gina as a mere drudge not even worthy of sentimental allocutions. It is, alas, only too likely that even Hedvig's death will, as Relling prophesies, mean nothing more to him than a new repertoire of fine phrases.

Gregers Werle, like Parson Brand, is a man with a mission. But he is the idealist even more fatally run to seed than Brand's distorted image, the 'regenerated' Einar. The 'mission' which he conceives to have been laid upon him is almost as nebulous as Hjalmar's great invention, though it may possess[1] the merit —for what that is worth—of being self-imposed. He is the 'superior' person who, whenever he sees his fellow-men going the common rounds of their daily lives, immediately thinks that they ought to be doing something different and, of course, 'better'.[2] He does not stop at thinking, but proceeds to exhortations, which, as far as one can judge, are of a negative or very

---

[1] I say 'may possess' because, as we shall see, Gregers's fantasies over the wild duck are quite unoriginal and, for anything we know to the contrary, his grand mission may well have been imposed upon him by his dead mother.

[2] There is an obvious anticipation of this in Fru Linde of *A Doll's House*, whose activities, however, seem to meet with the author's approval.

nebulous character: his victims are to rouse themselves, give up their old habits and assumptions, search their hearts, take moral soundings, judge themselves and their neighbours, all in the name of an 'ideal' which is not further defined. In the end, as Gregers himself comes to admit, his mission amounts to no more than being the self-invited thirteenth round the dinner-table, a cause of discomfort at the time and of calamity thereafter.

With both Gregers and Hjalmar Ibsen insists on the formative influences undergone in youth as he did with Brand and Peer Gynt. Gregers was the child of unhappily married parents, brought up in a divided home, where his mother filled him up with her wrongs, set him in incurable antagonism against his father,[1] made him abhor moral uncleanness as strongly as he everywhere suspected its existence and inspired him with the ambition to eradicate it. Hjalmar owed his education mainly to two foolish maiden aunts[2] who, on the one hand, by their adulation destroyed any personality he may have been born with —this, at any rate, is Relling's view—and on the other hand gave him a great conceit of his abilities, which the admiration of co-evals like Gregers and of others, won by his gift of the gab and his pleasing address, confirmed.[3]

Gregers's antipode is Relling, a medical man who, for all his practical psychology, has come down in the world, perhaps through dissipation. Where Gregers generalises, he considers every case on its merits; where Gregers dimly envisages a general good, his aim is the happiness of the individual; Gregers spreads *malaise* and disaster, he on the other hand brings ease and healing —at any rate to others: with himself, as his barely indicated love-affair with Berta Sørby suggests, he would appear to have

[1] Gregers's relations to his father are fully expounded in Freudian terms by Nissen, I., *Sjelelige Kriser* (1931), p. 98. Fru Werle's grievances may have been imaginary, at least in part.

[2] v, 90; Archer, VIII, 367.

[3] The most recent editor of Ibsen (Koht, H., Introduction to *The Wild Duck* in Centenary Edition, x, 10) believes that traits for Hjalmar Ekdal's character were contributed by an unsuccessful artist, Magnus Bagge, who once gave him drawing-lessons, Kristoffer Janson who was parodied as Huhu of *Peer Gynt*, and Edward Larssen, who took the earliest known photograph of Ibsen. The last identification is very likely in view of the fact that the figure who ultimately became Hjalmar is indicated in the early notes as 'E. L.'. Koht further draws attention (*ibid.* p. 23) to Mr Micawber, who seems to me much more plausible as a likely model for Hjalmar than his suggestion Alceste (of Molière's *Misanthrope*) for Gregers Werle.

been less successful. The guiding principle on which he acts will come up for consideration later. Though his readiness to talk about that principle and the pregnancy of his observations approximate him in some degree to the stage-*raisonneur* (such as Fjeldbo of *The League of Youth*, another doctor), Relling, positive and very clear-sighted, is rather a unique type in Ibsen's gallery of portraits: the schoolmaster Arnholm in *The Lady from the Sea* and the engineer Borghejm of *Little Eyolf* have none of his force and individuality. He was almost certainly suggested by the figure of Dr Borg, who in Strindberg's novel, *The Red Room*,[1] exhibits many of the same characteristics and fulfils a similar function.

Another sensible and balanced mind is that of Gregers's father. In view of two major points for which Ibsen admits only a purely subjective interpretation—the timber-fraud and Hedvig's paternity—a verdict of his character is difficult to reach (and is in fact unnecessary to pronounce). In general, he has received short shrift from the commentators, particularly the seniors among them, as an adulterer, domestic tyrant and swindler, whose main strength lies in his banking-account; but it is permissible to judge him much more favourably, as a man more sinned against (both by Old Ekdal and by his wife) than sinning, who certainly is not exempt from sins, but who voluntarily pays for them and uses tact and imagination—not to mention generosity—in the mode of payment. His contemplated marriage with Fru Sørby may strike a severe moralist as 'repulsive';[2] on the other hand, it is repugnant neither to natural nor to human law, it is entered upon under certain quite good moral guarantees, it injures none and it will undoubtedly subserve the lasting happiness and solid usefulness of the contracting parties. It is difficult to think—provided always that the general depressed level of the play is kept in mind—that Ibsen disapproved of this union, though something of the same sort for a Rebecca West or Arnold Rubek might have seemed definitely less desirable.

---

[1] *Röda Rummet*, 1879; it rightly caused a considerable literary sensation in Scandinavia. Ibsen knew it (Paulsen, J., *Samliv med Ibsen*, II, 1913, p. 224).
[2] 'Abstossend' is the epithet of Harnack, O., *Essais und Studien* (1899), p. 351.

*A propos* of the Copenhagen production, a warning was given not to repeat Hjalmar's mistake and take too sentimental a view of his father. He has certainly suffered shipwreck, either through the wickedness of others or through his own incompetence rather than through sheer criminality, but with his ungrateful cadging, his furtive drunkenness and his antics amid the Christmas trees in the attic, he is as despicable and ludicrous as he is pitiable. I cannot help thinking that Ibsen made a trifling mistake by putting in his mouth (twice)[1] the phrase: 'The forests avenge themselves.' It does not seem to me an expression at all consonant with his usual speech and is either farcically inappropriate or else cloudily portentous.

The remaining characters may be passed in review more summarily. The drunken reprobate Molvik, the servants and the book-keeper speak for themselves. Gina's vulgarity—perhaps a trifle overdone in Archer's translation?—is vulgarity of speech only: she is competent, loyal, considerate and affectionate without in any way advertising these qualities and, though with all the burdens of a household and a business on her she is overworked, she should not, I think, give the impression of a downtrodden slattern: otherwise Relling would have done something for her and even Gregers might have perceived that Hjalmar was not the only victim of the situation. Her friend Berta Sørby, the veterinary surgeon's widow, stands on a higher level of intelligence and culture, perfectly capable as she seems to be of holding her own in the best mercantile society of Norway.

For Hedvig Ibsen seems to have drawn on his recollection of his sister with the same name, the only member of his family with whom he maintained some sort of friendly relations and who followed his own career with sympathy. She is no childish heroine. There is nothing very unusual about her individuality or ways, except that she is, perhaps, a little young for her years in her continual absorption in make-believe and completely uncritical acceptance of her environment.[2] No more, I think,

---

[1] v, 35 and 104; Archer, VIII, 256 and 396.

[2] Bjørnson thought that she would have seen through Hjalmar before this and therefore refrained from her self-sacrifice. It will be remembered that she has not gone to school nor mixed with others of her age.

should be made of Relling's allusions to her puberty than an occasional proneness to a certain excited violence, which goes some little way to accounting for her suicide.[1]

## IV

The pathos of Hedvig's fate has led those for whom it is the most moving and the most arresting thing in *The Wild Duck* to look upon her as the heroine of the play and, as a not unnatural corollary, to identify her in some measure with the wild duck itself: for, after all, it is a not unusual practice to name a drama after its foremost character. Hedvig may be the most admirable personage presented in the play, but that in itself does not guarantee the validity of the theory; the virtuous Kent is not the hero of *King Lear*, nor the blameless Cassandra of *Agamemnon*; neither can it rightly be maintained that the play fundamentally is 'about' Hedvig, that her fate is the constant preoccupation either of the other personages or of the spectators: she is a victim like Ophelia in *Hamlet*, and almost an accidental victim.

The same, to be sure, can be said of the wild duck, but is there really any other close parallel between them? Does the wild duck's fate mirror that of her owner and, in doing so, give it a wider significance? They who incline to such a view remark that both of them live in a world of pretences for which they are not responsible and that they are the noblest, the least corrupted denizens of that world. Both perish. But further the parallel cannot be extended, and the dissimilarities are greater than the resemblances. Nothing goes to show that Hedvig has been wounded or maimed or even that the environment of pretence in which she has been brought up is marring desirable potentialities in her. We do not exclaim: 'What a nice, what a happy, what a noble little girl this would be *if she had not got* such a horrible home.' Nothing indicates a distortion in her nature except her reported playing with fire, which Relling expressly puts down not to anything in her environment, but to the stage which she has reached in her natural physical development.

---

[1] Relling's very positive pronouncement (v, 105; Archer, viii, 399) is intended to put the purposive nature of her act beyond doubt.

And where are we to find the application of the wild duck's plunge to the bottom of the sea and her recovery by Haaken Werle's incredibly clever dog?

Why does Hedvig shoot herself? Accident, as has been noted, should be ruled out. Hers is an intentional act, induced by the notion of sacrifice which Gregers has put into her head: to regain her father's love she is to offer up what she holds dearest in the world. She does not hesitate in designating as the sacrificial victim her pet, the maimed wild duck: she will get her grandfather, Old Ekdal, to shoot it dead. The construction that, on further reflection, as a conscious perseverance in Gregers's idea, Hedvig considered her own life to be even more precious than the wild duck must, I think, be rejected, even if unconsciously her act may conform to it. The act is a violent, perhaps hysterical one of self-destruction, the cause of it despair at Hjalmar's rejection of her as an interloper[1] and the manner suggested by the mocking rhetorical question she overhears: 'Hedvig, are you willing to renounce that life for me? [*Laughs scornfully*.] No thank you! You would soon hear what answer I should get.'[2]

Hedvig loves the wild duck partly because it has been wounded and is thriving again under her care, partly because it is the rarest, most aristocratic denizen of the attic and her very own property, partly because there are about it the romantic, fairy-tale associations of having lived its wild life a long way away and, at the time it was wounded, having 'been down in the depths of the sea'.[3] Even if Hedvig were capable of conceiving a 'symbol' —which, of course, she is not—there is nothing to suggest that the wild duck is a symbol to her in any deeper sense any more than that a boy's passion for his rocking-horse is a symbol to him of his pride of possession or love of mastery.

The other characters' attitude towards the bird is not quite so straightforward. For old Ekdal she is part, the most authentic part, of the surrogate wild life in which he can still see himself leading the primitive sportsman's existence where he had been happiest; for Hjalmar, similarly, one of the distractions enabling

---

[1] The terrible Racinian *réplique*; 'Er det mig?' 'Does that mean me?' (v, 96; Archer, VIII, 379).

[2] v, 102; Archer, VIII, 381.     [3] v, 50; Archer, VIII, 288.

him to escape from a reality that otherwise would depress him by its squalor and his own conviction of failure. But it is Gregers, with his proneness to read sermons in stones, who weaves speculative phantasies about the wild duck, not merely as one (if the most outstanding) of the elements in the make-believe wild life of the attic—which he dislikes as a sham and an obfuscation of reality—but in herself. It is not an exuberant imagination that makes him do this; significantly, the ideas are put into his head by others, first by his father, when, before the wild duck has ever been mentioned, he says *à propos* of Old Ekdal[1] 'there are people in the world who dive to the bottom the moment they get a couple of slugs in their body, and never come to the surface again', and then by Old Ekdal himself, who, after repeating the hunters' lore that, when a wild duck is shot, it plunges to the bottom and bites itself fast to the weed and rubbish there, recalls that this particular wild duck, having done this, was retrieved by an 'amazingly clever dog' belonging to Haaken Werle, who then made a present of the bird to the Ekdal family. Gregers immediately fastens on the parallel between this story and the carefree, naïve life of Old Ekdal, which was shattered by the action of his old partner, but continued in a kind of twilight, amid filth and rubbish, barely conscious, half dead. He sees himself as the incredibly clever dog who dives down and restores submerged creatures to light and renewed utility above. He does more than perceive analogies of this order, he voices them:

GREGERS. My dear Hjalmar, I almost think you have something of the wild duck in you.

HJALMAR. Something of the wild duck? How do you mean?

GREGERS. You have dived down and bitten yourself fast in the undergrowth.

HJALMAR. Are you alluding to the well-nigh fatal shot that has broken my father's wing—and mine too?

GREGERS. Not exactly to *that*. I don't say that your wing has been broken; but you have strayed into a poisonous marsh, Hjalmar; an insidious disease has taken hold of you, and you have sunk down to die in the dark.

---

[1] v, 15; Archer, VIII, 217.

HJALMAR.  I? To die in the dark? Look here, Gregers, you must really leave off talking such nonsense.

GREGERS.  Don't be afraid: I shall find a way to help you up again.[1]

It is clear that, to Gregers, Hedvig's wild duck is a symbol, which can possess, as the most thoroughgoing symbolists seem always to hold, an active property of its own in relation to what it is held to symbolise. For, in inducing Hedvig to kill her pet, he intends to destroy the bogus, 'lying' make-believe which poisons the atmosphere of her family.

We must, however, beware of identifying the calamity-fraught notions of Gregers Werle with Ibsen's own.  Like many another author, especially when a comparatively concentrated literary form, like the dramatic, enjoins economy, Ibsen could give prominence to a single phrase or object or concept (where in real life a number of rather similar phrases or objects or concepts would more usually occur), without necessarily attaching any unique and thus mysterious significance to the one chosen as representative; and an occasional, not over-recondite, coincidence or parallel[2] can have its uses for giving unobtrusive emphasis.  Because only the orphanage is mentioned during the eighteen hours or so in which *Ghosts* plays, we are not to suppose that Fru Alving had kept her late husband's memory alive in no other ways. Aslaksen (of *The League of Youth*) no doubt had many other stock-phrases besides 'the local situation', and Ballested (in *The Lady from the Sea*) was capable of painting other subjects than expiring mermaids.  Nor would Ibsen disdain a small telling phrase or *motif* which in its context suggests something bigger, more comprehensive and of wider applicability than itself, which 'strikes overtones' as some phrase it, such as Falk's killing of the song-bird in *Love's Comedy* and Nora's remark on coming out of her room to engage her husband in her great debate: 'Yes, I have changed my frock now.'  Many

[1] IV, 57; Archer, VIII, 300. There is a further allusion to this conversation, IV, 73; Archer, VIII, 333.

[2] Perhaps one can range under this head the mess which Gregers, with his doctrinaire determination to do everything for himself, makes of his room in trying to cope with an unfamiliar stove (V, 43; Archer, VIII, 272); this may imply some self-criticism of Ibsen, who, we know, insisted on sewing on his own buttons, but did it ineffectively.

others have done the same: one thinks of the purple carpet in Aeschylus's *Agamemnon*, which stands for the equality with the gods arrogated unto himself by the victorious leader of the Greeks.

Undeniably, however, Ibsen exhibits a liking for such overtones which does not characterise all tragedians, not even all poetic tragedians. However far we may go with Mr Wilson Knight in conceiving each of Shakespeare's plays as one 'extended metaphor', their allusiveness must be reckoned to a different order—unless we interpret Fortinbras and his share in *Hamlet* as representing all that part in the hero's nature which he aspires to perfect, but is temperamentally debarred from, or look upon Desdemona's handkerchief as a symbol of domestic disarray. At the beginning of the present chapter it was noted how the fortunes of Dr Thomas Stockmann constitute a parable of the unpopular reformer; and, of course, the two great 'dramatic poems'—to which different criteria apply than to a comedy like *An Enemy of the People*—are, by their nature, such elaborate parables of two different types of humanity that they are not infrequently referred to as 'allegories'. In *The Pretenders*, similarly, the contrast between three historical figures, King Haakon Haakonsson, Earl Skule and Bishop Nicholas, is carried so far and so deep as to embrace a universally valid commentary on leadership.

It is important to observe, nevertheless, that an ear insensitive to overtones can still derive the impression of a symphonic whole from the works just mentioned, perhaps even make out the essential themes. The fate of Haakon Haakonsson and his competitors, of Peer Gynt, of Brand and of Dr Stockmann can give us all the emotions we expect in great drama, even if we take no interest in leadership or Kierkegaardian ethics or municipal corruption. If we choose to regard the plays in question as being in their essence 'symbolic', as contributions to the elucidation of such general questions, we do so to some extent at our peril; as the author has furnished us in each instance with a complete and satisfying work of art we must not hold him responsible for the constructions it may please us to put upon it. The symbolism is, so to speak, detachable.

But the pervasiveness of the wild duck, the repeated references to it and the way in which so many of the human beings round about are preoccupied with it raise a presumption that this single small object, which is not even seen, possesses an importance of a novel order. After all, the play is called *The Wild Duck*. The wild duck and its associations can scarcely be dismissed *prima facie* as 'detachable' in the sense just argued. Should not a significance be attached to it greater than the aggregate of things which it means to the various personages who mention it, something overriding all the small 'lessons' and 'morals' which those who will can derive from almost any work of art, a significance for which the author himself can be made responsible? The same question presents itself more or less insistently with *Rosmersholm* and the 'White Horses' after which that play was originally named, with Ellida's love of bathing in *The Lady from the Sea*, with the vine-leaves in Løvborg's hair of which even so prosaic a person as Hedda Gabler makes mention, with the tower on Master Builder Solness's new house, with the great statuary group on which Rubek of *When We Dead Awaken* had founded his fame. Is any paramount importance to be attached to the fact that little Eyolf's crutch is seen floating after he is drowned or that the night on which John Gabriel Borkman dies should be a specially cold one? Has at the end of Ibsen's career the symbolism, in Mr Tennant's phrase,[1] become 'organic'—something, so to speak, without which the plays would fall to pieces as artistic and intellectual constructions, be nothing but trivial and rather painful anecdotes? Mr Tennant declares:

> Ibsen gave the play the name *Vildanden* and I maintain that it was not a title chosen because of the association such a name would arouse but because the wild duck is the chief protagonist of the play.... The play is not called *Vildanden* because Hedvig's fate was like that of a wild duck, nor because the wild duck, under the censorship of morals, conventions or religion, is the distorted expression of elementary urges. It is because the wild duck by its mere presence so affects the conditions of Gregers, Hjalmar and Hedvig by the various associations it suggests that it bears the sole responsibility for the final catastrophe.[2]

[1] Tennant, P. F. D., 'Critical Study of the Composition of Ibsen's *Vildanden*', in *Edda*, XXXIV (1934), p. 327.
[2] *Loc. cit.* p. 325; I have corrected some misprints.

We may say at once that, if Mr Tennant is right, *The Wild Duck* is all but unique among Ibsen's plays. Almost too obviously the lofty tower which Solness has constructed bears the 'responsibility for the final catastrophe'; but Løvborg's vine-leaves, Little Eyolf's crutch and Rubek's statue certainly do not, and the White Horses of Rosmersholm are only a minor item in Rosmer's and Rebecca's preoccupations. But, even for *The Wild Duck*, Mr Tennant, I think, overstates his case. The catastrophe, Hedvig's death, is brought about by Hjalmar's unkindness to her, which Gregers's doctrinaire interference unnaturally stimulates, and a play ending similarly could have been constructed by omitting the wild duck altogether (as indeed Ibsen seems at first to have conceived it) or by, so to speak, putting its various functions in commission instead of concentrating them in a single focus. Very likely, such a play would have been less effective than *The Wild Duck* we have. But the fact that Ibsen seems to have contemplated it at first goes some considerable way to proving that the symbolism again is 'detachable'.

In general, Ibsen was disdainful of symbolic explanations. Among all the contemporary critics of his play he seems to have preferred Edvard Brandes (Georg Brandes's journalistic brother) who consistently denied that symbolism; and he declared scornfully:[1] 'Yes, to be sure, the explainers. They don't always do their job well. They like symbolising,[2] because they have no respect for reality.' He added, to be sure: 'But if you really put a symbol into their heads, they turn it into something trivial and use bad language.' One will probably not be far out in concluding that for the plays as a whole—with the possible exceptions of the two great 'dramatic poems',—the interpretation on the plane of actuality is primary and sufficient, and that such 'symbols' as occur in them, like the sea in *The Lady from the Sea* or the wild duck in the play now under review, are added graces which conveniently (and perhaps poetically) resume in themselves from time to time a series of associations. But these

---

[1] *Auct.* Lothar, R., *Henrik Ibsen* (2nd ed. 1902), p. 126.
[2] Sometimes the 'symbolising' is no more than bad style, as when I. Nissen says that 'Dr Relling *symbolises* the recognition that once damage and lies have supervened it is often necessary to acquiesce' (*Sjelelige Kriser*, 1931, p. 78).

associations are always, to begin with, in the minds of the actors in the plays, and, if the spectator adopts them too, he does so at his own pleasure and risk, with no guarantee that the author himself accepts responsibility for their authenticity.

## V

If in one way (to put it at its lowest) the wild duck serves to hold together the play called after her, in another way Relling does so too. Whatever it is, his is a somewhat more limited function. For he has next to nothing to do with the sphere of which Haaken Werle forms the centre: his activities are confined to the Ekdal household. Not unlike Gregers Werle, he is a man with a mission, though he would probably have repudiated any such ascription to him other than the good physician's principle to do his best for his patients, for each according to his diathesis and complaint. In the play, he is called in to examine Hedvig after her suicide; but otherwise, his ministrations belong entirely to the psychological and moral realm; and, though he proceeds with professional empiricism, he acknowledges a therapeutic principle. It is formulated as keeping the 'life-lie[1] alive' in his 'patients', to maintain them, in other words, in the atmosphere of illusion where they thrive.

GREGERS. Oh, indeed! Hjalmar Ekdal is sick too, is he!

RELLING. Most people are, worst luck.

GREGERS. And what remedy are you applying in Hjalmar's case?

RELLING. My usual one. I am cultivating the life-illusion in him.

GREGERS. Life-illusion? I didn't catch what you said.

RELLING. Yes, I said illusion. For illusion, you know, is the stimulating principle.[2]

He has contrived to keep some glimmer of self-respect alive in his companion, the debauched theologian Molvik, by persuading

---

[1] The Dano-Norwegian *løgn* has a somewhat wider connotation, it seems, than the English *lie*. In one of Amalie Skram's novels a girl mutely hands over to her mother less than she has received, whereupon the latter exclaims: 'That is a lie.'

[2] v, 91; Archer, viii, 369.

him that his alcoholic outbreaks are the manifestation of the 'dæmonic nature' in him craving for satisfaction from time to time. He has not invented the notion of the 'hunting-ground' in the attic for Lieutenant Ekdal's benefit—the old man hit on it himself—but he encourages and approves of it. It is he, however, who has put into Hjalmar's head the belief that he has it in him to make a great discovery in the science of photography and thereby to redeem the decayed family honour. Relling's only concern is the happiness of his patient—though it may be noted that that happiness nowhere involves the unhappiness of others: but concepts like the good of society or the moral efficacy of the individual are not only excluded but repudiated.

Relling accordingly stands as the poles apart to the man of principle, Gregers Werle, who is in every way antipathetic to him. He rejects ideals in themselves;

RELLING. While I think of it, Mr Werle, junior—don't use that foreign word: ideals. We have the excellent native word: lies.

GREGERS. Do you think the two things are related?

RELLING. Yes, just about as closely as typhus and putrid fever;[1]

and particularly because the impossible demands which they make are the direct cause of individual dissatisfaction and unhappiness. 'Life would be quite tolerable', he exclaims at the very end of the play: 'Life would be quite tolerable, after all, if only we could be rid of the confounded duns that keep on pestering us, in our poverty, with the claim of the ideal.'[2] Pragmatically he is justified: as long as it was he who was in control of the situation in Hjalmar's house, all went well; but, from the moment he is ousted by the idealist, *malaise*, unhappiness and disaster ensue.

Relling being thus justified according to the most reliable test available, how far may we identify Ibsen's own attitude with his? 'Ideals' are seen as the hostile agent, standing in the way of human happiness. Has Ibsen finally come round to this view? If we make the identification of Relling and Ibsen, is there not a grave inconsistency between the position which the latter takes up in *The Wild Duck* and that to be inferred from the earlier plays, where truth, honesty, candour, straight-

[1] v, 92; Archer, VIII, 371.  [2] v, 106; Archer, VIII, 400.

dealing, the resolute facing of facts, everything indeed repugnant to the 'life-lie', seem to be exalted? Undoubtedly there is a great difference. But we have noted before, in connection with *Brand* and *Peer Gynt* particularly, how Ibsen could make his work embody two opposing points of view, could impartially scrutinise them and show them as issuing in similar results; he realised more and more clearly that everything, even truth,[1] was relative, that it was impossible to make universally valid demands,[2] and he was insistent that every factor must be weighed, all circumstances of an individual case taken into account. This is in a way a consequence of self-criticism. If Ibsen felt that he had been too hard on Brand, he redressed the balance by subjecting to similar castigation one who had none of the qualities of Brand, seeing himself or part of himself in both. Similarly he could see himself, the author of *Pillars of Society*, *A Doll's House* and *An Enemy of the People*, going about the world with the demands of the ideal in his pocket just like Gregers Werle among the cottagers at Højdal. Could he be sure that he had produced nothing but good? Were there not, to put it at its lowest, circumstances in which a Relling would be absolutely right in rounding upon him? The Lie, against which Falk so exuberantly declared war, may sometimes have its justification.

In the circumstances that must be taken into account in any verdict upon *The Wild Duck*, there is one of particular importance which has already been glanced at. The personages in the play are by comparison with their predecessors of a diminished stature, they are much more ordinary people. Is it fair, the inference seems to be, is it proper in the last analysis, is it profitable to ask such ordinary people to raise themselves to the moral level of a Thomas Stockmann or Helene Alving, not to mention a Brand and an Agnes? In other words, may not 'ideals' be a luxury and as such inaccessible to the great mass of humanity? The pragmatical test represented by *The Wild Duck* seems to return the answer Yes.

They who scan a work of art for ideals are themselves

---

[1] Note in this connection Dr Stockmann's exaggerated claim that very few truths have a life of more than twenty years (IV, 338; Archer, VIII, 135).

[2] Letter to C. Caspari of 27 June 1884 (*Breve*, II, 136).

idealists in the popular accepted meaning of the term: they attribute the best motives and await the highest in mankind. A conclusion like that to which Relling attains, in much of which Ibsen himself seems also to concur, is profoundly repugnant to them or if not repugnant, at least grieving. It is on that account, no doubt, that *The Wild Duck* has been called the most pessimistic of Ibsen's plays[1] and that the pessimism vulgarly attributed to all tragedies is confirmed in his case.

Before proceeding to a discussion of *The Wild Duck* as a tragedy and to a fuller consideration of Ibsen's pessimism, we might for a moment pause to ask whether the thesis that ideals are not for the common man is taken up again. Relling, it has been said, is a unique figure in Ibsen's gallery of portraits. In his next work he characteristically put this variant of the *raisonneur* in quite a different light with Ulrik Brendel, the peripatetic philosopher full of ideals and talk who does as little good to others as he does to himself. But Brendel is dwarfed by Rosmer and Rebecca, in whom there are potentialities of true greatness, and the scale of the figures is nowhere again quite so much reduced as in *The Wild Duck*. The protagonists of *Rosmersholm* and *When We Dead Awaken* certainly, of *Little Eyolf*, *The Master Builder* and *John Gabriel Borkman* almost certainly, are personalities of uncommon endowments, whose frustration stirs emotions again akin to that of Brand, Earl Skule and Bernick and of Mrs Alving and Hjørdis.

The mention of Hjørdis, however, gives one pause in calling to mind Hedda Gabler, who in a very similar fashion, when her own life has lost its meaning, plays with the lives of men; a diminution of stature in *her* case is undeniable; mere *ennui* has in her taken the place of Hjørdis's tragic despair. *Hedda Gabler* and *The Lady from the Sea* stand nearest to *The Wild Duck* from the present point of view. But *The Lady from the Sea* is a comedy to which another scale must be applied than those of tragedy and tragi-comedy, and in *Hedda Gabler* we may give Eilert Løvborg the benefit of taking him for a genius, even if we cannot, with some admirers, go so far as to look upon Hedda Gabler herself as a grand creature gone wrong.

[1] E.g. by Georg Brandes (in 1898), *Henrik Ibsen*, p. 145, English translation (1899), p. 99.

If these arguments are accepted, *The Wild Duck* will be seen to stand isolated at any rate among those plays to which we can attribute a tragic ending. This may be the 'novelty' to which Ibsen drew his publisher's attention, although by the 'method of procedure' he mentioned at the same time he much more probably meant that grouping of the personages and incidents round the doubly mysterious Wild Duck herself.[1]

## VI

If Hjalmar be regarded as a diminished, even less heroic, Peer Gynt and Gregers Werle as a smaller Brand who has fostered his idealism in similarly remote and barren tracts, the tragedy of *The Wild Duck* proceeds from an impact of these two characters, and the smash-up of Hjalmar's domestic felicity, with the death of Hedvig, has a two-fold cause. The catastrophe is most obviously induced by Gregers, who, presenting the demands of the ideal, first undermines the mutual confidence on which the Ekdal household is reared, replaces its security by disquieting doubts about its past and its future, turns a collectively and individually happy family into an unhappy one, and also puts the idea of a blood sacrifice into Hedvig's head. In the second place and more particularly, however, as we have seen, Hedvig's substitution of herself for the Wild Duck as the sacrificial victim is due to Hjalmar's thoughtless cruelty towards her. Such cruelty does not seem an obvious attribute of an easy-going, comfort-loving nature like his; but in the circumstances it proceeds naturally from his complete egoism, his inability to realise the bearings of the situation in which he finds himself and from the angry *malaise* engendered by his uncertainty.

Hjalmar has been very suddenly thrust into this situation through the interference of Gregers, and the situation from which the tragedy ensues is therefore fortuitous. It is not every Peer Gynt who runs up against a Brand, and most of the Peer Gynts of this world proceed happily to their obscure graves. If the second phase of Gregers's interference—his action upon Hedvig—had not supervened upon the first, all might still have been well, especially if the practised healer Relling had remained

[1] The grouping of *Ghosts* round the Orphanage is not unlike this, however.

at hand to soothe and guide. In fact we see the reintegration of
Hjalmar's shattered family life taking place before our eyes at the
beginning of the fifth act when he consents to sit down to lunch
and to postpone his removal from the house to a more convenient season. And Relling's bitter prophecy: 'Before a year
is over little Hedvig will be nothing to him but a pretty theme
for declamation',[1] from which it is impossible to dissent, indicates
that in so far as he is concerned that process of reintegration will
continue, though of course to a lesser completeness.

Besides the grotesque, the comic elements associated with the
attic menagerie and inherent in the character of Hjalmar and
his father, Ibsen thus had a double justification for describing
his play as a tragi-comedy and withholding the full designation
of tragedy: the fortuitous juxtaposition of Hjalmar and Gregers
and the evanescent effect on the former of the catastrophe that
overtakes him.

There is, however, another—at least one other—aspect from
which the 'tragedy' of *The Wild Duck* may be explored. The
catastrophe is undeniably the catastrophe of Gregers. He has
had a great chance of the sort for which he has been waiting, the
chance to have justice done to his old friend's family, which,
rightly or wrongly, he believes to have been outrageously
treated, and to raise at any rate some of his fellow men to that
high moral level on which he thinks that all should have their
being; and nothing but evil has ensued upon these selfless
efforts. Cannot, therefore, *The Wild Duck* be construed as the
idealist's tragedy? Undoubtedly it can (subject to the overriding consideration that it should be the idealist's, the active
moralist's, constant preoccupation to take the circumstances of
every case into account and that he must take full responsibility if
he fails to do so). But it seems as if Ibsen wished to minimise this
aspect of *The Wild Duck*—and by so doing to refrain from casting
a justifying glow around those activities of his own which
resemble Gregers Werle's. For one thing, he withheld from
Gregers not only the greatness and nobility with which he
endowed Brand, but all amiability as well: Gregers is animated
by no real love for mankind in general or of Tom, Dick and
Harry in particular, and no one cares for him. In the second

[1] v, 106; Archer, VIII, 399.

place, important as he is in the scheme of *The Wild Duck*, he never holds the centre of the stage: he is an ominous rather than a sinister figure, standing at the side, fatally involving others in the darkness of his personality. Moreover, his final exit deprives him of the last opportunity of assuming heroic stature: he expresses no regret—beyond the apology that he always acted with the best intentions—no contrition or repentance like that of Brand or Peer Gynt. He betrays no resolve, like Nora, to think things out in the light of fresh knowledge and, in a new life, make good the ill he has committed, turn himself into a real benefactor of his kind. If he really intends to commit suicide, he slinks off as one who just sees that he has no luck on his side. Neither in Gregers nor in Hjalmar does calamity induce a purgation—yet another card in the hand of those who contend for Ibsen's pessimism.

## VII

Ibsen called none of his works a tragedy. *Lady Inger* and *The Pretenders* are 'historical dramas' (*historisk skuespil*), *Brand* and *Peer Gynt* 'dramatic poems' (*dramatiske digter*), *Emperor and Galilean* is a 'world-historic drama' (*verdenshistorisk skuespil*),[1] *When We Dead Awaken* a 'dramatic epilogue' (*dramatisk epilog*); for the rest, with two exceptions, the simple term 'play' or 'drama' (*skuespil*) sufficed, which, an unusually modest tyro, Ibsen had adopted for *Catiline*. In fact, however, he wrote very little which does not fit into the tragic category, and the exceptions prove almost all to be in one way or another ambiguous exceptions: there are commentators who advance good reasons for denying or heavily qualifying the happy ending of *Love's Comedy*, in spite of its title, and of *The Lady from the Sea*; the right triumphs in *The Pretenders* without the sacrifice of the just man, but more consistently than for him sympathy is engaged for 'God's step-child', Skule, who perishes; Little Eyolf meets with a violent death in the play called after him, and the tone of the whole remains as sombre as that of *Rosmersholm* or *The Wild Duck*, so that the reconciliation of Alfred and Rita Almers and their resolve to begin a new life of social usefulness shed but a watery gleam over the conclusion;

---

[1] The component halves are each called *Skuespil*.

in *Pillars of Society* (as in *The Feast at Solhaug*) great and perilous matters are at issue, and, though this time the little boy gets away with his life, he (with others) comes nearer to losing it than is exactly compatible with comedy; Dr Stockmann, the enemy of the people, comes off worst in the first round of his fight against the 'compact Liberal majority'. The fact that Lady Inger, the two heroes of *The Vikings in Helgeland* and Mrs Alving are left alive need hardly invalidate the generalisation that Ibsen is pre-eminently a tragedian. Indeed, the only play later than *Olaf Liljekrans* that raises no serious doubt about its exclusion from the category of tragedy is *The League of Youth*.

Up to a point every tragedy must be pessimistic, and dramatists whose preferences lie with tragedy are pessimists, since they exhibit 'heroes', men and women of superior abilities, coming to grief by a process which is made to appear inevitable. Ibsen accordingly must, like his brethren, suffer the presumption of being a pessimist. Paradoxically enough, however, a common ground for the imputation in his case is one that should lessen it on considerations proper to tragedy in general. It is contended that he takes a 'low view' of humanity and that the men and women whose sad fate is unfolded in his plays precisely lack all superior abilities, that, in brief, they are not true heroes, that he is incapable of creating true heroes. Certainly, if the ascription 'heroic' be confined solely to those who, like Don Rodrigue the Cid, perform almost superhuman feats or, like Orestes, feel themselves called upon to cope with intractable situations or, like Lear, run through a whole gamut of torments, very few indeed of Ibsen's personages would qualify for it: none, indeed, after Haakon Haakonsson and Brand. His Hedda Gablers fail to do their duty, his Bernicks and Borkmans are swindlers, his Rosmers and Allmerses weaklings. But an argument so based is surely two-edged. If the personages whom Ibsen presents are no prehistoric champions strayed into the modern world, all the more credit is due to them for exhibiting will-power, endurance and resignation, and, on occasion, for repenting their trespasses. That his characters are 'low' does not make Ibsen a pessimist. Is Arnold Bennett a pessimist—and Dickens with his unrivalled gallery of 'low' portraits?

Where, however, 'lowness' connotes not merely lowly birth, defective breeding and small knowledge of the world, but an ignoble outlook which by its prevalence puts on an appearance of universality, there is rather better reason in identifying its presentation with pessimism. But, as has been pointed out, *The Wild Duck* stands unique among Ibsen's plays in the unrelieved earth-of-the-earthiness of the characters amid the illiberal life which they lead and in the apparent approbation with which the frustration of ideals is treated. Dr Relling is *par excellence*, however, the advocate of moral relativity; he is the last man to hold that what he prescribed for the Ekdal household or the cottagers of Højdal is a universal panacea.

All the same, Ibsen viewed humanity through no rose-tinted spectacles. Even if *The Wild Duck* be left out of consideration, a high proportion of the men and even of the women he presents are individually poor stuff and the society into which they coalesce seems to be fatally unable to rise above their highest common factor. Think of the hypocrite and knave Engstrand in *Ghosts* with his precious daughter, the hypocrite and fool Manders, and Oswald, who may be a good-for-nothing through no fault of his own, but none the less remains a good-for-nothing; think of the mixture of intrigue and bullying which characterises Peter Stockmann in *An Enemy of the People*, the malicious old rascal Morten Kiil, the sweepings of the educated class who people the newspaper office, the poltroons who vote solid at the public meeting—and so the list might be extended. There is scarcely a single play with a range of decent, kindly and intelligent folk.

Not that the majority of Ibsen's characters are in any notable degree villains, criminals or even considerable sinners; they are just stuff for the Button-Moulder's ladle. With Kierkegaard, Ibsen said: 'I do not complain that mankind is wicked, I complain that it is abject', and no doubt, as Sophocles felt that 'not to have been born is best', so he thought that the extinction of the human race could be no great calamity. In the notorious poem 'Til min Ven Revolutionstaleren'[1] he declared that, if he could, he would have torpedoed the Ark. Ibsen's tragedy is manifestly tinged with a deeper pessimism than that, shall we say, of Schiller or Voltaire or perhaps even Sophocles.

---

[1] vi, 371.

It is true, too, that for all the background of fjord, sea, waste upland, rain, snow and radiant glacier which Ibsen takes every befitting opportunity to suggest,[1] there is little to be seen in his work of serene or starry vault of heaven. None of his personages is sustained by any religious faith and in their misery they do not, as Chekhov's so often do, look forward in a selfless rapture to some happy future for mankind or even to a half-mythical Moscow. But neither does his work leave an impression, as does that of Hardy, of a vast constrictive universe which, by its very power and its indifference to what human creatures do or plan, puts on an appearance of hostility. His Boyg is a much more narrowly localised monster, whom one can evade if one cannot overcome. Ibsen may be an unmetaphysical genius, as indeed most great dramatists seem to be; the fact acquits him of the charge of postulating a universe whose creatures are doomed to ineluctable misery. He may have known of Schopenhauer and Hartmann, but he did not subscribe to their constructions.[2]

Existence, as Ibsen exhibits it, is a strenuous and hazardous business, to live and be happy involves perpetual exposure to evil chance and constant struggle either with rivals (as in *The Pretenders*) or with character (as in *Peer Gynt* and *Brand*) or with the conventional restrictions of present-day society (as in *A Doll's House*) or with a crushing misfortune (as in *Little Eyolf*) or with the 'trolls within' (as in *The Master Builder*, indeed in all the last plays from *Rosmersholm* onwards); but the strenuousness of the strife, before which only two of Ibsen's figures lay down their arms, not only breeds in a Nora or a Brand or a Rebecca West strength, even nobility of character, but betrays also a conviction that the prize is attainable. Except Hedda Gabler and Rosmer all believe that it may be possible for them to survive and be happy, and their fate may weaken that conviction in others, but does not destroy it. 'Life would be tolerable,' says Relling, 'if. . . .'

[1] He often produced a comparable effect by the lighting which he prescribed. Writing to Lindberg about *The Wild Duck* he observed: 'I lay great weight on the lighting in this piece. I have wished it to correspond to the fundamental mood which prevails in each of the five acts' (*cit.* Centenary Edition, x, 36).

[2] He asked himself the question, nevertheless, whether human evolution might not have taken the wrong path (*Efterladte Skrifter*, III, 1909, p. 142).

# THE MASTER BUILDER

(*Bygmester Solness*)

# 1892

## I

*THE WILD DUCK* was followed at the normal two years' interval by *Rosmersholm* (1886), *Rosmersholm* by *The Lady from the Sea* (1888), and *The Lady from the Sea* by *Hedda Gabler* (1890). *Rosmersholm*, in re-echoing the great constitutional struggle of Left and Right in Norway, seems to represent something of a return to the social dramas preceding *The Wild Duck*. Its directly political message, however, amounts to 'a plague o' both your houses', and the drama turns on whether or not Rosmer and Rebecca can find any grounds for remaining alive. After *Rosmersholm* the outside world, in which political parties clash and newspapers write about it, ceases to exist for Ibsen's characters and for Ibsen himself even more completely than it had done in *The Wild Duck*: the dramas henceforward are all inner dramas, as indeed Rosmer's had been, of the inhibited personality contending with its inhibitions.[1] In *The Lady from the Sea* the struggle ends in victory,[2] but *Hedda Gabler* is steeped in gloom with the same (if fewer) macabre flashes of sardonic humour as *The Wild Duck*.

A couple of months after the publication of *Hedda Gabler* in February 1891, the author told his German translator, Elias,[3] that he had conceived the idea of a new play in vague outline

---

[1] This is true, I think, even of *Little Eyolf*, though it affords a partial exception to these generalisations since at the end the outside world is called on, rather sketchily, to redress the balance of the inner world.

[2] Even this is denied by many critics. Hans, for instance (*Ibsens Selbstporträt in seinen Dramen*, 1911, p. 173), contrasts the 'defeat' of Ellida Wangel in her effort to free herself from a Philistine, loveless environment with Nora Helmer's victory. It is curious that up to this time outdoor scenes in Ibsen's plays are generally associated with comedy, and *The Lady from the Sea* takes place entirely out-of-doors: to be sure, the later *When We Dead Awaken* has no indoor scenes, and the fresh air actually kills John Gabriel Borkman.

[3] Repeated by him in 'Christianiafahrt' in *Neue Rundschau*, xvii, ii, 1462.

but nothing more is known about the further elaboration of this idea, as a twelvemonth or so later, he destroyed all the preliminary notes except the mournful little poem 'De sad der, de to', to which further reference will be made later. A further longish gap of time ensued: not till 9 August 1892 did Ibsen, then established after twenty-seven years' absence in Christiania again, begin on what appears to have been the first draft[1] of *The Master Builder* (*Bygmester Solness*) which was completed in six weeks;[2] rather less time was given to the fair copy, and that went off to Gyldendal's at Copenhagen before the end of October:[3] from this, with very few alterations, was printed the first edition, published first in London on 6 December 1892 and sent out from Copenhagen and Christiania on 12 December 1892.

## II

Two hanks of 'pre-history' furnish the warp in the fabric of *The Master Builder*. One concerns the early professional career of the Master Builder himself, Halvard Solness; the other, his earliest meeting with Hilda Wangel.

Solness appears to have made some professional reputation quite quickly, since he received the commission to build the church tower at Lysanger, a place remote from his home.[4] It was just a little after the time that his great opportunity had come to him: his wife's old home had burned down and, as with it the reason for leaving intact the large estate round it had disappeared, it was broken up into building plots on which Solness put up the 'homes for men and women' that made him the most successful man, locally, in his profession. The set-up of his drawing office—two rooms, it seems, in his own house and a staff of two men and a girl—forbids us to picture him as an architect of outstanding eminence, but in the circumstances of

---

[1] Now in the University Library, Oslo; the haste in which it was written is manifest, and many corrections were made in ink and pencil, though none is substantial.

[2] Act I on 20 August, Act II on 6 September, Act III on 19 September.

[3] It is now in the Royal Library at Copenhagen.

[4] It is not known, nor is it material, where exactly the scene of *The Master Builder* is laid. It seems to me probable that in all the later 'urban' plays of Ibsen, *The Wild Duck*, *Hedda Gabler*, *The Master Builder* and *John Gabriel Borkman*, he had Christiania in mind.

a comparatively small community, he is obviously much sought after and financially as prosperous as he could wish. His home-life, however, is unhappy. The accident to which he owed his prosperity involved the death of his two children and the sterility of his wife Aline: his wife's mind, too, has sustained a grave injury, though there are no grounds for thinking it actually deranged.

Not unconnected with this half of the *donnée* is the other. For it was on completing the church tower at Lysanger, when Solness finally decided to devote himself to domestic architec-ture, that he had first encountered Hilda Wangel. So intoxi-cated with that decision and the convivial celebrations following on the inauguration of the tower that the episode quite passed out of his mind,[1] he had taken her, then a little girl of twelve or thirteen, into his arms, kissed her over and over again and promised in ten years' time to make her a princess and give her a kingdom.

The actual drama of *The Master Builder* begins in the evening of this anniversary day with the sudden and completely un-expected arrival in the Solness house of Hilda Wangel, insistent on the execution of the promise Halvard Solness had made her. Before her entry, there have been two scenes of exposition (in which the pre-histories are scarcely glanced at). They show that not everything is well with the outwardly prosperous, well-balanced architect Halvard Solness, who is both 'at the head of his profession' and in the prime of life.[2] First, they draw attention to the kind of tyranny which he exercises over his small staff: attached to his service he has a decayed architect Brovik, and Brovik's son Ragnar, who are extremely useful to him in certain branches of his vocation which he does not seem to have mastered himself,[3] and he is determined to keep them even by illegitimate means; one influence over them he exercises through his clerk, Kaja Fosli, Ragnar Brovik's *fiancée*, who is slavishly devoted to her employer and whose devotion he ensures

---

[1] It is possible to argue that the episode (like Solness's alleged singing on the builders' scaffold) took place entirely in Hilda's imagination; but that would be an unnecessary complication, and eventually Solness seems to accept her story.

[2] '...a man no longer young, but healthy and vigorous' (VI, 4; Archer, X, 191).

[3] VI, 15; Archer, X, 216. It is insisted that he is not professionally qualified, and always scrupulous to call himself 'Master Builder' rather than 'Architect'.

by a show of affection which he does not really feel.[1] Solness knows the whole situation to be thoroughly false and reprehensible, all the more so as his relation with Kaja obviously distresses his wife; but, as he explains to the physician and friend of the family, Dr Herdal,[2] he welcomes the consequent pangs of remorse as 'salutary self-torture', a form of expiation for the unhappiness which, on other grounds too, he has brought upon his wife; he feels, too, that some mysterious agency drives him along a certain line of conduct and that he must go on in his dealings with the Broviks and Kaja as he has begun. Further, the Broviks serve as a reminder and safeguard of what he most fears, his supersession by the younger generation.

With a striking *coup de théâtre*, upon the words 'Yes, just you see, doctor—presently the younger generation will come knocking at the door.... Then there's an end of Halvard Solness',[3] a knock is heard at the door and Hilda Wangel enters. Solness has not the least idea who she is, but the reintroduction is effected by Herdal, who met her during the recent summer holidays. Arrangements are made for Hilda to stay the night, and, left to themselves, she and Solness take up the remainder of the act with the reconstruction of the events of ten years ago, culminating in Hilda's demand to have the kingdom then promised her handed over at once and Solness's avowal ' *You* are the very being I have needed most'.... [4]

The remaining two acts take place on the following day.[5] A conversation between Solness and Aline at the beginning of

---

[1] The scene between Kaja and Solness may be a sly piece of malice on Ibsen's part, to mislead the audience into thinking that the author of *Hedda Gabler* had advanced one step further on the road to the fashionable drama of adultery.

[2] It is, I think, important for the actor of the part to realise that the revelation of the psychical turmoil beneath the energetic, blunt, normal exterior of Solness should astound Herdal as much as it does the spectator (cf. VI, 18; Archer, X, 221). This was admirably achieved in his rendering of the part by the late Norman McKinnel. In a more recent English production both Solness and Hilda Wangel were as mad as hatters from the start, so that none but madmen could take any further interest in them.

[3] VI, 20; Archer, X, 224.      [4] VI, 34; Archer, X, 255.

[5] Many of Ibsen's plays roughly observe the same time scheme: the action begins one day and is concluded the next (*Ghosts, Rosmersholm, The Lady from the Sea, Hedda Gabler, Little Eyolf, When We Dead Awaken*); *A Doll's House, The Wild Duck* and *An Enemy of the People* only slightly exceed this measure; in *John Gabriel Borkman* the action is continuous, in fact the time taken to act it slightly exceeds the time represented, since Act II is supposed to begin just before Act I has finished.

Act II completes the recapitulation of the pre-history, but the remainder of the Act is principally made up of Solness's resolve, promoted and abetted by Hilda, to start a new chapter of his life. He clears up the unsatisfactory position in his office by consenting to encourage Ragnar Brovik and allow him to begin in practice on his own account; he dismisses Kaja. He makes up his mind to mark the fresh start by a symbolic act akin to that with which the chapter just closing was inaugurated; he will climb to the top of the tower of the new house which is on the eve of completion and, as he has not done since the ceremony at Lysanger, with his own hand hang the customary wreath on the weather vane at the top.

The latter decision greatly alarms Mrs Solness, since her husband has become liable to vertigo and, at the beginning of the third act, she thinks she secures Hilda's aid in dissuading him from so perilous an undertaking. But Hilda secretly and overtly abets Solness: to the incredulity of Ragnar Brovik and his young friends, he climbs the tower, crowns it with his wreath, waves to Hilda as he promised, turns giddy and falls to his death.

## III

A great deal of personal experience went to the composition of *The Master Builder*. In the course of his talk with Elias some two months after the publication of *Hedda Gabler* about its successor, Ibsen remarked[1] that it was still very vague in his mind except for an 'experience' and a 'woman's figure'; from his further confidences it emerges fairly clearly that the 'figure' must have been that of Fräulein Emilie Bardach,[2] a Viennese girl whom he met and daily consorted with during his summer holiday of 1889 at Gossensass in the Tyrol, and that it subsequently developed into the personage of Hilda Wangel.[3] About the complementary 'experience', it is impossible to be so explicit:

[1] Elias, J., 'Christianiafahrt', in *Neue Rundschau*, XVII, ii, 1462.

[2] Ibsen's letters (in German) to Emilie Bardach were first published by Brandes in *Henrik Ibsen*, being vols. XXXII and XXXIII of *Die Literatur*; a photograph of Fräulein Bardach is given (facing p. 84).

[3] 'Merged' would be an apter word than 'developed', since, of course, Hilda Wangel had already been created for *The Lady from the Sea* (1888) and is substantially the same character as that of the later play.

undoubtedly each, Ibsen and Fräulein Bardach, had been greatly attracted to the other and flattered by the attraction engendered, as in the circumstances would be most natural— he a European celebrity, she an agreeable girl of eighteen; in retrospect, at least, each believed that only the other had been deeply in love, which is also natural enough, since the direct relations between them had scarcely survived their summer holiday. Still, more than seven years later Ibsen wrote to his friend: 'The summer in Gossensass was the happiest, loveliest in all my life. Can scarcely think of it. And yet must do so all the time.'[1] The affair remained purely ethereal, but it equally certainly left a deep impression on the author. The most affecting thing about it was his persuasion that he was beloved[2] and that the main spring of the joy of life, against which his devotion to his life work had so strictly barred him, could still run fresh.

Emilie Bardach seems to have been a rather overstrung and, at the same time, a commonplace, specimen of the *Backfisch* of her time and country.[3] Only one unusual trait emerges, the ambition to which she confessed of stealing other women's husbands away from them 'like a little bird of prey'. This must presumably have been an entirely speculative programme, which a young person of eighteen guarded by her mother and the Austrian equivalent to Mrs Grundy could scarcely have begun to carry out. Perhaps some reflection of Emilie Bardach's merely cerebral erotic occupations and her professed unscrupulousness in stealing men is to be seen in Hedda Gabler and the latter trait, too, in Hilda Wangel. But Fräulein Bardach apparently did not see much of herself in the heroine of *The Master Builder*,[4] and her youthful freshness, imaginative intrepidity and ease in coping with middle-aged gentlemen are probably her chief contribution to the last-named character.

---

[1] *Die Literatur, ut cit.* p. 112.

[2] According to Gosse (*Ibsen*, 1907, p. 202) he told a young colleague that he might love as much as he liked, and welcome; *he* was in better case because he was loved.

[3] This emerges from her Journal, printed in extract and translated by Rouveyre, A., 'Le Mémorial Inédit d'une Amie d'Ibsen', in *Mercure de France* (15 July 1928), 257.

[4] She did, however, after its publication send a photograph of herself to the author, subscribed, to his annoyance, 'The Princess of Orangia' (cf. vi, 27; Archer, x, 240).

Very general traits they are, shared with countless young women, like Helene Raff, the Munich painter, who became friendly with Ibsen immediately after his Gossensass flirtation, or like the Norwegian pianist Hildur Andersen, to whom he dedicated and presented his draft manuscript.[1] In this connection, I am tempted also to name Fru Johanne Dybwad, whom he may have had in mind when he 'created' Hilda Wangel for her to act in *The Lady from the Sea*, the only character, besides Aslaksen of *The League of Youth* and *An Enemy of the People*, to occur in two different plays.[2]

A deeper mark was left on *The Master Builder* by another woman friend of the author and an experience of a more searching nature than the flirtations or friendships just alluded to.[3] In the autumn of 1891, Laura Kieler, the model used by Ibsen for Nora Helmer, came into his life again. The lady, it will be remembered, had first become known to Ibsen as a writer;[4] and though she was otherwise much taken up by her duties as a wife and mother—not to mention by the upheaval of their catastrophic interruption—she had continued to exercise her pen from time to time. A convinced opponent of the aestheticism and the social radicalism propagated by Georg and Edvard Brandes, she had sharply attacked their like in a play *Men of Honour* (*Mænd af Ære*), which, approved in manuscript by Ibsen,[5] was published in 1890 and soon afterwards performed both at Christiania and Copenhagen. It met with some rough treatment, not least, as may readily be understood, at the hands of the Brandes faction, which was not slow to bandy personalities by raking up the 'true' substratum of *A Doll's House*.

[1] Facsimile of dedication in Koht, II, 357.

[2] Engelcke Wulff, later Friis, later Treschow, declared that she met Ibsen when she was nineteen at Sæby in 1887, that he talked to her there and, meeting once in the street at Christiania, called her 'min Hilde' (Centenary Edition, XI, 24). If the story and implication are accepted, Frøken Wulff was used for the original Hilda of *The Lady from the Sea*. One may mention here the history of old Goethe and young Marianne von Willemer of which Ibsen had recently read in a study by Georg Brandes.

[3] For almost the whole of this story I am indebted to Kinck, B. M., 'Henrik Ibsen og Laura Kieler', in *Edda*, XXXV (1935), p. 498.

[4] It is a little odd that without knowledge of this circumstance, several of the imaginative continuations of *A Doll's House* made the altogether unliterary Nora an authoress too.

[5] Cf. *Breve*, II, 174.

The serious charge in their counter-attack was the implication that, like Nora Helmer, Fru Kieler had been guilty of forgery.[1] Less serious, but still grave, was the implication that she had voluntarily forsaken her home and children. The battle joined, she mobilised her friends; Fru Linnell[2] wrote to Ibsen asking whether he could not intervene, and it was Camilla Collett's opinion that since, through *A Doll's House*, Ibsen had done so well out of Fru Kieler, he might contribute something in return. But no reaction was registered; Ibsen may well have thought that the world-wide sympathy for Nora engaged by his imaginative work could not have failed altogether to benefit the person with whom she was identified. At last, in November 1891, Laura Kieler sought, and obtained, an interview with her old friend himself, when, she alleges,[3] all the facts of the story which *A Doll's House* had presented in so distorted a fashion became known to him and the cruelty of her lot was made plain. Ibsen was deeply moved, as he always seems to have been when past memories were revived in him: he sobbed. But he refused to grant her request to conjure Georg Brandes—with whom he remained on excellent terms—to let the whole story rest. He declared that he *could* not intervene.

The long and harrowing interview had the most profound effect upon him, and it determined not merely the whole atmosphere of *The Master Builder*, but many of its episodes as well, to a considerably greater degree than, it would seem, the Gossensass episode can have done. For Emilie Bardach came to Ibsen as a complete stranger, whereas Hilda Wangel, like Laura Kieler, was an old acquaintance already linked to her friend by sentimental ties. Laura Kieler, throwing new light on the times and the circumstances when the ties between them had been formed, confirmed one of the most powerfully held tenets of Ibsen's tragic beliefs, the ineluctability of the past—a theory inapplicable to the case of Emilie Bardach. Similarly, the

---

[1] If it be true that she *had* once forged a document (though in circumstances rather different from Nora's) and had confessed as much to Ibsen, the difficulty in which it would place him in giving testimony on her behalf must not be left out of account.

[2] Fru Linnell was the recipient of the Rhymed Epistle to a Swedish Lady, of 1870 ('Ballonbrev', VI, 376).

[3] Nothing of this interview is reported by Ibsen himself.

interview with Laura Kieler was likely to confirm in Ibsen the general sentiment (totally foreign to his relations with Emilie Bardach) that a course of conduct decided upon in a grave crisis can go forward against a better judgement and even to the limit of catastrophe by its own momentum—the sentiment which has swelled and crystallised in Solness to the conviction that invisible 'helpers and servers' aid him on his onward path and demand sacrifice even of moral integrity in return.[1] Further, according to her son's testimony,[2] Laura Kieler was recognisable in the personality of Hilda Wangel, whereas, as has been said, Emilie Bardach did not similarly see herself. Gerard Gran, who probably knew nothing of the interview between Ibsen and Laura Kieler, pronounced[3] Hilda to be 'Norwegian in all her being, her figure built up of observations and impressions after his return home'.

Lastly, though some conscientious scruples had induced Ibsen to break off the relation with Emilie Bardach, it had in the main been a joyous one, even if shot here and there with the melancholy of the autumnal setting in which they parted; but Laura Kieler had stirred in the depths of Ibsen's bosom a profound sense of guilt—guilt not only towards herself—and the sense of guilt permeates the whole of Halvard Solness's personal tragedy.

A personal model for Kaja Fosli, it is said,[4] existed and, ever since the Gossensass idyll became common property, speculation has naturally been rife on the possible parallels between Susannah Ibsen and the Master Builder's wife, Aline Solness. If there was a parallel at all,[5] it did not go very far; one may hazard the Hibernian assertion that if it had gone far it would never have been drawn at all. For Ibsen was the last man in the world to advertise, however indirectly, any domestic infelicities of his own, more particularly if he might be held responsible for them. Susannah Ibsen was a cultivated, mentally alert woman whose intellectual companionship of her husband seems always to have been uncommonly close. Though at this

[1] It has been pointed out that there was a clear literary example of this accessible to Ibsen in Schiller's *Wallensteins Tod*.

[2] Kinck, *ut cit.* p. 532.     [3] Gran, II, 301.

[4] Seip, Introduction to Centenary Edition, XII, 20.

[5] Seip, who obviously had access to much unpublished material, says so (*loc. cit.* p. 20).

time she was beginning to suffer from the rheumatoid arthritis
that eventually crippled her, no one who met her felt, to my
knowledge, on leaving her that he had 'just come up out of
a tomb', as Hilda (quite justifiably) did after her talk with
Aline Solness at the beginning of Act III.[1] Nevertheless, it is just
possible that about the time when *The Master Builder* was
written, there was some marital disagreement or at any rate
temporary coolness; and it may be—though this is not a necessary inference—that Fru Ibsen had been hurt by her husband's
intimacy with Fräulein Bardach[2] and that his cutting short the
relation was due to his realisation of this. Magdalene Thoresen,
Susannah Ibsen's stepmother, who visited her and her husband
in 1894, reported that they seemed to be living quite separate
lives;[3] that, however, is the only printed testimony of the kind
with which I am familiar, unless one ranges with it the twelve
short lines of 'De sad der, de to':

> De sad der, de to, i så lunt et hus
> Ved høst og i vinterdage.
> Så brændte huset. Alt ligger i grus.
> De to får i asken rage.
>
> For nede i den er et smykke gemt,—
> Et smykke, som aldrig kan brænde.
> Og leder de trofast, hænder det nemt,
> At det findes af ham eller hende.
>
> Men finder de end, de brandlidte to,
> Det dyre, ildfaste smykke,—
> Aldrig *hun* finder sin brændte tro,
> *Han* aldrig sin brændte lykke.[4]

---

[1] VI, 68; Archer, X, 327.

[2] Elias's evidence goes against this (*loc. cit.* p. 1461).

[3] *Breve fra Magdalene Thoresen 1855–1901* (1919), p. 240.

[4] VI, 413; Archer's translation runs: 'They sat there, the two, in so cosy a house,
through autumn and winter days. Then the house burned down. Everything lies
in ruins. The two must grope among the ashes. For among them is hidden a jewel—
a jewel that never can burn. And if they search faithfully, it may easily happen
that he or she may find it. But even should they find it, the burnt-out two—find
this precious unburnable jewel—never will *she* find her burnt faith, *he* never his burnt
happiness' (X, xxi). I own that, whether the poem be related to Ibsen's private
life or to the existing *Master Builder*, I cannot guess what this 'unburnable jewel'
may be, since it is not the wife's burnt faith or the husband's burnt happiness.

The poem may be an immediate personal effusion though the fact of its publication speaks against such an assumption; on the other hand, it may be no more than the lyrical summing-up of the sentiment which was to be disengaged from the play shaping itself in Ibsen's imagination[1] just at that moment of time (18 March 1892)—the proto-*Master-Builder*[2]—though admittedly it could not accurately be called a lyrical summing-up of the sentiment disengaged by the play in its ultimate form.

## IV

The final question of this order is: How far, if at all, should Ibsen be identified with Halvard Solness?

In the play, we see a successful artist-craftsman still at the height of his powers, grown old enough to fear the competition of his juniors and eminent enough to apprehend a reversal of fortune; he has long lived alienated from his wife; he is excited and stimulated to fresh endeavour by a young girl, who frankly admires and loves and believes in him; and at the same time he becomes so acutely conscious of the extent to which the personal happiness of himself and of others has been sacrificed to his professional advancement as to embark upon the reorientation of all his life and ambition. That this may also describe Ibsen in 1892 is an attractive hypothesis and *prima facie* plausible.

Ibsen spoke of Solness as a man he was 'somewhat akin to'[3] and used at times to look upon himself as a Master Builder.[4] Plainly, too, at the time of writing this play he was at the height of his reputation, but, while conscious of his powers, he must also have been aware that, at the age of sixty-four, they would begin to wane before long. He had recently undergone notable stimulation through his friendship with Emilie Bardach and

[1] 'It is said', Archer remarks (x, xx), 'to have been his habit, before setting to work on a play "to crystallize in a poem the mood which then possessed him".' The poem was dated by Ibsen himself and bore the sub-title: 'Første forarbejde til "Bygmester Solness"' ('first preparatory study for *The Master Builder*').

[2] With the *motif* of the fire, which was worked into the final form.

[3] Koht, II, 352.

[4] Koht (II, 351) reports that, on an acquaintance's noticing him in contemplation of the houses in a street and asking him whether he was interested in architecture, Ibsen had answered: 'Yes, it is really my own job [*vak*].'

other young girls. On the other hand, the evidence about alienation from his wife seems to be too slender to be admitted, and there are no grounds for believing that he felt himself so unduly favoured by fortune in his professional career that a turn of the tide was to be feared.[1] At two further important points the parallel definitely falls away.

In 1891 Knut Hamsun delivered before several Norwegian audiences a lecture, girding at the hegemony of his great seniors (like Ibsen himself, Bjørnson, Lie and Kielland) and accusing them, in especial, of insufficiency in two matters to which the juniors attached high importance, namely lack of psychological penetration and an unwillingness to explore the occult and the irrational in human nature—as he, Hamsun himself, had so strikingly done in *Sult (Hunger)*. Ibsen attended one of these lectures and, it seems, gave it his full attention. Nevertheless, it is most unlikely that the man who had just given *The Lady from the Sea*[2] and *Hedda Gabler* to the world should feel he had fallen so badly short in Hamsun's *desiderata*; nor can any evidence be adduced that he ever experienced jealousy of others' artistic and professional successes or dreaded his supersession by 'the younger generation knocking at the door'.

Indeed, Solness's uneasiness *vis-à-vis* the younger generation has been interpreted in precisely the opposite sense. In his interesting book *Ibsens Selbstporträt in seinen Dramen* (1911), Dr Wilhelm Hans points out that, as a rule, the younger writers of the time, young people in general, were enthusiastic partisans of Ibsen, whom they did not look upon as an obstruction, but rather as a leader. The year of *The Master Builder* (1892) saw, for instance, the height of the Ibsen boom in Great Britain; in Germany, Gerhart Hauptmann and his like were forging to the front; in France, the Théâtre de l'Œuvre was about to establish itself largely on a repertoire of Ibsen's plays. In Dr Hans's view[3]

---

[1] The evidence here is obscured by the Norwegian use of the word *lykkelig* to denote both 'lucky' and 'happy'. Ibsen insisted, and in public too, that he had *not* been 'lykkelig'; but the context shows that he meant he had not been 'happy'.

[2] Hamsun, however, had relegated *The Lady from the Sea* to 'the higher lunacy' (Introduction to Centenary Edition, XI, 41).

[3] *Op. cit.* p. 196.

Ibsen felt, not that he was being superseded, but that he was being called to a task for which he was not equal, that of leading the younger generation upwards and onwards—just as *Rosmersholm* betrayed his despair at his inability to found that third party in Norwegian politics, the aristocracy of the spirit, which he believed to be so urgently necessary—and that his failure, due to temperamental shortcomings, to take the lead increased the sense of personal insufficiency which was always apt to haunt him and which had found expression in Gregers Werle of *The Wild Duck*.

The second important point at which the parallel between Solness and his creator Ibsen seems to break down is the resolve to close a chapter and, if possible, enter upon a new phase of activity. If Solness, instead of perishing at the end of the play, were to remain alive, his dissatisfaction with the pass to which he has been brought would clearly involve a break with the past even greater than that on which he had resolved when on Lysanger church tower he spoke to the Mighty One and said 'I will never more build churches for thee—only homes for human beings'.[1] With Ibsen, however, though there is still projected into all his subsequent creations a sense of guilt such as can scarcely be dissociated from dissatisfaction, there is, after *The Master Builder*, no violent break and no obvious reaching after new forms, new ends and new effects, but rather the reverse.

A further elucidation of this proposition will involve a brief consideration of Ibsen's last plays and of the general question of guilt in his work as a whole.

The few words with Elias early in 1891 about the new play and the 'woman's figure' round which it was to crystallise suggest that, just as *Brand* had been a self-purgation after the events of 1864, he may now have intended to 'purge' himself of his flirtations (such as that with Emilie Bardach) which by then had come to irk him as perhaps a trifle unworthy and disloyal. But on top of this comes something of quite a different order, the revelation made through Laura Kieler a few months afterwards, that he had no mere peccadilloes for which to atone: a much more serious *catharsis* was called for, so serious that it was not completely effected by a single work.

[1] vi, 80; Archer, x, 353.

## V

The last four plays with which Ibsen ended his career—*The Master Builder, Little Eyolf, John Gabriel Borkman* and *When We Dead Awaken*—are very alike in several respects. They all re-introduce, rather after the style of *Pillars of Society* and *A Doll's House*, a minor love story by way of rudimentary sub-plot which, except in *The Master Builder*, gives some contrasting tones to the sombre hues of the principal theme. Not only is the time of action strictly concentrated but the retrospective technique has been further developed. What took place in the past is now shown to have been more important and even more dramatic than what goes forward during the progress of the action, as cannot be said, say, of *Hedda Gabler* or *The Wild Duck*, and through these earlier occurrences so much virtue has gone out of the main characters that Bernard Shaw could aptly entitle the chapter of *The Quintessence of Ibsenism* which deals with them 'Down Among the Dead Men'. More than that, either in their imagination[1] or in reality, they have all been great sinners and labour under a sense of guilt. Borkman stands apart from the others in that he appears actually to have been a criminal in a big, but not in a heroic, way, repenting not because he has committed his crimes, but because he has committed them un-successfully, while he remains quite unmoved by the greater sin imputed to him, that of having with his ambitious plans 'killed the love life'[2] of the woman who stood closest to him.

With the other three heroes of the final group the guilt is always associated with some malfeasance in the private sphere. Most nakedly does this appear in *Little Eyolf* (1894), where Alfred Allmers has his conscience pricked to writing about Human Responsibility and, in the end, starting a ragged school by reminiscences of past sensuality, which first brought his son into the world and then caused his incurable deformity. That he married the wrong woman, Rita, rather than the cooler Asta —a complicated business in itself—comes in as a side-issue.

[1] It is a prime piece of evidence that unhappy Aline Solness, with every excuse for putting the blame for her wretchedness on her husband's shoulders, says expressly and with evident surprise at the suggestion, that he owes her no requital (VI, 39; Archer, X, 265).

[2] VI, 196; Archer, XI, 246.

*When We Dead Awaken* (1899) once more shows a hero with two women and the choice of the 'wrong' one, but here the interest swings round definitely from other issues to that of the private life and its justifiable demands.

As has been seen, the erotic appeal leaves John Gabriel Borkman unmoved,[1] and in *Little Eyolf* the antinomy of spirit *versus* flesh seems without any great difficulty to be resolved in favour of the spirit: both Allmers and Rita decide henceforward to live for duty. But *When We Dead Awaken* agrees with *The Master Builder* in subjecting the other side of the argument to a more thorough and by no means damaging scrutiny. The hero, Arnold Rubek, a sculptor, is like Solness (and Ibsen) an artist-craftsman at the height of his fame. Like Solness he is married, and his married life does not give him very much. As Solness is confronted by Hilda Wangel (and as Ibsen was confronted by Laura Kieler), so Rubek is suddenly and unexpectedly confronted by Irene. She served as his model for the main figure in the masterpiece to which he owed his name, and after doing so had been dismissed. Evidently some non-professional relations had subsisted between them, but Rubek had refrained from 'touching' her, partly because he wanted to keep free of anything that might stand between himself and his devotion to his art, and partly because he shared Rosmer's notions about the absolute innocence needed for the production of great and enduring work. Irene, on the other hand, had so ardently wished for a union with Rubek that, when he went away from her, she had gone to pieces morally, mentally and physically. At the same time as his easy life with his frivolous young wife Maja has brought home to Rubek what his austere devotion to his calling has for long withheld from him and as his meditations on the lost years have raised doubts in him about the essential value of the art to which these lost years were devoted, Irene reappears to enforce the realisation of what he lost in not keeping her by his side and to show him the catastrophic ruin which he brought upon herself by his refusal. The cumulative effect of these realisations is decisive; Rubek—whom no valid obligations attach to Maja, as Solness might be held to be

---

[1] One cannot withhold a sneaking sympathy from the eloping couple Erhart and Fanny Wilton: but they cannot rank as a recommendation of hedonism.

attached to Aline—begins a new life, which, however, is immediately brought to an end from natural causes.

Though the resemblances between Rubek and Solness and the situations in which they find themselves are obvious, there are some equally notable differences. Rubek enjoys greater freedom of action than Solness and he has a positive awareness of what he has missed in life. However, the first of these differences should perhaps be minimised: we may, with Hilda,[1] conclude that he is no longer under any vital obligations to his unpleasant wife and that what keeps him in his joyless and somewhat sterile existence is a sick, chronically hypertrophied conscience—such as cannot, I think, be diagnosed in Rubek. For the full realisation of the real guilt which he has incurred, crushing though it is, comes upon Rubek suddenly, whereas Solness has been so long and so cruelly tormented as already to be very near the limits of sanity at the time that the play about him begins.

Another source of misery springs in Solness's bosom (as it does in Rubek's), the belief that, despite the heavy sacrifices extracted by his career, that career has fallen short of expectations. This may be inferred from the disappointing sequel to the challenge which he declares he hurled at the Almighty from the church-scaffolding at Lysanger[2]—the equivalent of a Bedford Park in Oslo or Stavanger savours somewhat of an anticlimax—as well as from Hilda's indignant incredulity that her Master Builder cannot climb as high as he builds.[3] Is this disappointment a personal confession of the author too?

Meditation on the discrepancy, in all its aspects, between desire and performance, or 'dream' and 'deed', had, as was seen in the discussion of *Love's Comedy*, become chronic with Ibsen. He seems to have envied the man, who, like Mortensgaard in *Rosmersholm*, 'never wills more than he can do';[4] but his envy was probably as deeply shot with contempt as that of Mortensgaard's critic, Ulrik Brendel, who, after his failure to assimilate

---

[1] Hilda may be thought to change her mind (VI, 69; Archer, x, 335), but her compassion for Aline and unexpected unwillingness to leave her does not of itself touch the relation between Solness and his wife.

[2] VI, 80; Archer, x, 353.  [3] VI, 62; Archer, x, 315.

[4] V, 189; Archer, IX, 153; compare Hilda's definition of 'a really vigorous, radiantly healthy conscience', 'so that one *dared* to do what one *would*' (VI, 53; Archer, x, 300).

dream and deed, goes out into the night, neither repentant nor unhappy; and, in any event, while scrupulously keeping the further horizon open, Ibsen set himself, in each play, a limited objective and made sure of attaining it. Not even *When We Dead Awaken* imposes the conviction that, for any reason, he felt a violent dissatisfaction with his literary career as such.[1]

That a man may dispassionately approve of the quality of his life-work is far, however, from being the same thing as his thinking he was right in taking up that life's work. A judge may look back with complacency on his legal career while sincerely believing he would have done better to devote himself to the violoncello. So Ibsen might quite well satisfy himself that he had successfully married *drøm* and *daad* and at the same time think that his ambitions had been wrongly directed. There are some indications that he wrestled with the idea during the last decade of his active life and that the equivalent to Solness's discovery—'building homes for human beings—is not worth a rap'[2]—was no merely transitory mood of discouragement. *When We Dead Awaken* contains most of such indications, with Rubek's virtual retirement, at the very outset, from his profession and his later resolve to start quite a new life.

At the time of *Love's Comedy* Ibsen had realised that he was put into the world to be a playwright, even if that should mean being a third-rate human being; and like Brand, he had resolved to give up all—notably *livsglæde*, the joy of life—to his vocation. Georg Brandes had buoyed him up with the demonstration that by applying his aesthetic talents in a certain way he could help his fellow creatures, and in *Pillars of Society*, *A Doll's House* and their successors his talents had been so applied. But by the time of *The Wild Duck* it had been borne in upon him that his fellow creatures did not want the kind of help he could give, the kind

[1] By this I mean that Ibsen probably considered his plays to be in their own way as good as they could be. He thought—as who would not?—that they might here and there show undesirable features, like the *soupçon* of animality in Rubek's portrait-busts, and he regretted what concentration on his work had debarred him from; but that is all. The above, however, is not the view of Fibiger, A., whose unimpressive argument, *Henrik Ibsen, en Studie over Guds-Linien i hans Liv* (1928), is meant to show how *When We Dead Awaken* is a palinode from first to last and that its author looked upon himself as having played the traitor to his best self in everything which he had undertaken since *Brand*.

[2] VI, 80; Archer, X, 253.

of truth which his plays proclaimed and that the reformer might in fact do an infinity of harm, not least to those about him. Ibsen gave up plays with a message, though the vocation of the playwright still remained. Now, however, in *The Master Builder* and its followers the vocation itself is called into question once more. What shall Ibsen now do? Like Solness on the church tower at Lysanger, defy God—that is to say, bury his talents?— or carry on with purely aesthetic exercises, knowing them to be of no good except for filling his pocket?—or try something completely new at the age of sixty-four? The uniformity of the last plays supplies the answer that their author was content to suspend judgement, while submitting (after his own fashion) the evidence to further scrutiny, to give the benefit of the doubt to the assets in his private balance-sheet and to allow himself to proceed on the road along which the momentum of his past career was driving him.

## VI

To return now to the question of guilt:

It is almost a commonplace that guilt is closely associated with tragedy. There is scarcely one of the world's great tragic plays in which the central figure does not commit some grave, some recognisably grave offence which he has to *expiate*, and even in those tragedies in which 'tragic guilt' does not stand out as immediately obvious, as in Aeschylus's *Prometheus*, for instance, the ingenuity of man has been occupied in inventing some sort of constructive guilt; for, as Aristotle says: 'The change of fortune presented must not be the spectacle of a virtuous man brought from prosperity to adversity: for this moves neither pity nor fear: it merely shocks us.'

Though Ibsen may have characteristically hedged in refusing to give his compositions any more high sounding name than dramas, it is hard to withhold the term tragedy from most of them. But the debates about the end of *Brand* and the end of *Peer Gynt* show that at times the imputation of guilt affords particular difficulties. It may not be unreasonable to attribute tragic guilt to Hedda Gabler, who perishes after having, fairly directly, brought Løvborg to his death; but *Ghosts*, if it was to provide an instance of the two kinds of tragic guilt which

Kierkegaard postulated,[1] the hereditary guilt (which works the undoing of Oswald) and the 'ethical' guilt of his mother (who knew she was doing the wrong thing in returning to her husband), could only do so by splitting the person of the tragic hero; and the precise adjustment of the offence which Johannes Rosmer may have committed to the terrible punishment that overtakes him is by no means crystal clear.

'Tragic guilt' and 'guilt' can, however, be kept distinct even in tragedy. Though it may be difficult to justify the sufferings of a Mrs Alving or a Johannes Rosmer as *punishment*, both, certainly, are conscious of being miserable offenders. And questions of guilt, the consciousness of it and its opposite, 'innocence', always had a compelling fascination for Ibsen. Already Catiline and Lady Inger, for instance, come into the plays which they are to dominate weighted with a sense of wickedness; *The Pretenders*, under one aspect, can be looked upon almost as a Morality Play of the Good Conscience and the Bad Conscience; an outstanding feature of the stories of Peer Gynt and Brand—as it is of Consul Bernick's—is their acknowledgement of error and repentance. With Rosmer the consciousness of guilt had far-reaching ramifications, in that he holds the great, necessary work of which he dreams, the ennoblement of the human race, to be possible only for the utterly pure in heart and himself, consequently, debarred from undertaking it. A belief akin to this colours also the despair of Solness.[2] This, however, only constitutes one facet of the wider problem of guilt, innocence and responsibility to which everything else (on the moral plane) is subordinated in all Ibsen's last dramas.

## VII

The prominence given to the mood in which *The Master Builder* was written and what may therefore be called its lyrical quality prompt the question whether the self-revelation contained in it and in *When We Dead Awaken* is a constant phenomenon or

[1] On this see Stobart, M. A., 'New Lights on Ibsen', in *Fortnightly Review* (n.s.), LXVI (1899), p. 101.

[2] And John Gabriel Borkman could not execute his great economic projects, because he was involved in crime.

whether the interview with Laura Kieler in 1891 proved so seismic an experience as to effect a revolution in Ibsen's approach to his works. An adequate answer to the question would be long and complicated. Briefly, however, it may be said[1] that, detached as Ibsen almost invariably appears to be towards the personages which he created and towards the experiences which he attributed to them, the latter had, as he expressed it, been 'lived through' (*gjennemlevet*) by him too. Sometimes this was a purely imaginative process: there is, for instance, no suggestion that, even remotely, his own life, or even the life of his friends, had been confronted with problems like those of Mrs Alving in *Ghosts* or of Rosmer and Rebecca in *Rosmersholm*.

But Ibsen told Peter Hansen that all his writings 'had their origin in a mood and a personal situation',[2] and all through his dramas, perhaps from the time of *The Vikings in Helgeland*[3] onwards, there runs a thin, but tough thread of his own personal experiences, that perpetual fight against the demons within, which he identified with life in a famous poem, and that sitting in judgement upon himself, which, in the same place, he called the function of poetry:

> Leben, das heisst bekriegen,
> In Herz und Hirn die Gewalten;
> Und dichten: über sich selben
> Den Gerichtstag gehalten.[4]

We have seen how *Love's Comedy* already canvassed the question of the 'mission in life' which had again become so urgent in *The Master Builder* and how *Brand* and *Peer Gynt* effect

---

[1] It is the subject of Wilhelm Hans's interesting and intelligent *Ibsens Selbstporträt in seinen Dramen* (1911).

[2] 'Alt, hvad jeg digterisk har frembragt, har havt sit udspring fra en stemning og en livssituation' (*Breve* I, 212).

[3] If, as may plausibly be assumed, Hjørdis is modelled on Susannah Ibsen, he had heard the voice of his Valkyrie and her accents determined the rhythm of the play.

[4]
> 'What is life? A fighting
> In heart and brain with Trolls.
> Poetry? that means writing
> Doomsday-accounts of our souls.'
>         (Garrett, F. E., *Lyrics and Poems from Ibsen*, n.d., p. l.)

In his own Norwegian translation Ibsen equated 'Gewalten' with 'trolde' (VI, 412).

a clearing away of all the perilous stuff accumulated in the author's bosom by his and his fellow-countrymen's failure to achieve the heroic in 1864. For eight years Ibsen laboured at *Emperor and Galilean* in the fervent hope of constructing some grand metaphysical scheme to which he could wholeheartedly subscribe and to which he could align all his thought;[1] *An Enemy of the People* is the direct reaction to the outcry raised on *Ghosts*, and *The Wild Duck* a re-examination of the missionary function imposed by Georg Brandes; even *Rosmersholm* mirrors something of the same order as well as Ibsen's attitude to the political questions of the hour. Only the most obvious illustrations have been chosen, but they should suffice to substantiate the thesis that, whatever else they may be besides, Ibsen's plays are subjective expressions of his personal emotions and sentiments.

## VIII

On the other hand, the objectivity of *The Master Builder* must not be denied. Ibsen would never permit the 'reality' of his figures and stories to be called in question; and this play, where the question was so frequently raised and the word 'symbolism' so much bandied about, justifies him to the full. For *The Master Builder* was and remains the story, as Mr Desmond MacCarthy has put it, of an 'elderly architect who falls off his scaffold while trying to show off before a young lady'.[2] The tragedy attached to the fable is that of the sick conscience caught in an *impasse*; and it is not in itself affected by the question whether the sick conscience presented is that of the author in disguise or whether he conceived it purely through the strength of his imagination. The intensity with which the workings of that conscience and the oppressive sense of guilt under which it labours are expressed may, of course, derive from direct fellow-feeling; but that is not a necessary conclusion either, and, in any event, the energy of

[1] Hans finds many more subjective elements in the finished work than this; he sees a precursor of Gregers Werle in the Emperor Julian who, like Ibsen, has the presumptuous notion of stopping the progress of the world with his ink-stained fingers (*op. cit.* p. 103).

[2] Introduction to *Four Plays* (1941), p. ix. The most brilliant exposition of *The Master Builder* along these lines is that of Bernard Shaw in *The Quintessence of Ibsenism* (3rd edition, 1922, pp. 121 ff.).

the expression cannot by itself suffice to make either the out-come of a play appear tragic or the fable significant.

*The Master Builder's* poignancy resides mainly in the prolonged dialogues between Solness and Hilda Wangel at the end of the second and throughout most of the third act, a series (almost) of operatic duets, when their love for one another and its hope-lessness become increasingly plain to themselves and to the audience, for all the hopes of a fair dawn with which they play. Nothing but the kind of miracle that never happens can save Solness from his fall—not even the helpers and servers, now forgotten—and his full realisation of this, together with his resolve to 'do the impossible once again',[1] gives him the heroic stature he needs to lift the fable above the level of police-court and inquest news; the delighted talk of the lovers about what would follow the impossible miracle, high up on the Princess's balcony, reveals the abysmal suffering inflicted by imprison-ment in the flesh and the conditions which the flesh entails.

All this has nothing to do with symbolism, and when Edvard Brandes, in accordance with his unswerving belief, wrote a critique denying all symbolic admixture to the story, Ibsen expressed his cordial appreciation, particularly for the inter-pretation of the personages and for 'accentuating their quality of real flesh and blood';[2] and he is said,[3] on good authority, to have declared that the play quite straightforwardly presented men and women whom he had known, but, obviously, placed in a poetic light or had 'poetically coloured'.

## IX

This 'poetical colouring'—if no more be admitted—calls for some comment, since in places it seems to have been laid on very thick. What, for instance, are we to make of an architect, *a fortiori* a master-builder, who commits the extravagance of an enormously lofty tower on an ordinary dwelling-house? What are we to make of his 'helpers and servers' and of his hold over

[1] VI, 81; Archer, x, 356.
[2] 'at få deres egenskab af virkelighedsmennesker hævdet' (*Breve*, II, 199). Edvard Brandes's critique appeared in the Copenhagen newspaper *Politiken* for 22 December 1892.
[3] Centenary Edition, XII, 26.

Kaja Fosli? What are we to make of the nine lovely dolls which Aline continues to mourn and, last but not least, of Hilda's 'Kingdom', of her demands in general?

Aline Solness presents a problem, but it is, I fancy, a problem for the actress more than anything else. She is that humanly and artistically very 'difficult type', the person almost literally soured by adversity. Her afflictions have been many and real and perhaps unsurmountable, but she is quite submerged in them, it is clear that her husband derives no help from her and that the shudder of repulsion, not unaccompanied by a distant compassion, which Hilda Wangel feels after her *tête-à-tête* with her, is a natural and normal reaction.[1] About the dolls, I think that Professor van der Leeuw has said the wisest words.[2] The blow her whole being sustained through the catastrophe to which, by an accident, her husband happened to owe his prosperity was as terrible as anyone can sustain without going mad; and it is to avoid going mad that, by a species of self-protection, she cannot 'think' the catastrophe through to the end; her thought stops short at the only endurable loss she sustained; and it dwells on the dolls so as not to be sunk in sheer black horror.

If it be thought that this is a mere explaining away of a difficulty, it must be conceded that Solness's tower is not susceptible to such treatment. It cannot be explained away; it is the symboliser's most concrete datum; and there seems only one other example in Ibsen's constructions of such intractability. Anomalies like the changing colours of the baby's eyes in *The Lady from the Sea*, the vine-leaves in Eilert Løvborg's hair are carefully reduced to subjective imaginings—and for the White Horses of Rosmersholm Ibsen went perhaps to unnecessary lengths to provide a rationalistic explanation, in the white scarf which Rebecca is busy knitting through a considerable part of the action. But, frankly, the statuary group of 'Resurrection Day', as it emerges from the allusions to it in *When We Dead Awaken*, seems to be an impossibility, and we

[1] The loss of her home must be reduced, too, in the light of Dr Herdal's description of it as a 'grim old robbers' castle' (VI, 19; Archer, x, 222).

[2] 'Ibsen's Bouwmeester Solness' in *Omhoog* n.s., v (1922), p. 270. I do not mean to imply that the search for factual parallels is futile, such as those adduced by Archer (x, xxx).

have to choose between saying the same of Solness's tower and succumbing to the banality of supposing that he fell from the equivalent of a second-floor window.[1]

The subjective explanation, however, is fully valid for the 'helpers and servers', those forces outside himself to which Solness fancied that he owed the translation of his half-formed wishes into reality and which, by bringing down Aline's old home, turned his *mens rea* to cognisable guilt.

As for Kaja Fosli, whom he believes to have been sent to him by their agency, we may say that her relation to Solness is a not uncommon one of the weak personality suddenly and completely enslaved to the strong personality, with more than a tincture of the unconsciously erotic in it, and that Solness, perfectly aware of this, by means of hypnotic passes and things of the kind in which he only partially believes[2] and which he only pretends to conceal, deliberately exploits the relation for the sole purpose of keeping a tight hold on three very useful, underpaid subordinates.

This leaves us still with the large and important problem of Hilda Wangel's demands on the Master Builder and the nature of their relationship.

Hilda Wangel is more difficult, perhaps impossible, to interpret on a purely rationalistic basis. She is the same girl who figures in *The Lady from the Sea* and who there found so much, but especially the deeps of human nature, 'frightfully thrilling'.[3] Some great experience, real or imagined, transfigured her childhood and she now thrusts herself back into the orbit of her Master Builder in order to confirm, extend and deepen that experience. She is only interested in action and in the emotional experiences which action provokes; to sharpen the latter she has lived in her imagination to a degree which can justly be called morbid and which definitely reaches the limits of sanity.[4]

---

[1] In Strindberg's play *The Secret of the Guild* (1881) an architect is reputed to be unable to climb to the top of his own tower and is urged (by his wife) to do so.

[2] Ibsen took a distrustful interest in spiritualistic phenomena at this time, and he approved of the hypnotising gestures made by Fahlstrøm in acting the part of Solness (Koht, II, 353).

[3] She speaks of having lived with her father only recently; no word alludes to her stepmother or her sister.

[4] Hilda Wangel first met Aline Solness at a *sanatorium* (VI, 21; Archer, X, 228). There are other indications of deranged health, as in 'the quivering twitch of her

In her remote home at Lysanger Solness, the powerful, successful Master Builder, has been the greatest man whom she had met and in her imagination she evidently sees herself in some way, for short or for long, associated with his greatness. She will be the Valkyrie of this superman, urging him to further greatness, and in doing so she will achieve herself, attain that 'kingdom'[1] of freedom which she craves and from which she can, serene and secure, look down upon the world of men. What the mundane aspects, the mundane foundation or the mundane view of this relationship will be she does not greatly care.

But the tragedy of the Master Builder is her tragedy too. She finds her great man petty in many ways. He has given up building churches and church towers. He tyrannises over his pitiful staff. That might be remedied, and the way in which she takes in hand the relation of Solness to the Broviks shows how it could be done. Moreover, Solness is afraid of the younger generation; that, too, can be remedied by enlisting some of the feared enemy in her own person on his side in the struggle, if struggle there has to be. But this is not the worst. There is Solness's sick conscience, something no superman ought to own:[2] his gnawing remorse about a guilt which actually is no guilt[3] shows this. Hilda, true to her conception of herself as a Valkyrie, contrasts the sick conscience with the robust conscience of the Vikings of old who throve on banditry and rape, and who would have had as little compunction as the original Hamlet in setting fire to a house if they could gain an advantage thereby. Let Solness become such a Viking. But what then? What future is there in reality for him? What, more insistently, for her? He could go on being a Master Builder in

lips' (vi, 34; Archer, x, 255) and the abrupt alternations of wild excitement and apathetic defection. The nerve-specialist Aronsohn, O., *Das Problem im 'Baumeister Solness'* (1910), concludes that Solness is a certifiable lunatic and has grave doubts about Hilda. Did Shaw in *Candida* turn to farcical uses this situation in which all the protagonists are suspected of insanity?

[1] Is it the same thing as 'peace of soul' (*sjælefred*, vi, 51; Archer, x, 292)?

[2] In his treatment of the Broviks, Solness shows some of the *allures* of the superman, a type more completely developed (and condemned) in John Gabriel Borkman; Georg Brandes had become a great champion of Nietzsche, and Ibsen had doubtlessly followed his controversy with Harald Høffding on the subject in *Tilskueren* for 1889.

[3] The story of the crack in the chimney (vi, 52; Archer, x, 292) confirms this.

a Norwegian town with a young living mistress instead of an old dead wife.[1] But is that to be the end of the dream? An alternative would be to fly entirely into the land of make-believe and there build castles in the air. Is that work for the man who spoke to God from the top of a church tower and for the Valkyrie of such a man? There remains the last alternative, which becomes insistent by the end of the second act. As in *Rosmersholm*, there is no worthy solution but the double tragedy. And that does in fact supervene: for, to put the matter crudely, Hilda, one must suppose, goes completely out of her mind after the end of the play. But it is not impossible to argue that for two or three moments, when Solness undertakes to do the impossible once again and does it, Hilda and he set foot in her kingdom.

## X

The early acting history of *The Master Builder* shows more than the usual anomalies; William Archer obtained an advanced copy of the London edition in time to translate it, for a performance given to secure the copyright, at the Haymarket Theatre, London, on 7 December 1892;[2] and the first performance in the original was given by William Petersen's travelling troupe of Danish actors at Trondheim on 19 January 1893, the same day as the earliest performance in German. A month later, on 20 February 1893, it was presented at the Christiania Theatre, with Fallstrøm as Solness, Fru Wetter-Gren as Kaja, Johanne Dybwad as Hilda Wangel and Laura Gundersen as Aline Solness.

A notable performance was that given, in French, at Christiania in 1894 by Lugné-Poë and the Théâtre de l'Œuvre, which carried Ibsen away to high encomiums: 'that was the resurrection of my play', he told the gratified performers.[3] I do not know, however, whether any very special significance attaches to their interpretation, since Ibsen was always carried away on seeing his plays well done and never stinted whatever praise he bestowed.

[1] Cf. vi, 69; Archer, x, 330 f.
[2] This was to make assurance doubly sure, since the prior publication in London was undertaken to the same end. Elizabeth Robins created the part of Hilda.
[3] Koht, ii, 355.

*The Master Builder* is a good acting-play, even an exciting one, and as such has always maintained itself on the boards with moderate persistence. But it never rivalled the general popularity of *A Doll's House* or of *Hedda Gabler*; and the 10,000 copies of the first edition satisfied the demand of readers for long enough.[1]

For the first time the case for a symbolical interpretation became urgent—'*everything* in this play is symbolic', the Swedish critic Wirsén groaned[2]—and, rightly or wrongly, most critics seem to have felt that a deep-going exegesis of the play was necessary to its full enjoyment. These interpretations were of all kinds and, between them, covered most of the points touched on above,[3] besides incorporating some assumptions which were quickly found to be unacceptable. Thus, a Lutheran weekly in Norway[4] saw Bjørnson (who had already been cast for the parts of Stensgaard in *The League of Youth* and Stockmann in *An Enemy of the People*) in Solness and thought that the party-leader Sverdrup was represented by old Brovik.

A. B. Walkley (who was presumably the author of a squib commentators appear to have taken seriously, drawing a parallel between the careers of Solness and Mr Gladstone)[5] thought, on the whole, meanly of *The Master Builder*; but he admitted that it was of great historical interest as introducing symbolism into the modern theatre.[6] Though the generalisation requires a little rectifying in detail, it remains true that the appearance of *The Master Builder* coincides with the vulgarisation, through the medium of the stage, of that anti-realistic, 'symbolistic' movement in the arts, which had been gathering way for some dozen years, notably in French-speaking countries. Ibsen was thus,

---

[1] A precise estimate of its circulation and relative popularity in book-form is vitiated by the appearance of collected editions (the first in 1898).

[2] *Kritiker* (1901), p. 113.

[3] Even the point that Solness's professional career can be interpreted as Ibsen's was already made.

[4] *Lutherisk Ugeskrift*, I (1893), pp. 12 and 152; *cit.* Halvorsen, H. B., *Norsk Forfatter-Lexikon*, s.v. *Ibsen*.

[5] 'The Political Master-Builder', in *Saturday Review*, LXXVI (1893), p. 34. The article is anonymous. That it is a squib is shown by the equation of Hilda Wangel with John Morley, if by nothing else; it is essentially a belittlement of Gladstone.

[6] Walkley, A. B., 'Some Plays of the Day', in *Fortnightly Review* (n.s.), LIII (1893), p. 468.

rather unexpectedly—since he had been one of the arch-priests of the realistic church—standing shoulder to shoulder with Maeterlinck (his admirer) in the front rank of *les jeunes*. In this way, on the one hand, he facilitated an abandonment of their extreme position by the older realistic fanatics—Hauptmann slithers through *Hannele's Ascension* down to his *Sunken Bell*—and, on the other hand, he made his peace with those who refused to accept the preceding, harsher plays.[1] Did Ibsen, without being completely aware of it, solve with *The Master Builder* Solness's problems of building in a third style and so effectively steal the thunder of the younger generation?

[1] 'In fact, Dr Ibsen has remounted not a few rungs of the ladder he has been descending of late (the Bygmester's imagery is contagious) by the mere fact of dipping himself once more into the fantastic' (*Saturday Review*, LXXV, 1893, p. 241).

## NOTE TO THE READER

The author wishes to point out that since this book was first published, much new material on the subject has appeared. However, since this is a facsimile reprint, it was decided to retain the original bibliography.

# SELECT BIBLIOGRAPHY

## BIOGRAPHIES

BEYER, H. 'Ibsen.' *Norsk Biografisk Leksikon*, VI. Kristiania, 1934.

GRAN, G. *Henrik Ibsen Liv og Verker*. Kristiania, 1918.

KOHT, H. *Henrik Ibsen eit Diktarliv*. Oslo, 1928–9. English translation: London, 1931.

## GENERAL STUDIES

ANDRÉAS-SALOMÉ, L. *Henrik Ibsen's Frauengestalten nach seinen sechs Familien-Dramen*. Berlin, 1892.

BOER, R. C. *Ibsen's Dramas*. Haarlem, 1928.

BOETTCHER, F. *La Femme dans le Théâtre d'Ibsen*. Paris, 1912.

BOYESEN, H. H. *A Commentary on Ibsen*. London, 1894.

BRADBROOK, M. C. *Ibsen the Norwegian*. London, 1946.

BRANDES, G. M. C. *Henrik Ibsen*. København, 1898. (English translation in *Henrik Ibsen, Bjørnstjerne Bjørnson*: London, 1898.)

COLLIN, C. 'Henrik Ibsens Dramatiske Bygningsstil.' *Tilskueren*, pp. 601 ff. København, 1906.

DOWNS, B. W. *Ibsen: the Intellectual Background*. Cambridge, 1946.

DRESDNER, A. *Ibsen als Norweger und Europäer*. Jena, 1907.

FARINELLI, A. *La Tragedia di Ibsen*. Bologna, 1923.

FIRKINS, I. T. E. *Henrik Ibsen, a Bibliography*. New York, 1921.

GOSSE, E. *Ibsen*. London, 1907.

HALVORSEN, J. B. 'Ibsen.' *Norsk Forfatter-Lexicon*, III. Kristiania, 1892.

HANS, W. *Ibsens Selbstporträt in seinen Dramen*. München, 1911.

HØST, S. *Ibsens Diktning og Ibsen Selv*. Oslo, 1927.

LØKEN, H. *Ibsen og Kjærligheten*. Kristiania, 1923.

ROBERTS, R. E. *Henrik Ibsen: a critical Study*. London, 1912.

SAURÈS, F. A. Y. S. *Trois Hommes* (3rd edition). Paris, 1913.

SCHACK, A. *Om Udviklingsgangen i Henrik Ibsens Digtning*. København, 1896.

SHAW, G. B. *The Quintessence of Ibsenism*. London, 1891. (Augmented edition, London, 1913.)

TENNANT, P. F. D. *Ibsen's Dramatic Technique*. Cambridge, 1948.

WICKSTEED, P. H. *Four Lectures on Henrik Ibsen*. London, 1892.

WOERNER, R. H. *Ibsen*. München, 1900–10.

ZUCKER, A. E. *Ibsen, the Master Builder*. London, 1930.

### For 'Love's Comedy'

BAKKEN, H. S. 'Ibsens *Kjærlighedens Komedie*.' *Edda*, XXXI. Oslo, 1931.

BING, J. '*Kjærlighedens Komedie*.' *Festskrift til William Nygaard*. Kristiania, 1913.

BULL, F. 'Innledning' to *Kjærlighedens Komedie*. *Henrik Ibsens Samlede Verker* (*Hundreårsutgave*), IV. Oslo, 1930.

# SELECT BIBLIOGRAPHY

HERFORD, C. H. 'A Scene from Ibsen's *Love's Comedy.*' *Fortnightly Review* (n.s.), LXXVII. London, 1900.

HERFORD, C. H. 'Introduction' to *Love's Comedy*. The Collected Works of *Ibsen*, I. London, 1908.

LANDMARK, J. A. 'Ibsens Arbeidsmanuskript til *Kjærlighedens Komedie.*' *Edda*, XXVIII. Oslo, 1928.

ORDING, F. *Henrik Ibsen*. '*Kærlighedens Komedie.*' Kristiania, 1914.

## For 'Brand'

BERGGRAV, E. *Ibsens sjelelige Krise*. Oslo, 1937.

BEYER, H. *Søren Kierkegaard og Norge*. Kristiania, 1924.

BING, J. *Henrik Ibsens Brand*. Kristiania (n.d.).

BULL, F. 'Brand, Bruun og Freihow.' *Berggrav, ut supra*.

CHESNAIS, P. G. LA. *Brand d'Ibsen*. Paris (n.d.).

CHESNAIS, P. G. LA. 'Ibsen disciple de Kierkegaard?' *Edda*, XXXIV. Oslo, 1934.

FREIHOW, H. V. *Henrik Ibsens* 'Brand'. Oslo, 1936.

HERFORD, C. H. 'Introduction' to *Brand*. Collected Works of Henrik Ibsen, III. London, 1906.

KINCK, B. M. 'Dramaet *Brand*, Opfatninger og Tolkninger.' *Edda*, XXX. Oslo, 1930.

KOHT, H. 'Innledning' to *Brand*. *Henrik Ibsens Samlede Verker* (*Hundreårsutgave*), V. Oslo, 1928.

LARSEN, K. *Henrik Ibsens episke Brand*. København, 1907.

MARCUS, C. D. 'Ibsen och Göticism.' *Edda*, XXXI. Oslo, 1931.

PROZOR, M. 'Un drame de Henrik Ibsen, *Brand*.' *Revue des deux Mondes* (4th period), CXXVI. Paris, 1894.

STOBART, M. A. 'New Lights on Ibsen's *Brand*.' *Fortnightly Review* (n.s.), LXVI. London, 1899.

SVENSSON, S. 'Brand och den svenska Göticismen.' *Edda*, XXX. Oslo, 1930.

## For 'Peer Gynt'

ANDREWS, A. LE R. 'Further Influences upon Ibsen's *Peer Gynt*.' *Journal of English and Germanic Philology*, XV. Urbana, 1916.

ARCHER, W. 'Introduction' to *Peer Gynt*. Collected Works of Henrik Ibsen, IV. London, 1907.

BAKKEN, H. S. '*Per Gynt*, Replikk til Pål Kluften.' *Edda*, XXX. Oslo, 1930.

BERGSØE, V. *Henrik Ibsen paa Ischia*. København, 1907.

BULL, F. 'Innledning' to *Peer Gynt*. *Henrik Ibsens Samlede Verker* (*Hundreårsutgave*), VI. Oslo, 1931.

BULL, F. *Henrik Ibsens* '*Peer Gynt*'. Oslo, 1947.

EITREM, H. 'Den fremmede Passager i Ibsens *Peer Gynt*.' *Edda*, XVI. Kristiania, 1921.

KLUFTEN, P. 'Per Gynt.' *Edda*, XXX. Oslo, 1930.

LOGEMAN, H. 'Den store Bøigen.' *Edda*, VI. Kristiania, 1916.

LOGEMAN, H. *A Commentary on Henrik Ibsen's* '*Peer Gynt*'. The Hague, 1917.

LOGEMAN, H. 'The "Caprices" in Henrik Ibsen's *Peer Gynt*.' *Edda*, VII. Kristiania, 1917.

# SELECT BIBLIOGRAPHY

LOGEMAN, H. 'Bøigens Oprindelse.' *Danske Studier*, XIII. København, 1916.
PROZOR, M. *Le Peer Gynt d'Ibsen.* Paris, 1897.
QUILLER-COUCH, A. 'Ibsen's *Peer Gynt.*' *Adventures in Criticism.* London, 1896.
ROBERTS, R. E. 'Introduction' to *Peer Gynt.* London, 1912.
STAVNEM, P. L. 'Overnaturlige Væsener og Symbolik i Henrik Ibsens *Peer Gynt.*' *Afhandlinger viede Sophus Bugges Minde.* Kristiania, 1908.
STURTEVANT, A. M. 'Aase and Peer Gynt.' *Modern Language Notes*, XXIX. Baltimore, 1914.
ZUCKER, A. E. 'Goethe and Ibsen's Button-Moulder.' *Publications of the Modern Language Association of America*, LVII. Menasha, 1942.

## For 'A Doll's House'

ARCHER, W. 'Introduction' to *A Doll's House. Collected Works of Henrik Ibsen*, VII. London, 1907.
FEILITZEN, U. (*pseud.* 'Robinson'). *Ibsen och Äktenskapsfrågan.* Stockholm, 1882.
KOHT, H. 'Innledning' to *Et Dukkehjem. Henrik Ibsens Samlede Verker* (*Hundreårsutgave*), VIII. Oslo, 1933.
SPIELHAGEN, F. 'Drama oder Roman?' *Theorie und Technik des Romans.* Leipzig, 1883.
WULFFEN, E. *Ibsens Nora vor dem Strafrichter und Psychiater.* Halle, 1907.

## For 'The Wild Duck'

ARCHER, W. 'Introduction' to *The Wild Duck. Collected Works of Henrik Ibsen*, VIII. London, 1907.
LYNNER, V. E. 'Gregers Werle—og Ibsens Selvironi.' *Edda*, XXVIII. Oslo, 1928.
NISSEN, I. *Sjelelige Kriser i Menneskets Liv.* Oslo, 1931.
SEIP, D. A. 'Innledning' to *Vildanden. Henrik Ibsens Samlede Verker* (*Hunåreårsutgave*), X. Oslo, 1932.
TENNANT, P. F. D. 'A Critical Study of Ibsen's *Vildanden.*' *Edda*, XXXIV. Oslo, 1934.
WYLLER, A. '*Villanden.*' *Edda*, XXV (Oslo, 1936).

## For 'The Master Builder'

ARCHER, W. 'Introduction' to *The Master Builder. Collected Works of Henrik Ibsen*, X. London, 1907.
BRANDES, G. M. C. *Ibsen* (being *Die Literatur*, XXXII and XXXIII). Berlin (n.d.).
KINCK, B. M. 'Henrik Ibsen og Laura Kieler.' *Edda*, XXXV. Oslo, 1935.
LEEUW, G. VAN DER. 'Ibsen's Bouwmeester Solness.' *Omhoog* (n.s.), V. Amersfoort, 1922.
ROUVEYRE, A. 'Le Mémorial Inédit d'une Amie d'Ibsen.' *Mercure de France.* Paris, 15 July 1928.
SEIP, D. A. 'Innledning' to *Bygmester Solness. Henrik Ibsens Samlede Verker* (*Hundreårsutgave*), XII. Oslo, 1935.
WALKLEY, A. B. 'Some Plays of the Day.' *Fortnightly Review* (n.s.), LIII. London, 1893.

# INDEX

# INDEX